Reconsidering
AYN RAND

Reconsidering
AYN RAND

MICHAEL B. YANG, M.D.

WINEPRESS WP PUBLISHING

CONTENTS

CONTENTS

Part Two
The Philosophy

ACKNOWLEDGMENTS

Many thanks are due to the numerous friends and family members around the country who have encouraged and supported me in the writing of this book. I am especially grateful to Dr. John Robbins, president of The Trinity Foundation, who consented to read and comment upon one of the final drafts of this book. I have benefited from a number of his criticisms and suggestions. Of course, any errors that remain are entirely my own.

1

INTRODUCTION

"*Atlas Shrugged* changed my life." Thousands, perhaps millions, of people have spoken those words, and I was one of them. Eighteen years have passed since I overheard three seniors at my high school discussing a book called *Atlas Shrugged*. Its author was Ayn Rand. I was fourteen years old and presumed myself fairly well read, but her name was unfamiliar to me. The bits and pieces I snatched from my friends' conversation intrigued me. It sounded as if they were discussing philosophy, but they were also recounting stories with characters like John Galt and Cuffy Meigs. What kind of names were those? What kind of book was this? Out of curiosity, I purchased a copy.

"Who is John Galt?" Those are the opening words of a novel unlike any other I had ever read before. The plot was thrilling, and the ideas behind the story were inspiring and provocative. I had great difficulty limiting myself to just a few hours with *Atlas Shrugged* each day. Schoolwork was boring by comparison with my newfound love. When I finished reading the book, I felt pleasantly exhausted and joyously elated. I knew the course of my life had changed forever. I scribbled on the last page of the book: "December 27, 1981. Date of my intellectual rebirth."

In reality, I still knew very little about Ayn Rand or her philosophy, but the stories and the ideas contained in *Atlas Shrugged* had already brought me to a pivotal moment in my life. I knew that I wanted to be like the heroes of *Atlas Shrugged*, but I realized that I needed to learn more. So I devoured Rand's other writings, and within a short time, her ideas became the dominant influence in my life.

The experience I had was probably common to hundreds of thousands of readers who have felt the power of Rand's fiction. Since its publication in 1957, *Atlas Shrugged* has sold more than five million copies. Perhaps a measure of the book's continuing influence may be estimated from the results of a survey conducted jointly by the Library of Congress and Book-of-the-Month Club in 1991. The survey asked readers which books had made a difference in peoples' lives. The results found *Atlas Shrugged* placing second only to the Bible.[1]

While many readers have a profound knowledge of Ayn Rand, others have only a cursory familiarity with her name or her writings. Who was she, and why have her ideas become so influential?[2] Briefly, Ayn Rand was born Alice Rosenbaum. She immigrated to the United States from the Soviet Union in 1926. Despite difficult beginnings as a writer, she eventually gained international fame as the author of *The Fountainhead* (1943) and *Atlas Shrugged* (1957). She was a novelist as well as a philosopher, although for years few professional philosophers gave her much attention or respect. Her careful integration of fiction and philosophy was a unique accomplishment, and her novels served as a literary platform for portraying the practical consequences of the philosophical system she conceived: Objectivism. This philosophy is lived out by the heroes in her stories and had its most profound and dynamic expression in *Atlas Shrugged*.

What are the fundamental beliefs of Objectivism? Rand summarized her philosophy in this way:

> My philosophy, in essence, is the concept of man as a heroic
> being, with his own happiness as the moral purpose of his life,

---

[1] *Library of Congress Information Bulletin*, December 16, 1991, pp. 478–479.
[2] Two biographies of Rand have appeared in print. In 1962, Nathaniel and Barbara Branden wrote *Who Is Ayn Rand?* In 1986, Barbara Branden completed *The Passion of Ayn Rand*.

with productive achievement as his noblest activity, and reason as his only absolute.[3]

In contrast to the prevalent liberal tendencies of the era in which she lived, Rand was an advocate of *laissez-faire* capitalism and reason. She was not, however, a conservative in the typical sense of the word. Indeed, she was often anathema to the conservatives because she advocated rational selfishness as a virtue while denying the existence of God. Her name and her highly controversial ideas were familiar to many who grew up in the sixties and seventies. Today, eighteen years after her death, her ideas have penetrated every level of society, and her influence remains widespread. Even though her name may not now possess the same fame and recognition it once had, those who are sensitized to her name will hear it mentioned often. Perhaps one of her best-known students is the current chairman of the Federal Reserve System, Alan Greenspan. In addition, the Libertarian political movement, even though it was officially repudiated by Objectivism, remains one of the most visible results of Rand's influence.

Indeed, Ayn Rand's ideas have inspired whole movements. However, we should not lose sight of how she came to have such influence. She touched people one at a time through her fiction. Like many of those who adopted the philosophy of Objectivism, I was first attracted to Rand because of her novels. What appealed to me were the heroic, confident individuals she portrayed in *Atlas Shrugged* and *The Fountainhead*. There was an independent, intellectual streak in me that was drawn to Rand's characters, for they exemplified what I wanted to be. The beckoning call to live the full and uncompromising life of someone like Howard Roark or John Galt was difficult to resist.

Some people might find it odd to mix fiction and philosophy. But Rand's novels offered breathtaking adventure and suspense that was fully integrated with passages on philosophical issues. From

---

[3] "About the Author," *Atlas Shrugged.* The pages cited in the books by Ayn Rand are from the paperback editions. The exception is *Philosophy: Who Needs It.*

the stories, I learned about ideas that were the fountainhead of the courageous and productive lives that Rand had created in her fictional heroes. I also discovered the motives behind the contracted, destructive existence of her villains. As Leonard Peikoff has said, Ayn Rand was the preeminent salesman for philosophy:

> Who else could write a Romantic best seller such as *Atlas Shrugged*—in which the heroes and the villains are differentiated fundamentally by their metaphysics; in which the wrong epistemology is shown to lead to train wrecks, furnace breakouts, and sexual impotence; in which the right ethics is shown to be the indispensable means to the rebuilding of New York City and of man's soul?[4]

Indeed, there are intense thematic conflicts in Rand's writings. She pitted reason against faith and feelings. She upheld the existence of an objective reality, as opposed to the idea of an illusory and subjective world put forth by some philosophers. However, it seemed to me that Rand's views regarding these fundamental issues were merely preparatory to her explanation of the intense moral and political conflicts that have characterized much of man's history. The combatants in this struggle were the ethics of self-interest and the ethics of self-sacrifice. The idea that was the focus of Rand's praise was rational egoism. The object of her wrath was altruism.

Why did Rand find altruism so objectionable? The answer lies in what people mean by altruism and how they practice it. Ayn Rand defined altruism this way:

> The basic principle of altruism is that man has no right to exist for his own sake, that service to others is the only justification of his existence, and that self-sacrifice is his highest moral duty, virtue and value.[5]

---

[4] *Philosophy: Who Needs It*, p. vii.
[5] "Faith and Force: The Destroyers of the Modern World," *Philosophy: Who Needs It*, p. 74.

In her nonfiction works, Rand demonstrated how the ideas of altruism had historically been used to destroy man's soul and render him a malleable instrument in the service of the State (communism and socialism) or the Fatherland (Hitler's fascism). However, she did not end her analysis of altruism with political systems. She traced the idea of altruism to religion in general and Christianity in particular.

As far as Rand was concerned, all religions were merely variations on the theme of altruism. Instead of man living for the State, he lived for God. The Judeo-Christian heritage seemed to evoke her severest criticism. Christianity, she said, was an anti-life, anti-self philosophy and was thus incompatible with the life of a rational being. Through the strategic use of chapter titles, well-known sayings, and stereotyped characters that allude to Christian themes, Rand portrayed Christianity as chief perpetrator and originator of altruism.[6] Consequently, many people who read Rand's novels came to identify Christianity with all that is evil, not only in the fictional world of *Atlas Shrugged* and *The Fountainhead* but also in the real world that we inhabit. As a result, it was impossible to be a genuine student of Objectivism and not be an atheist.

The Fountainhead and *Atlas Shrugged* provided a foundation, but many students of Objectivism grew in their understanding of Objectivism and gained intellectual ammunition against altruism and Christianity through Ayn Rand's nonfiction works like *The Virtue of Selfishness*, *Capitalism: The Unknown Ideal*, and *Introduction to Objectivist Epistemology*. More serious students investigated the original sources: *The Objectivist* or *The Objectivist Newsletter*. Rand's former colleague, Nathaniel Branden, supplied other materials for consideration in his later best-selling books: *The Psychology of Self-Esteem* and *The Psychology of Romantic Love*. Even though Branden was removed from the Objectivist movement in 1968 as a result of a schism known as "the break," his writings in these books are a logical continuation of his original contributions to *The Objectivist* and continue to influence many who admire Rand. Simi-

---

[6] For example, chapter 5 in part 3 of *Atlas Shrugged* has this title: "Their Brothers' Keepers."

larly, while the Libertarians were never part of Objectivism, many Libertarian writers openly declare their admiration for Rand. George Smith, for one, has contributed much to the education of Rand's admirers through works like *Atheism: The Case against God*.

Indeed, I had absorbed the information presented in these key books and felt confident that Objectivism was right about Christianity and altruism. With time, however, I began to notice that the way many Christians lived did not fit the box that Rand had put them in. For example, some Christians were vibrantly confident and successful. They were also keenly aware of, and interested in, intellectual issues. All the while, they manifested genuine love and compassion toward other people. What could account for this discrepancy? If Christianity were an altruistic system, and if altruism could result in only self-abnegation, envy, and irrationality, such people as these should not exist. Furthermore, it was not so easy to attribute the "good" in these people to *reason*, and the "bad" to *faith*, as Rand often did.

This question and other factors prompted me to start examining the Bible during my first semester at Harvard Medical School. After all, I had never read the book myself. I had been relying on professional Objectivists and Libertarians to tell me what was in it. My goal in examining the Scriptures was to prove that my Objectivist mentors were right after all. I anticipated that my questions would be resolved, and my arguments against Christianity would be strengthened. Confidently, I said to myself, *I'll read the Bible, and then I'll be able to tell Christians exactly why they are wrong*.

So I began. At first, the Bible seemed like an odd collection of stories and puzzling statements that I had to wade through. I had to reserve judgment on many passages until I understood their context better. Other sections, particularly the ones that commented on moral conduct, antagonized me. Objectivism had taught me a rational, justifiable code of ethics. What use did I have for these ancient, religious beliefs? Nevertheless, I persisted. Soon, I began to recognize a few biblical passages as having been alluded to in Rand's works. However, they did not seem to say what Rand claimed they said. For example, in *Atlas Shrugged*, Rand, speaking through her character

Francisco d'Anconia, appears to demolish with ease the proverb that "money is the root of all evil." That saying, in the mind of many readers, owes its origin to Christianity. So, by implication, Rand was detracting the Christian view of economics and morality. However, I discovered that the Scriptures say nothing of the kind. Instead, the corresponding passage actually reads, "For the love of money is a root of all sorts of evil."[7] At first I was tempted to dismiss the misquotation, but soon I became quite uneasy about the enormous difference in meaning those few words make. Any thinking person can see that for himself. The passage warns against an attitude that would love and idolize money; it does not condemn the possession or rightful use of money. I became concerned that other errors might be lurking, somewhere. They were.

Many readers are also drawn to Rand's novels by the passionate, romantic relationships she conceived. Howard Roark and Dominique Francon. John Galt and Dagny Taggart. Who could forget their love? We will pursue the subject of love more thoroughly later, but it is worth stating here that Rand believed Christianity's anti-self philosophy had a devastating impact on man's view of sexuality. In *Atlas Shrugged*, John Galt asks:

> What is the nature of the guilt that your teachers call [man's] Original Sin? What are the evils man acquired when he fell from a state they consider perfection? . . . He was sentenced to experience desire—he acquired the capacity of sexual enjoyment.[8]

Obviously, Rand was under the impression that Christianity considered sexual enjoyment evil, regardless of what context it occurred in, since sex came about in a fallen, sin-infested world. Ironically, I discovered a number of scriptures that say quite the opposite.

> So husbands ought also to love their own wives as their own bodies. He who loves his own wife loves himself; for no one

---

[7] 1 Timothy 6:10.
[8] *Atlas Shrugged*, p. 951.

ever hated his own flesh, but nourishes and cherishes it, just as Christ also does the church.[9]

Loving your wife as you loved yourself? What an intriguing concept. I thought Rand had said the focus of Christianity was purely self-sacrifice. And what was I to make of the passion that was unabashedly sanctioned and encouraged in this proverb?

> Let your fountain be blessed, and rejoice in the wife of your youth. As a loving hind and a graceful doe, let her breasts satisfy you at all times; be exhilarated always with her love.[10]

Rand seriously misjudged the Christian view of sexuality.

These two errors, one a misquotation and the other a misinterpretation, disturbed me. How could someone as brilliant and intelligent as Ayn Rand have made these mistakes? To be sure, these errors were committed in the practical branches of her philosophy, but it was precisely those areas of her philosophy that initially drew the attention and admiration of most readers. I wondered if there were additional errors in the theoretical foundations of her philosophy. I was far from giving up hope in the philosophy I had learned from Rand, but neither was I about to let these discrepancies slip by. Rand had often warned her readers: "Check your premises." Now these words echoed in my mind. I began questioning the entire philosophy that Rand had developed and especially the way she and other writers characterized Christianity.

In that process of inquiry, I discovered I was not alone. Serious questions were being raised by other writers about Rand's ideas on reason and existence. Essays in *The Philosophic Thought of Ayn Rand*, edited by Douglas Den Uyl and Douglas Rasmussen, had challenged the meaningfulness and usefulness of Rand's famous philosophical principles: Existence exists, and consciousness is identity. On further scrutiny, Rand's distinction between faith and reason also seemed to break down. The analysis offered by the several authors

---

[9] Ephesians 5:28–29.
[10] Proverbs 5:18–19.

who contributed to that volume served as a springboard for my own thinking. Beyond this, I revisited the philosophical questions about God that Rand never adequately addressed. I began to grapple with the nature of scientific inquiry and its often reported conflict with Christianity. Moreover, I considered and weighed the evidences for the Christian faith. There was also the beginning of an examination of my own life and purpose.

That quest resulted in my acknowledging the truth and the reality of Christ—that he is the resurrected Savior and the Lord of all. I began that journey by reconsidering Ayn Rand and the philosophy of Objectivism, and I have continued to grow in my understanding of her philosophy in the years since I came to know Christ. I would like to share that journey with you in the following chapters. The topics flow from the practical issues of self-esteem and romantic love, to the more theoretical questions about reason, faith, morality, and the existence of God. The order of the contents follows the path that many people take to Objectivism. Most people are attracted to Rand *first* by her characters and stories and *only then* begin to understand and assimilate the ideas and philosophy behind them. Even then, most learn the philosophy from her fiction.[11] Therefore, it might be most fruitful to revisit the stories and ideas of Ayn Rand in the same order that they tend to influence people.

As I mentioned earlier, a Library of Congress survey found *Atlas Shrugged* second only to the Bible in its impact on readers. It amused me to think that I had been influenced by both books. Today, there are perhaps hundreds of thousands of people who still steadfastly adhere to Rand's ideas. There are perhaps millions more who have been influenced and shaped by her in some way. Some may have relegated Objectivism to a small corner of their lives. Others, perhaps, have become disillusioned and abandoned her philosophy altogether, but their lives were forever transformed by their encounter with Objectivism. And there is a new generation just beginning to discover her writings. I hope this small volume will speak to them all.

---

[11] *The Passion of Ayn Rand*, p. 388.

I lived through Objectivism, not as a noted figure of the movement, but as an ordinary person whose life was profoundly affected in trying to live out Ayn Rand's ideas. I am grateful for the temporary vision of strength and wisdom that Rand gave me at a crucial time in my life. But ultimately, that strength and wisdom failed, and the vision turned out to be an illusion. Nevertheless, that failure prepared me to receive the Living Truth, who is the only fountainhead of all genuine strength and wisdom.

PART ONE

THE FICTION
AND THE PRACTICE

2

ESTABLISHING
THE FOUNDATIONS:
A SYNOPSIS OF RAND'S TWO MAJOR NOVELS

Art is the indispensable medium for the communication of a moral ideal.

Ayn Rand, *The Romantic Manifesto*

A few years ago, Ayn Rand gave a series of private lectures on the art of fiction-writing. During a discussion period, she happened to remark that there was not a single word in her novels whose purpose she could not explain.

Nathaniel Branden, *Who Is Ayn Rand?*

Ayn Rand's fiction provides a wealth of material for discussion. In her nonfiction works, she often referred to examples from her fiction and quoted her own characters. Because the level of familiarity with her fiction varies between readers, we should establish common ground. What follows is a brief synopsis of her two major novels, *The Fountainhead* and *Atlas Shrugged*. While this summary is neither complete nor exhaustive, it does provide a basic framework for our discussion of her ideas. Readers familiar with Rand's work may wish to begin in the next chapter.

The Fountainhead

"Howard Roark laughed." These opening words of *The Fountainhead* tell us much about a talented yet fiercely independent architect. At the story's inception, Howard Roark has just been expelled from the Stanton Institute of Technology for insubordination. What crime did Roark commit? He refused to learn the *art* of architecture. While studying at the institute, Roark had excelled in the technical aspects of his profession, such as material science and structural engineering; however, his unconventional approach to the artistic side of architecture conflicted with the traditional views of his instructors and colleagues.

Roark's approach to art may be best described by this principle: Form follows function. The appearance of a building should conform to a design that results in optimal management of space and function. This concept has been attributed to architects like Frank Lloyd Wright and Buckminster Fuller.[1] Contrary to popular misconception, the appearance of a building that adheres to these principles need not be a visually plain, square box. Fuller's geodesic dome is one example of how a visually stimulating construct automatically follows from a structurally innovative design.

---

[1] It is interesting that Rand never mentions Fuller, who in many respects was more innovative than Wright.

Perhaps we should let Roark speak for himself. In his critique of the famous Greek Parthenon, Roark asks:

> The famous flutings on the famous columns—what are they there for? To hide the joints in wood—when columns were made of wood, only these aren't, they're marble. The triglyphs, what are they? *Wood*. Wooden beams, the way they had to be laid when people began to build wooden shacks. Your Greeks took marble and they made copies of their wooden structures out of it, because others had done it that way. Then your masters of the Renaissance came along and made copies in plaster of copies in marble of copies in wood. Now here we are, making copies in steel and concrete of copies in plaster of copies in marble of copies in wood. Why?[2]

Roark's professors are offended by his refusal to incorporate the artistic achievements of previous eras into his designs. Despite their advice and threats, Roark remains true to his own principles.

In contrast, Peter Keating is the epitome of compromise. Keating, a graduating senior from Stanton Institute, is not an incompetent architect, but he frequently sabotages his own creative abilities by borrowing the ideas of others. Keating takes no chances on his own solutions; instead, he relies on well-worn designs that are acceptable to society. He takes the safe way out. For example, he imposes Renaissance and Gothic structures on modern buildings that are desperately crying out for an identity of their own. Ironically, Keating occasionally asks for Roark's advice and receives it. Keating would then incorporate Roark's ideas into his own design. Somehow, Keating realizes that Roark's unconventional standards work, even if the rest of the world will not acknowledge it.

After Keating's graduation and Roark's expulsion, their lives take different paths. Keating joins the prestigious architectural firm, Francon & Heyer, while Roark struggles to find and keep commissions. Shortly thereafter, Keating is catapulted to international fame by winning the Cosmo-Slotnick competition for designing the "World's Most Beautiful Building." However, it is not a glory that

---

[2] *The Fountainhead*, pp. 23–24.

Keating could claim as his own, for he had not won the competition alone. He had asked for Roark's anonymous help once again.

Why did Roark assist Peter with the competition? Because he was generous? No, it was because some aspects of the building that Peter had designed posed an intellectual challenge to Roark, and that challenge stirred Roark's interest. Roark desired no recognition for his involvement. Perhaps he even loathes to see his name attached to a building that is the product of compromise. However, Roark's love for solving architectural problems prompted him to suggest changes in Keating's design that vastly improved the final product. Ironically, the rave reviews for Keating's winning design emphasize "the brilliant skill and simplicity . . . the clean, ruthless efficiency . . . the ingenious economy of space . . ." all tempered and made acceptable by the inclusion of a Renaissance façade.[3] What society would not accept from an innovator like Roark, it was willing to receive from a second-hander like Keating.

Meanwhile, Howard Roark continues to struggle. Even though he receives requests for a number of preliminary architectural drawings and actually prepares plans for several buildings, he fails to secure enough contracts to stay in business. Part of the reason for his failure is his steadfast adherence to the artistic integrity of his designs. Despite great financial stress and professional need, Roark remains true to his judgment. Does he consider himself a selfless martyr? Far from it. After turning down a contract that he desperately needed, Roark says, "That was the most selfish thing you've ever seen a man do."[4] Out of money and out of time, Roark leaves the architectural world and becomes a common quarry worker.

Connecticut. The air is filled with the staccato sound of jackhammers interrupted only by the deafening roar of dynamite. Francon's granite quarry bustles with activity. This is where Roark has come to perform an honest day's work—for a season. A rock is a rock, and the raw steel of hammer and chisel lay in his hands. This is reality. There would be no need for compromises here. By coincidence, this is also where Francon's daughter, Dominique, has come

---

[3] *The Fountainhead*, p. 189.
[4] *The Fountainhead*, p. 198.

to live in her father's country home. Disillusioned by the absence of rational men in the world, this beautiful and intelligent young woman has come to Connecticut to rest and to escape. One day, she visits her father's granite quarry and discovers Howard Roark. From the moment their eyes meet, it is clear what they mean to each other.

> "Why do you always stare at me?" [Dominique] asked sharply. . . .
> "For the same reason you've been staring at me," [replied Roark.]
> ". . . [I]t would be better if you stopped looking at me when I come here. It might be misunderstood."
> "I don't think so."[5]

By the time Dominique meets Roark at this point in the story, she has already become a creature of emotional repression.[6] She has given up on life and the hope of ever finding beauty and perfection in an irrational world. When she does find something that approximates beauty and perfection, she loathes sharing it with anyone because it hurts her to think that such perfection has been seen and touched and appreciated by the imperfect and the irrational. That explains why she destroys a statuette of the Greek god Helios earlier in the story. She does it so that no one would ever gaze upon its beauty again. Now here was Howard Roark in the flesh. How would Dominique respond to a man who represented perfection? It is ironic that love would come to her in a twisted way—in a passionate, but rape-like encounter with Roark.

Soon afterwards, Roark receives the opportunity he has been waiting for. Roger Enright, a multimillionaire, asks Roark to design his new house. Roark abruptly leaves Connecticut and Dominique in order to pursue this possibility. However, the subsequent debut of the Enright House does not bring the lasting success that Roark had hoped for, and life settles into the same old pattern. There are occasional breakthroughs, but on the whole, jobs remain scarce. Through

---

[5] *The Fountainhead*, pp. 208–209.
[6] Ronald Merrill, *The Ideas of Ayn Rand*, pp.48–49; *The Fountainhead*, pp. 144–145.

the years, Roark struggles to succeed. During this period, Rand explores and reveals Howard's character even as she reveals the inner workings of the man who most zealously opposes him: Ellsworth Toohey.

Ellsworth Toohey writes for the Wynand newspaper, the *New York Banner*, and his column, "One Small Voice," gives him enormous power to shape and mold public opinion. Rand characterizes him as a preacher of collectivism and altruism. Through Toohey, Rand illustrates how ideas can enslave a society. She shows how Toohey gains that power over the masses by destroying the self-esteem and confidence of individuals.

> I shall rule. . . . If you learn how to rule one single man's soul, you can get the rest of mankind. It's the soul, Peter, the soul. . . . It must be broken. Drive a wedge in, get your fingers on it—and the man is yours. . . . Make man feel small. . . . Kill integrity. . . . Preach selflessness. Tell man that he must live for others. Tell men that altruism is the ideal.[7]

Now it is clear why Toohey has to destroy Roark. As long as one independent and unsubmissive man remains alive, he threatens Toohey's reign. Therefore, Toohey uses whatever influence he has, both public and private, to keep Roark from succeeding as an architect. But Roark doesn't even grant Toohey the satisfaction of distracting him. When Toohey asks, "Mr. Roark, we're alone here. Why don't you tell me what you think of me?" Howard replies, "But, I don't think of you."[8]

However, Toohey isn't the only person who is trying to defeat Roark. Dominique also struggles against him but for very different reasons. Experience has taught her that rationality, integrity, and beauty have no chance in an irrational world. Because of her great love for Howard, Dominique wants to see her beloved removed from the world of architecture, where compromise and envy would always be part of his life. It would be better for him to work in

---

[7] *The Fountainhead*, p. 636.
[8] *The Fountainhead*, p. 389.

some other capacity—in a mundane job that posed few challenges to his moral or intellectual integrity. Perhaps he could return to work at the quarry. At least they would be free to live and to love.[9] But Roark was never one to shrink back from challenges; otherwise, Dominique would not have loved him so.

Several years have passed since Peter Keating's triumph at the Cosmo-Slotnick competition. However, Keating is now slipping professionally. He desperately needs another success to boost his image. Now, he is given the opportunity to submit a workable design for Cortlandt Homes, a low-cost building project for the poor and underprivileged. None of the other architects have succeeded in meeting the efficiency standards within the financial constraints demanded by the project. Cortlandt Homes looms as a tantalizing puzzle, and the person who solves the riddle would win instant recognition and eternal gratitude from the public. In desperation, Keating again asks for Roark's help. Roark agrees to design the building for Keating; however, his motivation is neither to help Keating, nor the poor. Neither reason is sufficient inducement for Roark. Roark accepts the job because he *wants* to do it and because the task represents a supreme challenge to his abilities. He wants to see *his* design built. That the homes would benefit the poor was of secondary importance.

Roark agrees to help Peter Keating on one condition: Keating could take the credit, but the building has to be constructed as designed. No alteration is permitted. Despite his pledge to Roark, Keating eventually succumbs to pressure from the other architects on the advisory committee and accedes to certain deviations from the original design. An alteration in the façade here, the addition of a balcony there, and soon the artistic integrity of the building is lost. Roark takes matters into his own hands and dynamites the not-yet-completed building complex. After all, it is his creation and the contract has been violated. Even though the poor desperately need the building, it seems to Roark that their needs do not justify a demand on his mind that results in the theft and violation of his efforts. "It is said that I have destroyed the home of the

---

[9] *The Fountainhead*, pp. 465–467.

destitute. It is forgotten that but for me the destitute could not have had this particular home," says Roark.[10] The crime results in a dramatic trial pitting the rights of society against the rights of the individual.

In the end, Roark is cleared of *moral* wrongdoing. (The civil matter of repaying the cost of the demolished project was considered a different issue.) But of course, Roark has to win. In the words of Henry Cameron, Roark's mentor:

> And I know that if you carry these words through to the end, it will be a victory, Howard, not just for you, but for something that should win, that moves the world—and never wins acknowledgment. It will vindicate so many who have fallen before you, who have suffered as you will suffer.[11]

Roark stands for the inviolable rights to his own mind, and triumphs.

Atlas Shrugged

Atlas Shrugged begins by asking, "Who is John Galt?" This question catches most readers off guard. Did Ayn Rand intend this as a gimmick? Or was this Rand's version of an often-repeated curse with a religious connotation. The book jacket hints at part of the truth. "This is the story of a man who said he would stop the motor of the world—and did. Is he a destroyer or a liberator?"[12]

The theme of *Atlas Shrugged* is the role of man's mind in existence. What would happen, Rand asks, if the men of intelligence and productive ability were to vanish? The analogy is drawn from the story of Atlas, the Greek mythological giant who bore the world on his shoulders. What would happen to the world if Atlas were to shrug? The answer is obvious.

Rand begins by introducing us to the Taggart and d'Anconia families. Taggart Transcontinental Railroads is the nation's great-

---

[10] *The Fountainhead*, p. 685.
[11] *The Fountainhead*, p. 694.
[12] *Atlas Shrugged*, book jacket.

est railroad. The two Taggart children, James and Dagny, and their close friend, Eddie Willers, grow up to assume responsibility for the railroad their ancestors had built. However, James could not be more different from Dagny and Eddie in his approach to life and to the operation of the railroad. James Taggart is an incompetent railroad president and a politician who manipulates people and swindles favors. He is what Rand calls a "pull-peddler." In contrast, Dagny and Eddie act with intelligence and competence; they are the genuine leaders of their beloved and besieged railroad. Rand takes us back to their childhood—their formative years. During those summer months on the Taggart estate, we are also introduced to Francisco Domingo Carlos Andres Sebastián d' Anconia, a close childhood friend of both Dagny and Eddie and heir to the world's greatest copper empire.

The values and attitudes that these four children display during their early years laid the groundwork for the kind of people that they were to become. Even as a youth, James Taggart despised achievement. He appears more concerned about "spiritual" things, while Dagny and Francisco appear to care only about the material realm. At least, that is the way the conventional thinking of our culture would make us believe. The following exchange is typical of their differences. James asks Francisco once: "Don't you ever think of anything but d'Anconia Copper? It seems to me that there are other things in the world."

To which Francisco replies, "Let others think about them."[13]

Francisco, Dagny, and Eddie lead adventurous lives during their summer months together. They explore junkyards, build elevators, and steal rides on trains. While having fun, they are educating and positioning themselves to become the future leaders of industry who will bear the burdens and responsibilities of the world just as Atlas also bore the earth on his shoulders. Growing up together, a romantic relationship eventually develops between Francisco and Dagny. They consummate that love one summer during Francisco's college years.

---

[13] *Atlas Shrugged*, p. 95.

After his father's death, Francisco assumes control of d'Anconia Copper. Despite his business success, he grows visibly preoccupied as a result of some disturbing information given to him by a friend he had met while in college. At Patrick Henry University, Francisco had befriended two other students: Ragnar Danneskjöld and another man whose identity is later revealed as John Galt. After graduation, the three friends pursued different careers, but they continued to nurture a deep friendship. John Galt worked as a physicist-inventor-engineer at the Twentieth Century Motor Company. When the founder of the company dies, his liberal heirs take over and impose a new management philosophy based on Marxism and socialism. However, no one voices any objections to the policy change except Galt. At the end of a company meeting, Galt finally had enough. He rises to proclaim that he will put an end to altruism once and for all by stopping the motor of the world.[14] It is as though the altruist is saying: The man of the mind with productive ability is the enemy, and we want to enslave him for our purposes. And John Galt answers: I will take him out of your way.

Thus Galt is the first to understand the precarious state of the world and the destructive influence of altruism. He communicates this newfound revelation to his friends, Ragnar and Francisco, and their former philosophy professor, Hugh Akston. He invites them to join him in a strike—a strike that would gradually involve the withdrawal of many productive men from the world. For Galt believes that the sanction of the victims—the concession by the men of ability to the idea that their lives belong to others—is what makes the morality of altruism work. Galt's task involves educating these special men and inviting them to no longer sanction the ideas that work to their own destruction. However, the timing of the invitation has to be perfect. Only men who have been pushed to the limit by the looters and the altruists would be sufficiently receptive to Galt's message and be willing to join the strike.

Moreover, Galt and his friends would have to choose their course cautiously if they want to avoid detection. Galt finds new work as a common laborer, but he places himself in a strategic position to ob-

---

[14] *Atlas Shrugged*, p. 626.

serve and discover which key figures should be approached and invited to withdraw from the world. Bankers like Midas Mulligan, composers like Richard Halley, industrialists, writers, and neurosurgeons soon begin retiring and vanishing from society. At first, their disappearance goes unnoticed, but over years, civilization begins to crumble in their absence. John Galt is at work as both destroyer and liberator, the avenging angel and savior of the world.

Ragnar takes a different path. He becomes a pirate on the open seas, confiscating the cargo from American welfare-relief ships destined for the ports of foreign socialist states. This cargo, he believes, represents stolen goods taken from productive members of society to fatten the cache of looters and moochers. Ragnar characterizes himself as the antitype of Robin Hood and what that medieval character has come to mean in our society. Instead of taking from the rich to give to the poor, Ragnar takes back from the thieving poor what rightfully belongs to the rich and productive.

Of the three friends, Francisco has to be the most cautious. He has a great copper empire in his hands. If he simply resigns from his company, the wealth of his industrial empire could sustain the socialist machinery for years. Consequently, he has no alternative but to destroy his assets systematically. However, if he dismantles d'Anconia Copper too quickly, his plans might be discovered. The solution? He would play the part of an irresponsible heir squandering the wealth left to him by his ancestors. The most difficult aspect of his theatrics is that he cannot reveal his intentions to Dagny, the woman he loves. For as yet, her understanding and experience of the issues involved are insufficient to bring her into the strike. With great anguish and suffering, Francisco leaves Dagny without explanation and begins to play the part of a playboy. Disillusioned and heartbroken, Dagny nevertheless continues with her work at the railroad and rises to the rank of vice president in charge of operations. Eventually, business ventures bring her into contact with Henry Rearden, a steel industrialist who supplies the rails for Taggart Transcontinental.

Rearden is already married, but unhappily so. His wife, Lillian, is a person of spiritual sensitivity in the likeness of James Taggart.

Her hatred of all things material causes her to despise even her husband and his business accomplishments. Consequently, their marriage has become a sham. Only Rearden's sense of honor regarding his marriage vows keeps their relationship intact and prevents him from initially acting on his romantic feelings toward Dagny Taggart.

Meanwhile, Dagny and Rearden have become engaged in a desperate race to build a railroad branch to Colorado. Ironically, they call it the John Galt Line. Against seemingly insurmountable odds, they complete the construction on time and begin supplying desperately needed transportation to the nation's most productive region. The first run of the Taggart Comet on that stretch of rail is described vividly and brilliantly by Rand. The reader feels the rush of excitement and the rhythm of the train as it travels at one hundred miles per hour. And on the night of their triumph, Rearden and Dagny consummate their desire for each other—a fitting celebration of their achievement.

After the success of the John Galt Line, Rearden and Dagny continue their affair. They take a well-deserved vacation together traveling through the countryside. One day, they happen upon the deserted factory of the Twentieth Century Motor Company and discover the dilapidated remnants of a mysterious motor. The motor had been designed to convert atmospheric static electricity into useful energy at virtually no cost. Who could have invented such a motor? Why was it left to rust and decay? Will they be able to reconstruct it? Dagny has the motor transferred to a vault and hires a promising young scientist named Quentin Daniels to reconstruct it.

Meanwhile, men of the mind continue to disappear from the world. With each succeeding economic disaster, the looters issue new government regulations that only make matters worse. Ragnar continues his piracy while Francisco works to dismantle his empire. James Taggart marries a waitress out of pity, not love.

In the midst of this fascinating and complex plot, Rand effectively interjects philosophical ideas. For example, at James Taggart's wedding, a woman of high social status glibly comments that "money is the root of all evil." This invites Francisco d'Anconia to defend money as the root of all good.[15] Later, Francisco engages Rearden in a conversation about the morality of altruism and contrasts it with the morality of rational self-interest. He even finds opportunity to speak of romantic love as an act of self-exaltation, not self-denial.[16] As a result, Francisco and Rearden grow in mutual understanding.

Despite the temporary success of the John Galt Line, Taggart Transcontinental continues its decline. Dagny grows weary and withdraws to a cabin in the forests of Woodstock, which bears some resemblance to Thoreau's Walden Pond. Francisco, believing the time has come for Dagny to join the strike, approaches her. As he broaches the subject, the radio broadcasts news of a major disaster on the Taggart Railroad System, and Dagny feels compelled to return and save her railroad. Francisco never has a chance to finish his appeal.

Soon afterwards, Dagny receives a letter of resignation from Quentin Daniels. She senses that Daniels will be the next man to disappear from earth—to be reclaimed by the destroyer. Miraculously, Dagny is able to reach Daniels by phone, and he promises to wait until they can meet personally. But she arrives in Utah too late. John Galt has already claimed his next victim. Galt and Daniels are taking off in Galt's monoplane even as Dagny arrives. Dagny manages to secure another plane and follow them into a secret valley in the mountains of Colorado. There, the people on strike have formed a new society called Atlantis.

Atlantis seems like heaven. After crashing her plane in the valley and regaining consciousness, Dagny opens her eyes and sees the face of John Galt. It is the face of the ideal man she has always dreamed of. During her monthlong stay in the valley, Dagny learns much. She begins to grasp the philosophical issues that are driving the world to destruction, and her personal life also begins to sort itself out. Francisco, as Dagny discovers, has never been a playboy; he has been faithful to her. However, Dagny now loves John Galt, and she cannot give him up for either Francisco or Rearden. To do so would be an act of self-immolation.

---

[15] *Atlas Shrugged*, pp. 387–391.
[16] *Atlas Shrugged*, p. 460.

At the end of her month in Atlantis, Dagny remains unconvinced that the world should be forsaken and permitted to self-destruct. The men of Atlantis allow her to return to the world because she entered the valley as a "scab," as one uninvited and unconverted. Galt follows her back into the world to watch over her. Dagny wonders where he watches her from. Eventually, she discovers his name on the payrolls of her own company. One night, in the subterranean caverns of the Taggart Railroad terminals, they find each other and make love.

Meanwhile, the world crisis continues, and governments turn to the airwaves to allay the fears of the people. One evening, as the world gathers by television and radio to hear a government report on the world crisis, Galt interrupts all frequencies of the communication spectrum and overrides the official broadcast. "This is John Galt speaking." In a dramatic monologue, he offers an explanation for the erosion of civilization and attributes it to the morality of altruism and the philosophy of irrationalism. Galt explains his view of life and offers his philosophy as the antidote to the prevailing worldview. He describes a world grounded in reality, where reason is the only method of gaining knowledge and dealing with other men, and where morality is based on the virtue of rational self-interest. In conclusion, he invites men everywhere to remain victims of altruism no longer:

> The world you desired can be won, it exists, it is real, it is possible, it's yours. But to win it requires your total dedication and a total break with the world of your past, with the doctrine that man is a sacrificial animal who exists for the pleasure of others. . . . [Y]ours is the battle for any achievement, any value, any grandeur, any goodness, any joy that has ever existed on this earth.[17]

After this stunning announcement, the looters' government becomes hypervigilant in its search for John Galt. "Calling John Galt! . . . Can you hear us, John Galt?" The potential savior of the world is hailed on all frequencies. Surely, Galt can make their failed policies work. Dagny, in a moment of weakness, seeks out John

---

[17] *Atlas Shrugged*, p. 993.

Galt at his home, unaware that government agents have her under surveillance. As a result, Galt is captured and arrested.

The government attempts to install Galt as a puppet ruler over them. They want him to devise a plan that will forestall the disastrous consequences of their policies. But Galt refuses to cooperate. With few options left, they take him to the remote State Sciences Institute and torture him. Galt's friends rescue him in a daring raid. As they fly to safety, the lights of New York City suddenly go out. The twelve-year ordeal to stop the motor of the world is finally over. For Galt had once said to his companions that when the lights of New York go out they will know their task is complete. The blackout in New York symbolized the devastation taking place everywhere as Atlas shrugged.

The story concludes in the valley as Richard Halley's Fifth Concerto resonates from his piano.

> It was a symphony of triumph. The notes flowed up, they spoke of rising and they were the rising itself, they were the essence and the form of upward motion, . . . It was the song of an immense deliverance.[18]

Under the covering of this jubilant atmosphere, the former strikers begin work in their respective fields of expertise. Judge Narragansett considers the wording of a constitutional amendment that will protect economic liberty. Industrialists like Henry Rearden and Francisco d'Anconia and bankers like Midas Mulligan mastermind the rebuilding of a nation. The actress Kay Ludlow contemplates the film makeup she will use when she resumes her career. Ragnar Danneskjöld opens a treatise by Aristotle and ponders the ancient ideas that will be important in protecting the new world.

At the edge of the valley, John Galt and Dagny Taggart stand together looking into the night. With his hand, Galt traces the sign of the dollar over the expanse and says, "The road is cleared. We are going back to the world."[19]

---

[18] *Atlas Shrugged*, p. 1083.
[19] *Atlas Shrugged*, p. 1084.

3

SELF-ESTEEM, CONFIDENCE, AND HUMAN WORTH

There is only one source of authentic self-confidence: reason.

Ayn Rand, *The New Left*

"You think you're good, don't you?" [Francisco] asked.
"I always did," [Dagny] answered defiantly, without turning.

Atlas Shrugged

Thou hast made [man] a little lower than God, and dost crown him with glory and majesty!

Psalm 8:5

The thief comes only to steal, and kill, and destroy; I came that they might have life, and might have it abundantly.

John 10:10

C onfidence. Like sunlight signaling the start of a new day, it draws us and warms us. The heroes of *Atlas Shrugged* exhibit a confidence and rationality that appeals to many readers, especially the young. Early in the story, Ayn Rand vividly portrays the childlike innocence and adventuresome spirit of Dagny Taggart and Francisco d'Anconia.[1] It is not difficult to understand why many of Rand's admirers want to be like them. Francisco's character, in particular, resonated with me. Without his parents' permission, he shipped out at the age of twelve as a cabin boy on a freighter. Three months passed before Francisco was found. However, he was not disciplined for his actions; instead, his father merely asked if Francisco had performed his job well. Every boy dreams of an adventure on high seas without the risk of punishment.

One summer afternoon at the Taggart family estate, Francisco and Dagny built an elevator using a complex system of pulleys. Dagny's father examined Francisco's blueprints for the elevator only to discover that he had somehow invented a primitive version of differential equations. As if his intellectual acumen was not enough, Francisco excelled in sports too. On his first try at baseball, he hit a home run. There appeared to be no limit to what this boy wonder could do.

One story, it seems to me, exemplified Francisco's prodigious ability and quiet confidence. It was young James Taggart's birthday. He had just received a motorboat as a present but was having trouble learning to handle the machine. After exhausting the patience of his instructor, James snapped at Francisco, "Do you think you can do it any better?"

Francisco replied simply, "I can do it." The challenge was on. James and the instructor stepped off the boat for a moment onto the dock. Francisco exchanged places with them and briefly ex-

---

[1] *Atlas Shrugged*, pp. 92–93.

amined the controls. Before the instructor could reboard, Francisco had launched the motorboat out of the docks. The wind whistled in his ears as he skillfully guided the craft across the lake. Truly, "Francisco could do anything he undertook, he could do it better than anyone else, and he did it without effort."[2]

In contrast to remarkable heroes like Francisco, Rand also created twisted, irrational villains and timid victims—souls trapped in an existence of their own making. They seem almost subhuman, unconscious of their own creative potential and desirous of limiting others to the same level of existence. In *The Fountainhead*, we are introduced to such personalities. Peter Keating, for example, was the architect who forever sought the approval of others, constantly borrowed the ideas of colleagues, but never broke forth in confidence. He falls prey to Ellsworth Toohey, who knows only too well that the self-deprecating message he preaches to the likes of Keating is what permits him—Toohey—to ultimately control and manipulate people.

In contrast, Howard Roark was made of different stuff. He would not allow his mind to be manipulated by others. Eventually, he stood trial for believing that his life and ideas belonged to him and no one else. Roark was prosecuted for demolishing a housing project that had been conceived and designed by him but expropriated and defiled by others.

In his own defense, Roark argues:

Thousands of years ago, the first man discovered how to make fire. He was probably burned at the stake he had taught his brothers to light. He was considered an evildoer who had dealt with a demon mankind dreaded. . . . He had left them a gift they had not conceived and he had lifted darkness off the earth. . . . That man, the unsubmissive and first, stands in the opening chapter of every legend mankind has recorded about its beginning. . . . Adam was condemned to suffer—because he had eaten the fruit of the tree of knowledge.[3]

---

[2] *Atlas Shrugged*, p. 93.
[3] *The Fountainhead*, p. 679.

The conflict between the individual and society is a recurrent theme in Rand's works. The idea that the brilliant individual has to be sacrificed for the good of others was repugnant to her, and she identified that monstrous idea as *altruism*.

Altruism and Christianity: The Missing Link

Ayn Rand defines altruism as follows:

> The basic principle of altruism is that man has no right to exist for his own sake, that service to others is the only justification of his existence, and that self-sacrifice is his highest moral duty, virtue and value.[4]

For Rand, altruism doesn't mean merely helping other people. It means the sacrifice of a higher value for the sake of a lesser value, the sacrifice of oneself to others. According to her, the statists, collectivists, socialists, and fascists all advocate the morality of altruism. They do not hesitate to sacrifice individuals or whole nations to accomplish their objective. That is why civilization is on the brink of disaster. Howard Roark put his finger on the problem when he said, "The world is perishing from an orgy of self-sacrificing."[5]

If altruism is the problem, what then is the solution? Perhaps a change of morality is in order. Indeed, Rand believed she had found the antidote to altruism in her morality of rational self-interest. She called it the virtue of selfishness. Rand argued that each man is an end in himself and that "the achievement of his own happiness is man's highest moral purpose."[6] She would have us abide by the oath that John Galt took on the day he began his quest to stop the motor of the world:

> I swear—by my life and my love of it—that I will never live for the sake of another man, nor ask another man to live for mine.[7]

---

[4] "Faith and Force: The Destroyers of the Modern World," *Philosophy: Who Needs It*, p. 74.
[5] *The Fountainhead*, p. 686.
[6] "The Objectivist Ethics," *The Virtue of Selfishness*, p. 27.
[7] *Atlas Shrugged*, p. 993.

Many of Rand's insights into the workings of collectivism and altruism—at least what she meant by altruism—are quite right. Collectivism does deny the rights of the individual and sacrifices them in the name of society. However, Rand goes a step further by including Christianity under the banner of altruism. According to her, Christianity, like all altruistic philosophies, strikes at man's individuality and self-worth for the purpose of controlling and manipulating him. Therefore, any differences between Christianity and collectivism are ultimately unimportant and incidental. The two ideologies are merely different sides of the same coin.[8]

Rand carefully crafted her fiction to forge and reinforce this link between Christianity and altruism in the mind of her readers. Her villains spew forth volumes of collectivist rhetoric and season it with the salt of religious jargon. For example, James Taggart chastises Francisco d'Anconia for not paying more attention to "spiritual" things, all the while Taggart himself is plotting the destruction of his competitors through the use of government regulations. Henry Rearden's mother voices her concern over his preoccupation with work and complains about his neglect of family and community. "I knew he'd grow up to be the most selfish creature on God's earth," she said.[9] Perhaps no character more exemplifies the classic preacher of faith and of altruism than Ellsworth Toohey. He was the incarnation of pure evil. For Rand, Toohey is the consummate example of a class of people she called Witch Doctors.

In the opening essay of her book *For the New Intellectual*, Rand explains that human beings, by nature, require an integrated view of life. Whether they understand that need or not is irrelevant. Subconsciously or consciously, a person will eventually adopt a philosophy. The Witch Doctor's genius is that he provides a complete system of thought, even though it is an evil philosophy calling for self-sacrifice and self-abnegation. However, in order to persuade men to accept such a philosophy, the Witch Doctor has to first destroy

---

[8] "The Objectivist Ethics," *The Virtue of Selfishness*, pp. 14–15.
[9] *Atlas Shrugged*, p. 42.

their sense of self-worth. Once an individual's sense of identity and self-esteem has been erased, he may be persuaded to reject his own reason and follow the dictates of others.[10] And one of the methods that the Witch Doctor uses to accomplish this is guilt.

Nathaniel Branden, Rand's former colleague, once called this process of inducing guilt a strategy in brainwashing. In *The Psychology of Self-Esteem*, he writes:

> [This strategy works] on the premise that a guilt-ridden mind is less inclined to critical, independent judgment, and is more susceptible to indoctrination and intellectual manipulation. Guilt subdues self-assertiveness. The principle involved is not a new discovery. Religion has been utilizing it for many, many centuries.[11]

Thus, both Rand and Branden attribute the evils of altruism and collectivism to religion and Christianity. Any sense that I had in my teenage years that religious beliefs could be beneficial began to evaporate under the steady barrage of this kind of writing. The last vestiges of that belief disappeared after I read *The Ominous Parallels*, written by Leonard Peikoff, Ayn Rand's intellectual heir. It was a book that Rand had recommended with great enthusiasm.

The History of Altruism

In *The Ominous Parallels*, Peikoff attempts to document the similarities between the Weimar Republic (the pre-Nazi German State) and the current political situation in the United States. First, he describes how the ideas of altruism had come to dominate the German cultural psyche over a period of centuries. This cultural permeation by altruism, according to him, was a precondition for Hitler's subsequent success in mass indoctrination.

How did this process begin? According to Peikoff, the altruistic mentality had its roots in religion. Augustine, a key figure in the formation of Western thought, had written, "And all that you

---

[10] *For the New Intellectual*, pp. 17–18.
[11] *The Psychology of Self-Esteem*, p. 142.

[God] asked of me was to deny my own will and accept yours."[12] Martin Luther, the leader of the Reformation in Germany, also urged self-denial and obedience. Allegedly, these early attempts to inculcate blind obedience crescendoed over the centuries. Peikoff claims, "Christianity prepared the ground. It paved the way for modern totalitarianism. . . ."[13] According to Peikoff, Immanuel Kant, the philosopher who formulated the most consistent philosophical theory of self-sacrifice, "is the heir and perpetuator of centuries of Christianity. . . ."[14] Christianity, it seems, cultivated a people who would follow Hitler blindly.

There is no doubt that Peikoff documents some challenging similarities between religion and Nazism. Indeed, Hitler acknowledged, "Faith is harder to shake than knowledge. . . ."[15] Consequently, he organized the Nazi movement by emulating the Roman Catholic Church-State.[16] Hitler also encouraged his followers to view him as divine. Goering, one of Hitler's top generals, said:

> Just as the Roman Catholic considers the Pope infallible in all matters concerning religion and morals, so do we National Socialists believe with the same inner conviction that for us the Leader [Hitler] is in all political and other matters concerning the national and social interests of the people simply infallible.[17]

Some of Hitler's followers actually claimed, "Adolf Hitler is the true Holy Ghost!"[18] Obviously, if Hitler was divine, no one could

---

[12] *The Ominous Parallels*, p. 69.

[13] *The Ominous Parallels*, p. 69.

[14] *The Ominous Parallels*, p. 76.

[15] *Mein Kampf*, pp. 337–338 as quoted in *The Ominous Parallels*, p. 49.

[16] It should be noted that Roman Catholicism differs significantly from biblical Christianity as taught by the Protestant Reformation. Interested readers may wish to consider the fundamental biblical issues that distinguished the Reformers from the Roman Catholic Church-State.

[17] Herman Goering, *Germany Reborn* (London, 1934), as quoted in Melvin Rader, *No Compromise* (New York: Macmillan, 1939), pp. 191–192 as quoted in *The Ominous Parallels*, p. 50.

[18] Eugene Lyons, "Dictators into Gods" (*American Mercury*, March 1939), as quoted in Peter Viereck, *Metapolitics* (New York: Capricorn, 1965), p. 289 as quoted in *The Ominous Parallels*, p. 50.

disagree with him. "[T]he wishes and the selfishness of the individual must appear as nothing and submit."[19] After centuries of
being indoctrinated with the ideas of altruism, the German people
recognized, as Hitler did, that the supremacy of the Aryan race
lies in its willingness to sacrifice everything for the Fatherland.[20]
And that meant, of course, acquiescence to Hitler's plans for the
Third Reich.

Thus Peikoff attributes the atrocities of Nazism to the altruism
that Christianity had earlier taught the German people. If that were
indeed the case, was there any good to be found in Christianity?
Yes, but Peikoff attributes any beneficial elements in Christianity
to the influence of the Greeks.[21] For example, Aristotle, who lived
three centuries before Christ, had taught that man should be a
lover of reason and a lover of self. By implication then, Christianity's
teaching that men should love their neighbors as themselves must
have been derived from Aristotle.

However, it never occurred to Peikoff, or myself for that matter, that Moses had taught this concept of self-love and love for
others as a commandment of God over a thousand years before
Aristotle.[22] Christ's teachings owe nothing to Aristotle. However,
in Peikoff's mind, Christianity is an ethical system based on mixed
premises, and its inclination toward self-sacrifice outweighs any
positive view it has for self-love. As Peikoff explains, the medieval
moralist who accepted Christianity was caught in a contradiction:

> He urged man to forget his self—in order to save his (true) self;
> to do his duty, scorning personal happiness—in order to experi-
> ence the latter forever; to despise his own person, mind and
> body—yet love his neighbor as himself.[23]

True love for others, it seems, requires a man to ask his neighbor
to do as he had done—reject personal happiness. The Germans,

[19] *Mein Kampf* (no pages given) as quoted in *The Ominous Parallels*, p. 65.
[20] *Mein Kampf*, p. 297 as quoted in *The Ominous Parallels*, p. 66.
[21] *The Ominous Parallels*, pp. 68–69.
[22] Leviticus 19:18; Luke 10:27.
[23] *The Ominous Parallels*, p. 69.

indoctrinated with this concept of self-abnegation, were thus prepared to accept the dictatorship of Hitler.

Yet Peikoff also discerns a difference between the ethics that Jesus taught and the one taught by the philosophers of altruism.[24] (In this context, it should be noted that the philosopher Immanuel Kant was not a Christian.) First, Christian love does not seem to consist solely of self-denial but includes positive action toward others. Jesus had called for men to love God first and then to love their neighbors out of the context of that relationship with God. The modern philosophers gradually reversed this teaching and elevated the status of other men and society above God, thereby granting legitimacy to collectivism and totalitarianism. Inadvertently, Peikoff touches upon a major difference between Christianity and altruism that I was to understand fully only years later. Namely, who or what is the object of worship? Is it the Creator, or is it the creature—*e.g.,* society or other men?[25] Christian ethics is information revealed by God that prescribes moral conduct appropriate to man and to the governments instituted among men. Neither the individual nor society is sovereign. Both are God's creation and subject to his law. On the other hand, the ethics of altruism and totalitarianism was devised by philosophers who taught the priority of the state over individuals. Unfortunately, Peikoff did not pursue this line of inquiry. He assumed, as Rand did, that God and society were interchangeable and that the self-sacrificial elements of Christianity represented a slippery slope that could end only in evil. I too shared in that assumption and accepted Peikoff's conclusions uncritically. It was only years later that I began to appreciate the difference between Christianity and collectivism.

Indeed, the difference between Christianity and totalitarianism is significant, and one should not assume their similarity just because Hitler expressed admiration for the order of the Roman Catholic Church-State or because his followers called him the Holy Ghost. Hitler's own appreciation of the difference is underscored

---

[24] *The Ominous Parallels*, p. 70.
[25] See chapter 9 on morality and government.

by his comments at a special gathering shortly after the rise of the National Socialists to power in Germany. Herman Rauschning was present at the meeting and reports part of the conversation in his preface to *The Ten Commandments*, edited by Armin Robinson.[26] According to Rauschning, Hitler viewed Christianity as a Jewish sect, and he planned to stamp out Christianity just as he planned the eradication of the Jews. Hitler said, "After the destruction of Judaism, the extinction of Christian slave morals must follow logically. I shall know the moment when to confront, for the sake of the German people and the world, their Asiatic slave morals with our picture of the free man, the godlike man." Hitler wanted to abolish Christian morality and replace it with his own. He said he was waging war against "the curse of so-called morals, idolized to protect the weak from the strong in the face of the immortal law of battle, the great law of divine nature. Against the so-called ten commandments, against them we are fighting." Instead of submitting to the laws that a sovereign God had prescribed for all men, Hitler wanted to rule over his fellow man. He saw his fascism as a revolution against Christianity, not as a logical continuation of it. Thus, the difference between totalitarianism and Christianity is immense.

Not only did Peikoff fail to notice this disparity, but he also failed to report other historical facts that would have made any reader hesitant to accept his thesis that Christianity spawned Nazism. For example, how does Peikoff explain the formation of the Confessing Church in 1934 at the Barmen Synod? There, the regional German churches separated themselves from the national church; the latter had become an instrument of Hitler's fascist policies and no longer adhered to the message of the gospel.[27] The Nazis silenced and imprisoned a Protestant scholar and minister named Dietrich Bonhoeffer for attempting to expose the evils of the Nazi Reich. Eventually, Bonhoeffer was hanged for his role in an assassination attempt on Hitler.

---

[26] *The Ten Commandments*, pp. xi–xiii.

[27] Dietrich Bonhoeffer, *Meditating on the Word*, translated by David McI. Gracie (Cambridge, MA: Cowley Publications, 1986), p. 29.

Other examples abound. How do we explain the likes of Corrie ten Boom and the Protestant Huguenot villagers of Le Chambon, France, who rescued and evacuated Jews during the Second World War?[28] For their role in saving Jews, the Israeli government has acknowledged them and many others as "The Righteous among the Nations." Ten Boom and the villagers of Le Chambon all believed in the God of the Bible and did what they could to resist Hitler's plan of domination and genocide. If totalitarianism was the logical consequence of Christianity, these believers should have been among the first to join the ranks of the Gestapo. But they didn't, because they acknowledged another sovereign. Their concern for other people flowed from their understanding of God's word and his love for people. A church bulletin printed at Le Chambon during Nazi occupation and Vichy rule contained this Scripture verse that served as a sober reminder of the truth. "If someone says, 'I love God,' and hates his brother, he is a liar; for the one who does not love his brother whom he has seen, cannot love God whom he has not seen."[29] Understanding this truth, these believers willingly risked their lives to save others. It is curious that Peikoff neglects to mention these heroes of Christianity. Whether it was due to ignorance or deliberate suppression of the historical facts, Peikoff's omission helped uninformed readers like myself make an unjustified mental link between Christianity and the unspeakable horrors of Auschwitz.

The Psychology of Altruism

While Peikoff illustrated the deleterious effect of Christianity on whole peoples, Nathaniel Branden focused on individuals. Several psychological case studies in his book *Breaking Free* were devoted to demonstrating the devastating psychological consequences of Christianity. The following excerpts are part of a

---

[28] See Corrie ten Boom, *The Hiding Place* (Uhrichsville, OH: Barbour Books, 1971) and the documentary film *Weapons of the Spirit*.
[29] 1 John 4:20; see *Weapons of the Spirit*.

conversation that Branden had with a young Roman Catholic man named Alfred.

> ALFRED: I remember my mother helping my brothers and sisters do their homework. If they didn't see something, she practically would beat it into them. She really knew how to swear.[30]
>
> ALFRED: What we were taught mostly was the virtue of humility. It's better to walk with your eyes looking down. Don't ask questions. Don't argue with your elders. Be super-respectful with the priest. . . . Or else you'll burn in hell.[31]
>
> BRANDEN: All right, close your eyes, take a deep breath and relax. You're talking to the priest right now. You're looking up at him. He's angry. What are you feeling?
>
> ALFRED: Like he's out to get me—no, not just him, but something else, something immense is out to get me, to hurt me or crush me or. . . .
>
> BRANDEN: What have you done wrong? What sin have you committed?
>
> ALFRED: Just the sin of being me, I guess. Like it was a sin to see too much, a sin to lift your eyes off the ground. . . .[32]
>
> ALFRED: Then your own sense of guilt and unworthiness works against you, undermines you, disarms you, makes you feel: Christ, I am a sinner, they were right, I'm no good, I'm contaminated, I'm unclean, I can't set myself against them, I can't fight them, I'm out of the race, I'm disqualified. . . . That's the trap, isn't it?[33]

The magnitude of the oppression that Alfred felt was genuine. Branden's presentation of stereotypical Roman Catholic oppression is something many of us have encountered. However, the question is not so much whether anyone has ever been abused

---

[30] *Breaking Free*, p. 28.
[31] *Breaking Free*, p. 31.
[32] *Breaking Free*, p. 32.
[33] *Breaking Free*, p. 37.

within certain churches as it is whether biblical Christianity actually teaches the exploitation and repression of people. Alfred's plight
is lamentable. However, it is obvious that neither his mother nor
his priest understood Christianity; otherwise, they would have
informed him of God's forgiveness and his power and promise to
restore. "'Come now, and let us reason together,' says the Lord,
'Though your sins are as scarlet, they will be as white as snow;
though they are red like crimson, they will be like wool.'"[34] If only
Alfred had known of Paul's writings. "There is therefore now no
condemnation for those who are in Christ Jesus."[35] Of course, I
never knew such verses exist either, and it was all too easy for me
to disregard Christianity on the grounds of the oppression by the
Roman Catholic Church. However, several experiences helped me
to see Christianity in a different light. In college, I met several
confident Christians whose character seemed quite at odds with
the picture that Objectivism had presented. One person, in particular, influenced me without ever speaking a word to me.

An Unconventional Christian

While in college, I had participated in some laboratory research
in the Department of Neurosurgery at The Johns Hopkins Medical
School. Through my mentor, Dr. Henry Brem, I became acquainted
with another neurosurgeon named Benjamin Carson. Even though
I never actually spoke with Dr. Carson, something about his presence and demeanor impressed me from the start; I was surprised
to learn that he was a Christian.

I knew his story from the articles that had appeared in the
medical school newspaper.[36] He grew up in the ghettos of Detroit,
went to Yale University, attended the University of Michigan Medical
School, and subsequently completed his neurosurgical training at

---

[34] Isaiah 1:18.

[35] Romans 8:1.

[36] See also *Gifted Hands: The Ben Carson Story* (Grand Rapids, MI: Zondervan,
1990). It should be noted, however, that the particular church to which Dr.
Carson belongs differs from the historic Protestant Reformed faith on a number of issues.

Hopkins. Still a young man in his early thirties, he had already become the chief of pediatric neurosurgery at Hopkins. One Saturday in September of 1987, he organized and led a multidisciplinary team in performing a historic operation that allowed the separation of Siamese twins joined at the back of the head.

Dr. Carson attributed his success in life to God's provision and love. He was always beaming; his face shone with confidence. Calm and soft-spoken; gentle with power. Nothing of the manipulative nature of Ellsworth Toohey or the secondhand intellect of Peter Keating. Now, I am not suggesting that Dr. Carson is perfect, but his strength and confidence exploded my stereotyped image of the Christian as weak and pathetic. It was an image that I had learned from Rand.

Objectivism had implied that a consistent Christian would be so overwhelmed by an evil and destructive philosophy that he could not possibly succeed in life as a productive, intelligent, and happy person. Christianity was based on faith and feelings as opposed to Objectivism, which was based on reason and facts.[37] However, I came to realize that I could not merely attribute the success of someone like Dr. Carson to *reason* and his failures to *faith* as Rand had a tendency to do in her psychological analysis of people. Either there was much more to this business of faith, or Benjamin Carson had coped with a massive contradiction, and incredibly well, at that.

A Crack in the Edifice

In fact, over the years, Ayn Rand occasionally hinted, perhaps unintentionally, at the existence of positive values in Christianity. But her tone was so overwhelmingly antitheistic and her positive comments on Christianity so brief and sporadic that the reader often fails to take note of them. When contrasting Kant's version of altruism with Christianity, Rand observes: "[Kant's] version of morality makes the Christian one sound like a healthy, cheerful,

---

[37] See chapter 8 on reason and reality for a thorough discussion of what reason and faith actually mean.

benevolent code of selfishness. Christianity merely told man to love his neighbor as himself; that's not exactly rational—but at least it does not forbid man to love himself."[38] Christianity: A code of selfishness? Coming from Rand, that seemed like an extraordinary admission. But there was more to come. In November of 1981, Rand delivered a speech at the New Orleans meeting of the National Committee for Monetary Reform. The title of the message was "The Sanction of the Victims."[39] In the question and answer period following, a member of the audience asked:

> What do you reply when someone says to you, "You hate the poor and disadvantaged, don't you?"

Rand replied:

> No one has ever come close enough to me to say such a thing. I don't hate the poor. I just don't think that they are the best things in life and that one should tailor everything for their convenience. And here I'd like to quote a really interesting person, if you've heard of him. The Reverend Ike. He is a black evangelist, and a remarkable one because he preaches not suffering and submission but success. And he tells his congregation that every man can succeed in what he understands—what he can do. Reverend Ike's statement about the poor is as follows: "The best way to help the poor is not to be one of them."

When I first heard that exchange, I was amused. What a remarkable and effective way to silence one's critics! But even then I was troubled by this thought. Should I as an atheist and an Objectivist expect a Christian minister to say anything as reasonable as that? Didn't that preacher know about Adam's fall in the Garden of Eden? Doesn't the Bible speak against life, self-esteem, and prosperity? Was that evangelist an aberration or was he typical of Christians? Where did he learn that message of success? Years later,

---

[38] "Faith and Force: The Destroyers of the Modern World," *Philosophy: Who Needs It*, p. 78.
[39] Tape on file with author.

when I began to investigate this subject, I made some startling discoveries. In fact, there were many more preachers of the same success message.

Norman Vincent Peale, who authored *The Power of Positive Thinking*, is perhaps one of the best known preachers of success. I mention him not as an endorsement of his work or beliefs, but like the Reverend Ike that Rand mentioned, he serves as a popular reference point for the possibility that a message of confidence, personal worth, and success may be found in the Bible. Consider these two well-known verses that Peale often refers to. "I can do all things through [Christ] who strengthens me."[40] "If God is for us, who is against us?"[41] Both propositions emphasize the power of the omnipotent Creator and Savior to provide immeasurable strength and confidence when he is invited into a situation of weakness and doubt.

Even non-Christian success books seem to borrow some biblical principles. For example, in *Think and Grow Rich*, Napoleon Hill expounds on the basic principles of success, some of which are drawn from the Bible.[42] However, the similarities between his teachings and Scripture end rather quickly. Hill's notion of faith as "a state of mind which can be induced by autosuggestion" is radically different from Christian teaching.[43] It would be a mistake to equate the self-confidence that Hill and some success teachers advocate with the confidence that a person gains when he has come to know God and is known by God.

Nevertheless, the Bible does speak of the confidence that a person may have in God. The often-repeated story of David serves as an outstanding Old Testament example. Because of his confidence in Almighty God, the shepherd boy David confronts Goliath, the

---

[40] Philippians 4:13.

[41] Romans 8:31.

[42] Here are two chapter titles from *Think and Grow Rich* that illustrate the Bible's influence on Hill: "Whatever the Mind of Man Can Conceive and Believe, It Can Achieve" is loosely based on the proverb "For as he thinks within himself, so he is" (Proverbs 23:7). "Both Poverty and Riches Are the Offspring of Thought" can be traced to the verse "Death and life are in the power of the tongue" (Proverbs 18:21).

[43] *Think and Grow Rich* (New York: Fawcett Crest, 1960), p. 52.

Philistine giant, without fear. David says to King Saul, "Let no man's heart fail on account of him; your servant will go and fight with this Philistine."[44] When Saul expresses doubt about David's abilities, David recounts the goodness and faithfulness of God. "The Lord who delivered me from the paw of the lion and from the paw of the bear, He will deliver me from the hand of this Philistine."[45] David proclaims what he believes. Then he meets Goliath in battle and defeats him.

This is a far cry from the pessimism and the evasion of responsibility that I had been taught to expect from Christians. In reading Rand, I had come to believe that Christianity reduced people to the state of Nathaniel Branden's patient Alfred. They felt like and confessed that they were nothing. Religion had made them believe they were less than nothing. Just as Alfred tells us much about himself by his words, Rand's fictional characters also reveal much by what they say. Rand's villains issue lengthy denials and excuses that both prophetically predict their failure and reveal the smallness of their souls. They never seem to tire of repeating the excuse: "But I couldn't help it." In contrast, Rand's heroes speak with confidence. "Let's find out. . . . Let's make it. . . . You'll have it. . . . I'll take responsibility for it." Indeed, the power of words is one of the ways in which Rand communicated the radiant confidence of her characters.[46] Yet, as we have seen, the Scriptures also summon Christians to courage and confidence. This is apparent in the words of Christ. "If you shall have faith as a mustard seed, . . . nothing shall be impossible to you."[47] "Behold, I have given you authority to tread upon serpents and scorpions, and over all the power of the enemy, and nothing shall injure you."[48] And as Paul

---

[44] 1 Samuel 17:32.

[45] 1 Samuel 17:37.

[46] Once, while a screenwriter was working with Ayn Rand on the teleplay for *Atlas Shrugged*, he added the word *perhaps* to something Dagny Taggart said. Ayn Rand shouted at him for destroying Dagny's character. Dagny "*always* knows what she's doing—she doesn't use words like 'perhaps' or 'maybe'" (Barbara Branden, *The Passion of Ayn Rand*, p. 390).

[47] Matthew 17:20.

[48] Luke 10:19.

said, "In all these things we overwhelmingly conquer through Him who loved us."[49] Optimism is what we should expect from people who hold fast to the teachings of Christ.

What can we conclude thus far? At the very *least*, the Scriptures contain statements that lend encouragement and confidence to readers. However, if we simply stopped at such an acknowledgment, we still would not have gotten to the heart of the problem. Despite having a few kind words for Christianity, Rand believed that Christianity originated and propagated the philosophy of altruism. She tells us plainly that Christianity despises the material realm. It preaches self-sacrifice and advocates self-abnegation. It is the morality of death.[50] And of course, when a reader of *Atlas Shrugged* is told that Christianity is unconcerned with life on earth and the well-being of individuals, he naturally discards it as a viable option. But is Rand's view of Christianity correct?

A Mistaken Interpretation

In the climactic speech given by John Galt in *Atlas Shrugged*, Rand outlines the Christian "mythology" of Original Sin as she understood it:

> What is the nature of the guilt that your teachers call his Original Sin? What are the evils man acquired when he fell from a state they consider perfection? Their myth declares that he ate the fruit of the tree of knowledge—he acquired a mind and became a rational being. It was the knowledge of good and evil—he became a moral being. He was sentenced to earn his bread by his labor—he became a productive being. He was sentenced to experience desire—he acquired the capacity of sexual enjoyment.[51]

---

[49] Romans 8:37.
[50] *Atlas Shrugged*, p. 950.
[51] *Atlas Shrugged*, p. 951.

The Christian doctrine of Original Sin allegedly attacked man:

- As a rational being—one whose eyes were opened after eating from the tree of knowledge;
- As a moral being—one who could now choose good and evil;
- As a productive being—one who had to work in order to live; and
- As a sexual being—one who had acquired, as a result of the Fall, the capacity for sexual enjoyment.

Furthermore, as John Galt observes:

> It is not his vices that their myth of man's fall is designed to explain and condemn, it is not his errors that they hold as his guilt, but the essence of his nature as man [acquired as a result of the Fall]. Whatever he was—that robot in the Garden of Eden, who existed without mind, without values, without labor, without love—he was not man.[52]

Unfortunately, Ayn Rand completely misunderstood the Christian account of creation and Original Sin, and she misrepresented the events that transpired in the Garden of Eden. Even if Rand considered Christianity a mythology, her interpretation of the Fall cannot be validated by any serious examination of the biblical text. A cursory reading of the first three chapters of Genesis reveals a rather different set of propositions.

- God created the universe and man.
- The Creator demonstrated his care and love for man in the design of his environment.
- Man was given dominion over the whole earth, and he had creative, intellectual, and productive abilities.

---

[52] *Atlas Shrugged*, pp. 951–952.

- God provided a suitable and comparable companion for man.
- Man and woman were to love and enjoy each other.
- Man had the ability to choose good and evil.
- God had a plan of redemption even when man chose to disobey.

First, the Christian God created the universe and blessed it. "And God saw that it was good."[53] He did not intend the earth to be a place of condemnation. From the most distant star to the most complex living being on earth, all of creation was intended as a blessing. "God saw all that He had made, and behold, it was very good."[54] Even "the gold of that land is good."[55] Moreover, it seems absurd that a God who harbored hostility toward earthly life would subsequently bless Abraham by making him exceedingly prosperous or by making his physical descendants as numerous as the stars.[56] Nor can Rand's view of Christianity as a morality of death explain why Jesus healed physical diseases, fed the five thousand, and changed water into wine at a marriage feast.[57] Even the commandment to honor one's father and mother comes with a promise of long life and blessing.[58] All of these benefits occurred in the physical realm. Hence, the God of Christianity does not despise the material realm.

The Creator made man in his image.[59] He provided a marvelous environment for man to live in and endowed him with the gift of rationality. In addition, man was given dominion over every creature. In naming the animals, he was merely exercising a small part of his creative and intellectual abilities.[60] Man also began to

---

[53] Genesis 1:10.
[54] Genesis 1:31.
[55] Genesis 2:12.
[56] Genesis 12:1–3; 13:2, 6; 15:5.
[57] Matthew 9:35; 14:16–21; John 2.
[58] Exodus 20:12.
[59] Genesis 1:26–28; Psalm 8:3–6.
[60] Genesis 2:19.

cultivate the garden that had been entrusted to him, but that was only the beginning. The assignment he received was to completely fill and subdue the earth, thereby bringing all of creation to its maximum fruitfulness. Adam could think, he had dominion, and he engaged in productive work.

God also fashioned a woman out of Adam himself. She would be a companion suitable and comparable to him.[61] The Creator gave them the ability to procreate new life and the capacity for joy and intimacy. "And God blessed them; and God said to them, 'Be fruitful and multiply.'"[62] "And they shall become one flesh."[63] Thus Adam had values. He and the woman God gave him had the capacity for joy, even sexual joy.

Moreover, man had the ability to choose. Concerning Original Sin, Rand was mistaken when she said, "If man is evil by birth, he has no will. . . ."[64] In contrast, Christianity plainly asserts that man has a will, but he uses it for evil. God had given man specific instructions, yet man consciously and willfully disobeyed. He sinned as one undeceived. The rebellion and Fall of man set in motion an alien order on earth. Even then, God had a plan to restore man to all of his intended glory. Indeed, the process of redemption began immediately when God himself sacrificed animals in order to provide clothing for the fallen couple and to atone for their sins.[65] The promise of ultimate redemption was given when God proclaimed that the seed of woman, the Messiah, would one day crush the serpent's head.[66]

Whoever that man was in the Garden, he was not a robot. He had a mind. He possessed values. He engaged in productive labor. And he had a loving relationship with his wife and his Creator. He was man, the crown jewel of God's creation.

---

[61] Genesis 2:18.
[62] Genesis 1:28.
[63] Genesis 2:24.
[64] *Atlas Shrugged*, p. 951.
[65] Genesis 3:21.
[66] Genesis 3:15.

The Source of Human Worth: A Contrast in Views

Thus it may be seen that Rand's description of Christianity as a morality of death is quite unfounded. Let us reconsider Rand's definition of altruism:

> The basic principle of altruism is that man has no right to exist for his own sake, that service to others is the only justification of his existence, and that self-sacrifice is his highest moral duty, virtue and value.[67]

I submit, if this definition of altruism is correct, then Christianity cannot be altruism. For Christianity as taught in the Scriptures has never considered man a sacrificial animal, with no value and no right to exist for his own sake. The story of creation in Genesis shows that God placed high value on man and filled his life with purpose and meaning. (Of note, it was the Canaanites, whom the Hebrews drove out of the Promised Land, who practiced the most hideous form of human sacrifice. In contrast, it was God who commanded the Jews to set themselves apart from the way of corruption that surrounded them.) Christianity does not call men to self-immolation, but to believe the truth of the Scriptures so that they might be reconciled to God through the redeeming work of Christ. And out of that understanding and love for God, they are given a new heart and mind with which they may begin to love their fellow man and restore God's kingdom here on earth. Living with an abiding love is hardly the same as existing as a sacrificial animal. C. S. Lewis explains the difference in his book *The Weight of Glory*:

> If you asked twenty good men today what they thought the highest of the virtues, nineteen of them would reply, Unselfishness. But if you had asked almost any of the great Christians of old, he would have replied, Love. You see what has happened? A negative term has been substituted for a positive, and this is of

---

[67] "Faith and Force: The Destroyers of the Modern World," *Philosophy: Who Needs It*, p. 74.

more than philological importance. The negative idea of Unself-ishness carries with it the suggestion not primarily of securing good things for others, but of going without them ourselves, as if our abstinence and not their happiness was the important point. I do not think this is the Christian virtue of Love. The New Testament has lots to say about self-denial, but not about self-denial as an end in itself. We are told to deny ourselves and to take up our crosses in order that we may follow Christ; and to nearly every description of what we shall ultimately find if we do so contains an appeal to desire. If there lurks in most modern minds the notion that to desire our own good and earnestly to hope for the enjoyment of it is a bad thing, I submit that this notion has crept in from Kant and the Stoics and is no part of the Christian faith.[68]

Thus, when Rand describes Christianity as the equivalent of altruism, she is merely creating a straw man. Securing the good of others does not imply that one's own happiness cannot be secured at the same time. As the Scriptures say, "You shall love your neighbor as yourself."

Perhaps it is with this verse that Objectivism and Christianity can begin a dialogue. Rand often pointed out that a person's attitudes and actions depend on his view of himself. The crucial question in reference to the proposition "You shall love your neighbor as yourself" then becomes: How do you love yourself? The Objectivist and Christian views may be contrasted here.

Ayn Rand sees man as essentially a trader. The Objectivist morality of rational self-interest requires man to live as a trader in the realm of values and relationships just as he also lives as a trader in the realm of economics. John Galt makes this absolutely clear:

We, who live by values, not by loot, are traders, both in matter and in spirit. A trader is a man who earns what he gets and does not give or take the undeserved. A trader does not ask to be paid for his failures, nor does he ask to be loved for his flaws. . . . Just as he does not give his work except in trade for material values,

---

[68] *The Weight of Glory*, p. 3.

so he does not give the values of his spirit—his love, his friend-ship, his esteem—except in payment and in trade for human virtues, in payment for his own selfish pleasure, which he re-ceives from men he can respect.[69]

However, if we accept this view, then our primary focus in all relationships will be to ask: What does this person have to offer me? What if a person offers no values whatsoever to me? Am I not then justified in treating him indifferently? Why should I offer a person any semblance of respect until he demonstrates himself worthy of respect? What if he represents a negative value to me? What shall I do then? Examples from *The Fountainhead* and *Atlas Shrugged* illustrate what our response ought to be. When Ellsworth Toohey used his influence to deny Howard Roark professional op-portunities, Toohey was exhibiting pure evil. Toohey sought a nega-tive response from Roark by asking, "Why don't you tell me what you think of me?"

Roark replied simply, "But I don't think of you."[70]

Or consider Henry Rearden's opinion of the likes of James Taggart: "People like Jim Taggart just clutter up the world."[71] Of course, Rand would say that the evil exhibited by such characters deserves such a response. However, the tone of the dialogues suggests the intrinsic unworthiness of people who do not share in Objectivist beliefs. Even if a person does not exhibit the pure evil of an Ellsworth Toohey, we may be tempted to rationalize his irrelevance to our lives. The response may be one of indifference rather than condemnation. Moreover, what if a person once met my need but no longer satisfies my selfish pleasure? Should I not discard or ignore that person in the same manner as a worn-out appliance? Would that not be con-sistent with the Objectivist definition of a trader, a man who "earns what he gets and does not give or take the undeserved"?

In addition, the Objectivist belief in volitional consciousness adds an interesting perspective to this discussion on relationships.

---

[69] *Atlas Shrugged*, p. 948.
[70] *The Fountainhead*, p. 389.
[71] *Atlas Shrugged*, p. 87.

By volitional consciousness, Rand means that a man has to be man by *choice*. As we shall see in a later chapter, one implication of this concept is that a person can also become *nonman* by choice.[72]

From personal experience, I can testify that this view made it all too easy for my Objectivist friends and myself to think too highly of ourselves and consider other people as less than consistently rational creatures like us. They were subhuman and not worthy of my time or respect. (This view may be particularly appealing to young admirers of Ayn Rand, some of whom, on reaching the difficult adolescent years, may have been excluded socially and isolated because they were too intellectual or too individualistic.[73] Perhaps they took some comfort and strength in knowing that they were ostracized, as Howard Roark was, for being good and rational by the subhuman creatures surrounding them.) The temptation is ever present to distance oneself from others and think, *He or she is either irrelevant to my life or beneath me. Unless they rise to my level of rationality, understanding, and worth, they deserve only minimal or no consideration.*

To verify that this is not an isolated experience, the reader is invited to consider the circumstances behind the ousting of the Brandens from the Objectivist movement and Rand's gradual but sure isolation from former friends.[74] Whatever Rand may have said about the generosity that arises between men from having learned rational self-interest, the reality is that Rand taught that we have no unearned obligations toward each other. And that does not beget patience, understanding, or generosity.

Where then does true personal worth come from? The Christian view holds that genuine worth is a gift of God. The Psalmist writes, "Thou hast made [man] a little lower than God, and dost crown him with glory and majesty!"[75] All men are endowed with that glory through God's gift of his divine, rational image.[76] Perhaps

---

[72] See chapter 9 on morality and government.

[73] Dagny Taggart once considered getting D's instead of A's in school in order to increase her personal popularity (*Atlas Shrugged*, p. 100).

[74] *The Passion of Ayn Rand*, pp. 331–358, 385–389; see chapters 6 and 9 of the present book.

[75] Psalm 8:5.

[76] Genesis 1:27.

our coming to this understanding that the dignity of man is a gift
bestowed upon all men by the Creator can help us learn the balance of self-love and love toward others. Moreover, as C. S. Lewis
explained, Christianity also teaches that each person is an everlasting being created with a destiny that extends beyond our limited life span on earth. This perspective should not only give us a
proper recognition of our own worth but also the worth of others.
According to Lewis, "There are no *ordinary* people. . . . But it is
immortals whom we joke with, work with, marry, snub, and ex-
ploit—immortal horrors or everlasting splendours."[77] Such a view
helps us recognize that what we do on this earth has eternal implications. And if this view does prevail, we will not be able to look at
others as sacrificial animals that exist for our benefit. Nor can we
thumb our noses at them by calling them subhuman and treating
them indifferently. We are all made in the image of God and intended for high purpose and destiny.

However, the revelation of Scripture that teaches the immeasurable worth of every human being also exposes the human predicament of sin and failure. Knowing this truth ought to expunge
any notion of personal superiority. Each one of us has violated
God's laws. If we will not acknowledge that, then perhaps we will
at least acknowledge that we have all violated our own standards.
Relativism may claim that there is no right or wrong. However,
that is not the position of Objectivism. Rand argued, at least osten-
sibly, for moral absolutes, and that moral absolutism was partly
responsible for the attractiveness of her philosophy to many readers who cried out for a voice of certainty in uncertain times.[78]
Therefore, I have hope that what I say will not fall on deaf ears.
Despite our tendency to harden ourselves to the truth, I am
persuaded that honest introspection will show that none of us
can adhere to what we acknowledge as right (even if Objectivism were right) for a day, let alone a lifetime. And as Leonard
Peikoff admits, "To be evil 'only sometimes' is to be evil. To be

---

[77] *The Weight of Glory*, p. 19.
[78] "The Cult of Moral Grayness," *The Virtue of Selfishness*, pp. 75–79.

good is to be good *all* of the time, i.e., as a matter of consistent, unbreached principle."[79]

Who, among Objectivists, can claim to have fulfilled the requirements and demands of the Objectivist philosophy without exception? Who can say that in every waking hour of his life, he has remained in mental focus, never for a moment allowing himself to slip back into the stagnating swamp of subhuman existence and thereby acting immorally?[80] (If it is evil not to think—and Rand has said that the failure to think is indeed evil—then it is evil to not think for even five minutes.) Who can claim that he is able to justify his every action rationally, never acting on impulse or unidentified premises? How often have we assumed that we knew the reason for our actions, only to discover later that we had deceived ourselves? It was only with great powers of self-delusion that Rand claimed she had lived a perfect life.[81] If none of us can adhere completely to our own standards, is it not possible that we have failed to adhere to standards that supersede those of our own devising? Is it possible that the Bible is right in its observation that all have violated the laws of God, and therefore "all have sinned and fall short of the glory of God"?[82]

If a person answers in the affirmative, he need not despair, because the same source that reveals this truth about the human con-

---

[79] *Objectivism*, p. 266.

[80] "The Objectivist Ethics," *The Virtue of Selfishness*, pp. 25–26; *Atlas Shrugged*, p. 944.

[81] *Donahue*, May 1979. What Rand actually said, in response to a member of the audience who asked if Rand considered herself the perfect being, was: "I never judge myself that way. I judge myself in the following way: Have I absorbed and practiced all of the principles of behavior which I preach. And I would say 'yes' resoundingly." However, Rand admitted that early in her career she was influenced by Friedrich Nietzsche, whom she later regarded as evil. (See Ronald Merrill, *The Ideas of Ayn Rand*, pp. 21–40 and *Journals of Ayn Rand*, edited by David Harriman, p. ix.) But if, as Rand has said, thinking the thoughts of an evil philosopher like Kant is evil, then thinking the thoughts of Nietzsche is also evil. Therefore, by her own admission, Rand had at one point in her life committed evil. Moreover, it is doubtful that Rand always lived according to her own stated principles, even after she developed Objectivism.

[82] Romans 3:23.

dition also provides the way out. The plan of redemption as revealed in the Scriptures shows the greatness of God's love toward us. Christ invaded our fallen realm, lived a sinless life as a human being, and died to pay for the sins and failures of everyone who would receive him. In doing so, he satisfied the justice of God. Jesus is the Messiah of Israel and the Savior of the world. And by his resurrection, he proved that he has indeed triumphed over the human predicament.

This last point requires emphasis because Rand failed to comprehend the significance of Jesus' death and resurrection. During an interview in 1979 on *Donahue*, Rand responded to Phil Donahue's question about Original Sin by saying:

> Look, if you take Jesus Christ as an ideal human being—and that is properly the view of Christians—what do you do with your ideal human being? You put him on the cross, you torture him and murder him, for the sake of those who are less virtuous. Is that a proper example to set? . . . [You murder him] for the sinners to redeem their sins, as you said. I think that is a monstrous idea. If I were a Christian, I would resent it enormously. The ideal men are to be appreciated and followed and listened to—not crucified.[83]

It seemed to have escaped Rand's attention that there might be millions of Christians on this planet who worship Christ and revere his words. Their ideal man is appreciated and followed and listened to. While it is true that men crucified and murdered Jesus, it was Jesus, God himself, who chose to pursue the way of the cross.[84] He claimed that he had the authority to lay his life down and to take it up again. Rand seemed oblivious not only to the fact that Christ chose to *die* for those who are less virtuous, but also that he chose to *live* for them. The cross was not the end of the story. Christ's resurrection, his personal triumph over death, proved to his followers that eternal life was theirs for having placed their trust in him. Therefore, the believer can have confidence, regard-

---

[83] *Donahue*, May 1979; see also *"Playboy's* Interview with Ayn Rand," pamphlet, p. 10 as quoted in *The Ayn Rand Lexicon*, edited by Harry Binswanger, p. 411.
[84] John 10:18.

less of the circumstances he encounters, that Christ has secured the final victory for him. If Rand wished to regard the narrative of the Gospels as mythology, she should at least have considered the implications of the entire myth, not merely part of it.

Why then the need for us to come to the cross? Does not the cross speak of self-abnegation and self-sacrifice, as Rand had claimed? Unfortunately, Rand had a mistaken view of sacrifice. She writes:

> "Sacrifice" does not mean the rejection of the worthless, but of the precious. "Sacrifice" does not mean the rejection of the evil for the sake of the good, but of the good for the sake of the evil. "Sacrifice" is the surrender of that which you value in favor of that which you don't. If you exchange a penny for a dollar, it is *not* a sacrifice; if you exchange a dollar for a penny, it *is*.[85]

But consider this: Since the Fall of man, the human predicament was *already* one of spiritual death that would eventually result in physical death. Christ came out of love so that he might give birth to a people who would be called the children of God. The way of the cross is the pathway by which a person might exchange his life for the Life that God wants to impart to him. A lesser value is sacrificed for a greater value, not the other way around as Rand supposed. Moreover, yielding to the Living God does not turn us into blank and vapid personalities. The Bible shows how God can take the most ordinary of people and transform them into extraordinary sons and daughters. As Jesus said, "The thief comes only to steal, and kill, and destroy; I came that they might have life, and might have it abundantly."[86] Moreover, this "life" does not consist in a pie-in-the-sky afterlife only, as Peikoff's medieval moralist obviously thought, but may be received *now* even as believers invite God's kingdom to come into their midst and begin to rule and reign in all of life's circumstances through Jesus Christ.[87]

---

[85] *Atlas Shrugged*, p. 953.
[86] John 10:10.
[87] Romans 5:17.

Rational self-interest and self-preservation is something most of us are already acquainted with.[88] I might say we are blinded by it and therefore oblivious to the possibilities of much greater values. Like a child who is willing to exchange a twenty-dollar bill for a piece of candy because he does not know the value of the twenty, we too have difficulty seeing what is truly in our interest. The Scriptures appeal to genuine self-interest. For who can say that eternal life is not in a person's self-interest? Who can say that reigning in this life with a sense of God's divine purpose is a selfless endeavor? And if we acknowledge that God has something to say about what would truly fulfill us, then we see that the daily exchange of the old man within us for the new man that God desires in us is truly in our own interest. However, that process comes by way of the cross. "For whoever wishes to save his life shall lose it; but whoever loses his life for My sake shall find it."[89] And that proposition comes with extraordinary promises: "Therefore if any man is in Christ, he is a new creature; the old things passed away; behold, new things have come."[90]

Perhaps Lewis was right:

> [I]f we consider the unblushing promises of reward and the staggering nature of the rewards promised in the Gospels, *it would seem that Our Lord finds our desires not too strong, but too weak.* We are half-hearted creatures, fooling about with drink and sex and ambition when infinite joy is offered us, like an ignorant child who wants to go on making mud pies in a slum because he cannot imagine what is meant by the offer of a holiday at the sea. *We are far too easily pleased.*[91] (Emphasis added.)

We might be consumed by drinks—or any number of substitutes that *drinks* only symbolize—because we can't imagine the fullness of his Spirit and Truth dwelling in us. We move from one

---

[88] Objectivism's distinction between rational self-interest, whim-worship, and hedonism will be shown to break down in chapters 6 and 9.
[89] Matthew 16:25.
[90] 2 Corinthians 5:17.
[91] *The Weight of Glory*, pp. 3–4.

well-intended sexual relationship to another (as Dagny Taggart did) or forgo full commitment, because we cannot imagine the beauty of relationship and sexual fulfillment in a marriage for life with a spouse of God's choosing. And we cannot imagine the joy and expectancy that comes with following the Creator's plan and purpose for our lives.

It is only after we have received and experienced God's grace toward us that we can begin to share in his vision for others. Recognizing the inestimable worth of every individual, the believer in Christ comes with the Creator's heart of love toward those who live here and now. Defending the defenseless. Loving and touching even those who may be counted as enemies with the hope that God would yet change their lives, help them to see the truth, and bring them into vital relationship with himself. I suggest this view rather than the Objectivist view has greater power to change the world.

A Remaining Question

It is difficult to understand how Rand and her followers could have misunderstood and misrepresented Christianity to such a degree. I can only speculate on the reasons. Perhaps they were unaware of their own blindness as I was. Or perhaps it was because the confidence that we all seek flows first from the throne of God, and to acknowledge God as a source of confidence would also require us to recognize him as a source of authority. And the Objectivist accepts no authority but his own reason.

There is also something humbling about coming to the Creator of the universe and asking for help. To admit that there were challenges beyond my own abilities to handle was extremely difficult for me, and it remains difficult for anyone who believes in the self-sufficiency of man. This was an admission that Rand was unwilling to make, and perhaps it resulted in her distorted view of Christianity. However, in the final analysis, no matter how successful any of us may appear to be, our lives are filled with situations from which we need to be rescued and redeemed. Rand was no exception. There are times when we have to admit, "I can't do it, alone."

Despite God's great promise of his provision, we resist because we prefer to handle things our own way. My mind, my life. I will fashion, and I will make. Reflecting on the conflict within myself, I came to realize it was stubbornness borne out of myopia and ignorance rather than truth. Yet freely the Creator comes to each of us, offering his help and direction if only we will receive it. It is difficult to take that step to the cross in order to receive and acknowledge the power and reality of the resurrected Messiah. But if we will take that step, our eternal destiny will be secure and we will never have to face life with less than full confidence and assurance that God is indeed with us.

4

THE CODE OF COMPETENCE

Dagny, there's nothing of any importance in life—except how well you do your work. Nothing. Only that. Whatever else you are, will come from that. It's the only measure of human value. All the codes of ethics they'll try to ram down your throat are just so much paper money put out by swindlers to fleece people of their virtues. The code of competence is the only system of morality that's on a gold standard.

Francisco d'Anconia, *Atlas Shrugged*

Whatever you do, do your work heartily, as for the Lord rather than for men.

Colossians 3:23

N o one could ever accuse Objectivism of advocating a lax work ethic. The driving discipline of young Hank Rearden, who labored to the point of exhaustion in the mines of Minnesota, impressed me at an early age. The scene is forever etched in my mind. "[Rearden] decided that pain was not a valid reason for stopping [work]."[1]

In contrast, Rearden's brother Philip was a man without ambition or career. He lived off of Rearden's generosity and associated with sundry organizations that represented ill-defined social causes. "There was something wrong, by Rearden's standards, with a man who did not seek any gainful employment, but he would not impose his standards on Philip. . . ."[2] Even when Rearden demonstrated an interest in Philip's activities and offered his financial support, his generosity was met with insult. Philip requests the contribution in cash and says, "[I]t would embarrass us, you know, to have your name on our list of contributors, because somebody might accuse us of being in the pay of Hank Rearden."[3] Such rudeness is apparently typical of mystics and religionists like Philip Rearden, while generosity of heart more befits a realist like Henry Rearden.

A dialogue between James Taggart and Francisco d'Anconia, it seems to me, best illustrates the disagreement between the two opposing camps.[4]

> "Don't you ever think of anything but d'Anconia Copper?" Jim asked him once.
> "No."
> "It seems to me that there are other things in the world."

---

[1] *Atlas Shrugged*, p. 36.
[2] *Atlas Shrugged*, p. 46.
[3] *Atlas Shrugged*, p. 48.
[4] *Atlas Shrugged*, pp. 95–96.

"Let others think about them."

"Isn't that a very selfish attitude?"

"It is."

"What are you after?"

"Money."

"Don't you have enough?"

"In his lifetime, every one of my ancestors raised the production of d'Anconia Copper by about ten per cent. I intend to raise it by one hundred."

"*What for?*" Jim asked, in sarcastic imitation of Francisco's voice.

"When I die, I hope to go to heaven—whatever the hell that is—and I want to be able to afford the price of admission."

"Virtue is the price of admission," Jim said haughtily.

"That's what I mean, James. So I want to be prepared to claim the greatest virtue of all—that I was a man who made money."

"Any grafter can make money."

"James, you ought to discover some day that words have an exact meaning."

Obviously, Francisco was not serious about going to heaven. As one of the main protagonists of the nonbelieving Rand, he would not have believed in an afterlife. However, his comments about virtue are revealing. According to Francisco, virtue is to be found in the act of making money, and productive work is what he means by making money. Indeed, Objectivism emphasizes three cardinal values: reason, purpose, and self-esteem. And the corresponding virtues are rationality, productiveness, and pride.[5] As the quote chosen for the beginning of this chapter indicates, Objectivist morality stresses the importance and priority of competence and productive work. Unlike the lofty, mystical theories about virtue, spirituality, and heavenly rewards, here is a system of morality that is visible, measurable, and down-to-earth. The code of competence is Rand's gauge of rationality and virtue.

Rand expands on this view. "Productive work is the central *purpose* of a rational man's life, the central value that integrates

---

[5] "The Objectivist Ethics," *The Virtue of Selfishness*, p. 25.

and determines the hierarchy of all his other values."[6] "'Productive work' does not mean the unfocused performance of the motions of some job. It means the consciously chosen pursuit of a productive career, in any line of rational endeavor, great or modest, on any level of ability. It is not the degree of a man's ability nor the scale of his work that is ethically relevant here, but the fullest and most purposeful use of his mind."[7] In *Atlas Shrugged*, we find rational men and women who live according to the code of competence. They set goals and attain them. They confront opposition and overcome all obstacles. For highly motivated and idealistic readers with dreams of achievement and fulfillment, this was a vision they could identify with and share in. I, for one, came to agree with Rand that productive work should be the central integrating purpose of a person's life. But is such a view tenable?

Productive Work as Central Purpose

Few people would question the importance of productive work as it relates to the goal of human survival. Ancient man foraged and hunted for his food. Progress has brought some stability to life through innovations in agriculture, industry, and trade. However, for most of mankind's history, work was looked upon simply as a means to the survival of an individual and his community. In contrast, the efficiency and productivity of labor in a modern, industrialized society has reached such a high level that for the majority of men living in the West mere physical survival is no longer the primary, much less the sole, motivation for work. However, work continues to be important because, as Rand suggests, it provides an outlet for the creative and productive exercise of one's mind. We can certainly agree with the general tenor of Rand's statement about the importance of work, but can we agree with her claim that productive work serves as the central integrating purpose of a rational person's life?

---

[6] "The Objectivist Ethics," *The Virtue of Selfishness*, p. 25.
[7] "The Objectivist Ethics," *The Virtue of Selfishness*, pp. 26–27.

For me, this question first surfaced when I reconsidered Rand's own view of the relationship between rationality and productive work. "Reason is the source, the precondition of his productive work—pride is the result. Rationality is man's basic virtue, the source of all his other virtues."[8] It seems to me that this passage makes reason and rationality more basic than productive work. Why then, I wondered, is a life of rational contemplation—since rationality is the virtue from which all other virtues and values flow—not the central purpose of a man's life? Is it not *reason* that decides which values ought to be pursued and how much effort should be allotted to the pursuit of each value? However, the acceptance of reason does not automatically make productive work the chief aim of a rational person's life. Productive work may simply be one of the many values pursued by a rational person. It may even be a means to some other end. The more I thought about this question, the more I came to see that disagreements concerning the place of productive work in a life may have more to do with disagreements about what constitutes the life of a rational being than whether productive work is generally worthwhile.[9]

Other writers have also commented on this difficulty in Rand's theory. In *The Philosophic Thought of Ayn Rand*, J. Charles King writes, "It is, however, much too narrow to say that productive work is the central purpose of the life of anyone who is rational."[10] King develops the example of a young man who works diligently to amass a fortune before he reaches the age of thirty. When he turns thirty, however, he invests wisely so as to generate a comfortable and perpetual source of income, for he plans to spend the rest of his life improving his golf game. Thus we see that golf, not productive work, becomes the central purpose of the young man's life after age thirty. In fact, it may well have been the central purpose of his life *before* age thirty. All along, the young man may

---

[8] "The Objectivist Ethics," *The Virtue of Selfishness*, p. 25.

[9] See chapter 9 on morality and government for further development of this theme.

[10] J. Charles King, "Life and the Theory of Value," in *The Philosophic Thought of Ayn Rand*, edited by Douglas Den Uyl and Douglas Rasmussen, p. 117.

have been amassing his fortune in preparation for unrestricted golfing. We ask ourselves: Is such a person irrational? Obviously, the golfer is neither a parasite nor a looter who takes advantage of other men. He has earned the opportunity to enjoy golf for the rest of his life. He appears to be rational and moral in the conduct of his life. However, assuming that the golfer does not subsequently pursue a professional career in golf, it is clear that productive work has never been the central purpose of his life. And because productive work is essential to Objectivism's definition of a rational man, the hypothetical golfer must be considered irrational and immoral. While King finds no reason to convict him of irrationality, Ronald Merrill, a writer sympathetic to the Objectivist position, does.

In *The Ideas of Ayn Rand*, Merrill explains:

> Has [the golfer] really done anything wrong? Yes, he has, by the standards of Objectivist ethics. Again, it's not what he has that counts, nor even what he does, but what he is. By living in idleness, he is diminishing his productive capacity and ability, and thus acting against his own life. In reality skills decline if not practiced—business skills, not just golf! Knowledge is forgotten or becomes obsolete if not used; ability and ambition decay if not presented with new challenges. And that matters, because—in reality—fortunes are vulnerable to inflation, depression, and confiscation.[11]

It seems to me that Merrill is quite mistaken. To begin with, he has not answered King's primary objection. Productive work need not have been the central purpose of the young man's life in order for him to perform productive work. For the ten years during which our hypothetical golfer labored to amass a fortune, golf—not productive work—was the central purpose of his life. Let us demonstrate this truth in another way. Suppose the young man in retirement does not spend all of his time on golf. Instead, he continues to spend an hour a day in his area of expertise. Would that

---

[11] *The Ideas of Ayn Rand*, pp. 116–117.

satisfy Merrill's complaint that he lives in idleness? Probably not, since business skills decline if not practiced sufficiently. Would two hours be better? What about six or eight? It simply does not matter how many hours the man works. Productive work would still not be the central purpose of his life; golf would be. And the young man merely works to maintain some of his business skills.

Furthermore, no amount of work or skill can render an individual invulnerable to inflation, depression, and confiscation. A person may lessen the impact of inflation and depression by diversifying his investments. But no one can guarantee against confiscation by the state or the financial implications of unexpected natural disasters. A person may guard his future to a certain degree, but that cannot be the entirety of his focus. Moreover, who is to say how much energy should be devoted to protecting one's future as against enjoying life today?

Let us think about this problem using a slightly different example. Suppose the young man's interest is not golf, but cooking. He had worked in investment banking, but now he uses that fortune to finance years of study at a culinary institute. His sole interest in becoming a gourmet is so that he might enjoy a variety of exotic cuisines. However, it is possible that he may develop into a chef capable of working at New York's finest restaurants. At the very least, he could always find a job at the nearest fast-food establishment. In this respect, he may safeguard his future even if he were to lose all of his skills in investment banking and suffer bankruptcy. Consequently, we see that a person may protect himself against the charge of irrationality if he chooses a retirement activity as the central purpose of his life that has some potential value to other individuals. Even though he chooses the activity simply because he enjoys it, the activity would enable him to earn a living, should that become necessary. Surely that would satisfy Merrill.

Thus we can see that the argument against golf appears plausible only because golf is unlikely to make the man any money. In addition, an argument against cooking could only be sustained if we insist that the young man is best suited for a career in business and has no right to squander his skills in pursuit of a dream. But notice what has occurred: The rationality of a behavior has now become dependent upon either the market value of that behavior to others or our perception of what an individual is best suited to accomplish during his lifetime. How odd that a philosophy of individualism should wind up making the opinions and actions of others paramount to its test of rationality. As we shall see in chapter 9, this concept of productive work as *right* and *moral* action will return to plague the Objectivist theory of individual rights.

The difficulties with Rand's too narrow view of rationality and productivity can be demonstrated with one final example. What if a man considered the welfare of his family as the central purpose of his life? What if he saw his professional career solely as a means to the end of sustaining his family? According to Objectivism, such a person would be irrational as well. Indeed, Rand had stated in an interview that placing friendship and family ties above productive work was immoral.[12] However, we must remember that rational contemplation is more basic to productive work in the hierarchy of values. *Reason* determines the amount of time that one devotes to various activities, including productive work. But that is precisely where the problem lies. Every person has a different concept of what it means to be rational. The family man may be perfectly reasonable in desiring a balanced life. Unlike Henry Rearden, he may not be burdened by an irrational and unloving family. Therefore, he may find it quite desirable to nurture a growing relationship with his loved ones. Even though he enjoys the rewards of productive work and the challenges of a career, he may reasonably conclude that none of those would be worthwhile without his loved ones. To him, family and friends take priority over productive work, and he may be willing to forgo certain advancements in his career if they should interfere with his concern for personal relationships. Indeed, he may discover that the peace and love he receives at home actually enable him to become even more efficient and productive at work. Thus we may come to agree with King that "the

---

[12] *"Playboy's* Interview with Ayn Rand," pamphlet, p. 7 as quoted in William O'Neill, *With Charity toward None*, footnote number 177, p. 193; compare footnote number 26 in chapter 6 of the present book.

difference is a difference in *taste*, a difference in the kind of life and activity Rand admires and desires, as opposed to the kind of life and activity our hypothetical golfer [or the family man] likes and admires. But that difference is one of taste, not one of failure to abide by some objective standard."[13]

If our reasoning has been correct, then Objectivism has failed to substantiate its claim that productive work ought to be the central purpose of a man's life. The relative importance of productive work in peoples' lives, as we have seen, may represent differences in *taste* and *priorities*. And Objectivism has yet to validate its particular set of priorities.[14] Therefore, Objectivism cannot object to a Christian's set of priorities anymore than it can object to the priorities of the golfer, the cook, or the family man. Moreover, it cannot object to the Christian's greater interest in spiritual matters than materialistic concerns, *as long as* the believer is competent, diligent, and self-supporting. However, as a matter of principle, such a distinction between the spiritual and the material is entirely artificial and unnecessary.

The Spiritual versus the Material

In her fiction, Rand used her extraordinary literary prowess to illustrate the consequences of accepting the soul-body dichotomy. Those characters who were inclined to be spiritual, those who claimed to be motivated by love and selflessness, were the least likely to engage the concerns of the material realm. Philip Rearden couldn't hold a job. Lillian Rearden was passionless in her sex life. James Taggart managed his railroad irresponsibly and expected the government to bail him out. The reason for these characters' lack of interest in the material realm has to do with the philosophy they had accepted. The traditional sources of spirituality or morality, Rand believed, taught a dichotomy between the spiritual and the material realms. They emphasized other worldly concerns at

---

[13] J. Charles King, "Life and the Theory of Value," *The Philosophic Thought of Ayn Rand*, pp. 118–119.
[14] See chapter 9 on morality and government.

the expense of concern with this world. They renounced the physical realm as evil. In doing so, Rand felt that such belief systems abdicated any claims to possessing a philosophy that was relevant to life on earth.

In contrast, Francisco and Rearden confronted the material realm and mastered it. In Rand's eyes, they accomplished something of genuine value through their focused pursuit of productive work. Their philosophy was geared to life on earth. However, this is not to say that Francisco and Rearden had no spiritual concerns. In *Atlas Shrugged*, Rand tried to convey to us the process by which the rebirth of man's spirit may occur. Her philosophy was an attempt to defend her nontraditional version of spirituality. For Rand recognized that religion continued to hold a monopoly on morality and spirituality. Unless modern man, who has mastered the material realm through technological innovations, was able to put forth a defensible and coherent view in such matters, he would always be at the mercy of religion.

Excerpts from the *Journals of Ayn Rand*, edited by David Harriman, show us what Rand had in mind as she wrote *Atlas Shrugged.*

> Man has wrested existence from the mystic demons, but not consciousness—material reality, but not his mind. . . . Men have progressed in material production, but have not progressed in spirit—because the first was the province of reason, but the second is still the province of faith and emotion. There has been no *moral* progress, because the tool of all progress—the mind—was banished from morality.[15]

> Of course, that cheap snobbery about material production is based on a deeper philosophical error—on the vicious idea of "matter as sin" and spirit as its antagonist. And it's logical that if one accepts that idea (which represents the debasement of men and of the earth), then one considers the activity of preserving man's survival (material production) as low and evil. To be high, one must then starve to death—that's "liberating the spirit." Tie

---

[15] *Journals of Ayn Rand*, p. 664.

this to the clear exposition of the fact (as *clear* as you can make it) that the material is only the expression of the spiritual [where spiritual means thought].[16]

Here we must distinguish the *spiritual* (as Objectivist philosophy) from the *spiritual* (as religious or Christian philosophy). However, if *spiritual* means thought—and Rand agreed that was what it meant—then obviously one's thinking affects how one behaves and how one regards the material realm.[17] As the proverb says: "Sow a thought; reap an action." In this sense, *every* system of philosophy or religion is spiritual. (Whether a particular system of philosophy supports the existence of thought and truth is another matter altogether.[18])

What Rand meant by spirituality was also morality. All along, it had been her intention to create a philosophy that would justify her ethics of rational self-interest and her emphasis on transforming the material realm through productive work. One way Rand tried to demonstrate the superiority of her morality was to suggest that all of the competing religious moralities were unconcerned with the material realm. Indeed, this is one of Rand's basic assumptions. As an example, in *Atlas Shrugged*, she subsumes most religionists under the category "mystics of the spirit."[19] To me, this view seemed plausible initially, but I came to realize that it was a gross simplification and generalization of the problem.

Not all religious systems are the same. Some religions, to be sure, foster a sense of indifference toward the material realm or a hatred for rational thought. Rand's understanding of this kind of spirituality may be more accurate concerning the Eastern religions. Indeed, most of Rand's arguments against the anti-industrial and anti-intellectual mentality in her book *The New Left: The Anti-Industrial Revolution*, seem to have more to do with the teachings of Buddhism and Hinduism than Christianity. Notably, it was India,

---

[16] *Journals of Ayn Rand*, pp. 550–551.

[17] *Journals of Ayn Rand*, p. 551.

[18] See chapter 8 on reason and reality.

[19] *Atlas Shrugged*, pp. 953, 960–962.

with its religious admixture of Buddhism and Hinduism, that Dagny Taggart contrasted with America.[20] Buddhism, with its stated objective of avoiding pain, encourages the individual to extinguish all desire and follow a pathway of abandonment, release, and nonattachment to this reality. The Eastern religions, with their emphasis on transcendental meditation and spiritual experiences where one's identity is dissolved and merged into an irrational and indescribable ultimate reality, has been acknowledged by many as having contributed to the drug culture of the sixties, which Rand so vividly described in some of her works.[21] However, as I came to understand, these descriptions are not accurate of Christianity.

The Judeo-Christian Scriptures describe a rational God who has from the beginning been intimately involved with the details of life on earth. He created the universe and blessed it.[22] He created man and endowed him with the rational image. A mindless existence is not the proper one for man in Christianity. Man was given the ability and authority to dominate nature, and he was commissioned to bring it to maximum fruitfulness.

The Creator was also concerned about individuals and their life circumstances. He saved Noah and his family from the deluge.[23] He was concerned with Abraham and Sarah's earnest desire for a child.[24] He delivered the Hebrews from slavery in Egypt and brought them to a promised land full of milk and honey.[25] He taught them how to live a life of discipline and freedom. When the Babylonians invaded Judah and Israel and took their people into captivity, God helped them to prosper even in foreign lands. Eventually, many were given the opportunity to return home. Nehemiah led one such expedition that also rebuilt the walls of Jerusalem.[26]

---

[20] "The Anti-Industrial Revolution," *The New Left: The Anti-Industrial Revolution*, pp. 150–151.
[21] "Apollo and Dionysus," *The New Left: The Anti-Industrial Revolution*, pp. 57–81, specifically 69, 74–80.
[22] Genesis 1.
[23] Genesis 6–9.
[24] Genesis 15–21.
[25] Exodus.
[26] Nehemiah.

His spiritual concern for the welfare of his people motivated him to the down-to-earth task of rebuilding Jerusalem's desolate walls. There is no evidence here of a dichotomy between spiritual and material concerns.

As Rand said, "[T]he material is only the expression of the spiritual." Just as Objectivist thought governs the attitude and behavior of Objectivists regarding the material realm, Christian thought also affects the attitude of Christians toward the things of this world. However, the difference between the two systems is one of presuppositions and priorities. It is simply untrue to say that Christianity despises life on earth. Nowhere can this be seen more clearly than in the Incarnation. God invaded this fallen planet as the incarnate Christ. If to be spiritual implies a disinterest and nonattachment to this reality, and if to be spiritual means liberating oneself from the shackles of mortal existence by starving to death, then why would God, the ultimate in spirituality, come to us in flesh and blood? "And the Word became flesh, and dwelt among us."[27] The eternal, incorporeal God put on flesh and entered into the material realm that he himself had created. For what purpose? To be born in a lowly manger, to be suckled at the breast of a humble maiden, to dine with prostitutes and tax collectors, to touch the untouchables, to speak with the racially and morally impure, and to suffer physical death and torture for man's sins. He experienced all that man has experienced and more.

Contrary to what Rand supposed, in Christianity "liberating the spirit" does not mean starving to death. Jesus demonstrated a concern for the requirements of physical life on earth. He said, "For I was hungry, and you gave Me something to eat; I was thirsty, and you gave Me drink; I was a stranger, and you invited Me in; naked, and you clothed Me; I was sick, and you visited Me; I was in prison, and you came to Me."[28]

When his followers asked, "Lord, when did we see You hungry, and feed you, or thirsty, and give You drink? . . ." Jesus answered,

---

[27] John 1:14.
[28] Matthew 25:35–36.

"Truly I say to you, to the extent that you did it to one of these brothers of Mine, even the least of them, you did it to Me."[29] Indeed, with Christ's arrival on the scene of our circumstance, he brought hope and healing. Jesus demonstrated mastery over the material realm by feeding the five thousand, calming the storm, healing the sick, and resurrecting the dead. His parables and teachings do indeed speak of a future world to come, but he did not ignore the concerns of this world. "Thy kingdom come. Thy will be done, on earth as it is in heaven"[30] and "Give us this day our daily bread"[31] were not the prayers offered by some detached spiritual leader.

Even in the Resurrection, Jesus demonstrated no conflict between the spiritual and the material. His own resurrected body was one of flesh and bone. "See My hands and My feet that it is I Myself; touch Me and see, for a spirit [ghost] does not have flesh and bones as you see that I have."[32] And the promise to believers is that they would one day inherit a similar body. Paul writes: "So also is the resurrection of the dead. It is sown a perishable body, it is raised an imperishable body; it is sown in dishonor, it is raised in glory; it is sown in weakness, it is raised in power; it is sown a natural body, it is raised a spiritual body."[33] As marvelous as the human body is now, the resurrected body will be even more magnificent and will avoid the present imperfections. Furthermore, that body is destined to dwell in a glorious new Jerusalem.[34]

But here on earth, Christ encouraged his disciples in the use of their talents and promised rewards to those who were faithful to their task.[35] And his disciples continued to teach a spirituality that would transform peoples' lives and circumstances. If it was a code

---

[29] Matthew 25:37, 40.
[30] Matthew 6:10.
[31] Matthew 6:11.
[32] Luke 24:39.
[33] 1 Corinthians 15:42–44.
[34] Revelation 21:10–22:5.
[35] Matthew 25:14–30.

of competence that Francisco d'Anconia was looking for, he would have found it in the teachings of Christ and his followers.

- If anyone will not work, neither let him eat.[36]
- Whatever a man sows, this he will also reap.[37]
- Whatever you do, do your work heartily, as for the Lord rather than for men.[38]

Such teachings encourage competence and diligence in all that a person does. However, they do not constitute a code of competence that makes productive work the central purpose of one's life. The approach is one of order and balance. "Beloved, I pray that in all respects you may prosper and be in good health, just as your soul prospers."[39] And that prospect for genuine prosperity and wholeness flows from one source. "May the God of peace Himself sanctify you entirely; and may your spirit and soul and body be preserved complete, without blame at the coming of our Lord Jesus Christ. Faithful is He who calls you, and He also will bring it to pass."[40] These are not the idle words of spiritualists detached from this reality and ignorant of life's requirements, but the teachings of the most realistic of all realists—people who had seen reality from the point of view of the One who created it and mastered it.

---

[36] 2 Thessalonians 3:10.
[37] Galatians 6:7.
[38] Colossians 3:23.
[39] 3 John 2.
[40] 1 Thessalonians 5:23–24.

5

ROMANTIC LOVE:

OBJECTIVISM AND CHRISTIANITY

What is the nature of the guilt that your teachers call his Original Sin? What are the evils man acquired when he fell from a state they consider perfection? . . . He was sentenced to experience desire—he acquired the capacity of sexual enjoyment.

John Galt, *Atlas Shrugged*

The central thrust of this new religion [Christianity] was a profound asceticism, an intense hostility to human sexuality, and a fanatical scorn of earthly life. Hostility to pleasure—above all, to sexual pleasure—was not merely one tenet among many of this religion; it was central and basic.

Nathaniel Branden, *The Psychology of Romantic Love*

Let your fountain be blessed, and rejoice in the wife of your youth. As a loving hind and a graceful doe, let her breasts satisfy you at all times; be exhilarated always with her love.

Proverbs 5:18–19

P robably no subject attracts the attention of readers more than romantic love. Ayn Rand's portrayal of love had a profound impact on her admirers. Howard Roark and Dominique Francon. John Galt and Dagny Taggart. Who could forget their passion? For many readers, their relationships demonstrated what romantic love could and ought to be.

But what is their secret? Perhaps if we could learn the reason for their success, we might assure our own fulfillment in romantic relationships. Rand affirms that hope. Love may appear at first complex and mysterious, but in reality it is quite simple. However, what is simple is not simplistic. The key lies in understanding that romantic love, like all of man's other activities, begins with philosophy. Whether they are held consciously or subconsciously, a man's basic values and view of life shape his romantic choices as surely as they influence his political convictions. With his characteristic eloquence, Francisco d'Anconia expresses this view in *Atlas Shrugged*:

> Tell me what a man finds sexually attractive and I will tell you his entire philosophy of life. Show me the woman he sleeps with and I will tell you his valuation of himself. No matter what corruption he's taught about the virtue of selflessness, sex is the most profoundly selfish of all acts, an act which he cannot perform for any motive but his own enjoyment—just try to think of performing it in a spirit of selfless charity!—an act which is not possible in self-abasement, only in self-exaltation, only in the confidence of being desired and being worthy of desire.[1]

Since Rand had defined love as the response of a person to his highest values found in the person of another, naturally she con-

---

[1] *Atlas Shrugged*, p. 460.

cluded that a person's romantic choices reflect his own value and worth. Consequently, her character Francisco predicts:

> The man who is proudly certain of his own value, will want the *highest type of woman he can find*, the woman he admires, the strongest, the hardest to conquer—because only the possession of a heroine will give him the sense of an achievement, not the possession of a brainless slut.[2] (Emphasis added.)

Indeed, we find relationships based on these principles in *The Fountainhead* and in *Atlas Shrugged*. Confident, rational men and women discover each other and build relationships that appear to fulfill them spiritually, intellectually, and physically. Rand's vision of love awakens hope in us, perhaps because we long to experience the same intimacy in our own lives. However, Rand's view of love also carries with it a warning. Passion and joy may be the fruit of a love based on self-exaltation and self-enjoyment, but misery and torture await those who subscribe to a different philosophy: the philosophy of altruism.

Let us consider a man who regards love as an act of self-denial and self-sacrifice. Would not such a man view sexual enjoyment as a sinful activity and come to view genuine love as a "pure emotion of the spirit"?[3] Rand answers affirmatively. She believes that a man ruled by the principle of self-sacrifice could not desire the best that life has to offer; instead, "he will feel that depravity is all he is worthy of enjoying."[4] You see what has happened? The wrong philosophy has rendered him romantically and sexually impotent. Several stories from *Atlas Shrugged* illustrate Rand's theory especially well.

The Drama of Love

Henry Rearden rose from the coal mines of Minnesota to become the leading steel industrialist in the United States. His

---

[2] *Atlas Shrugged*, p. 460.
[3] *Atlas Shrugged*, p. 461.
[4] *Atlas Shrugged*, p. 461.

material success, however, is tarnished by his personal unhappiness, especially his marriage to Lillian. During their courtship, Lillian had exhibited an aura of grace, pride, and purity that appealed to Rearden. He could not completely identify his feelings for her, but she seemed to stand for everything he had hoped to achieve. Yet, within months of their marriage, that appearance gave way to an ugly reality.

Lillian, as Rearden came to realize, was an altruist. She regarded the spiritual realm as distinct from and superior to the material realm. For her the material world held little value, so it should not surprise us that she had no capacity for sexual pleasure. Lillian considered sex an ugly blemish, a part of man's animal nature, to be tolerated not celebrated. While she never resisted her husband's sexual advances, she was absent in spirit during their lovemaking. Frustration and bewilderment beset Rearden as their marriage became a torturous affair. Eventually, he came to the conclusion that "women were pure and that a pure woman was one incapable of physical pleasure."[5]

After years of agony, Rearden begins an affair with the beautiful and brilliant Dagny Taggart. After their first sexual encounter, the deep struggle that had consumed his soul surfaces with these words:

> What I feel for you is contempt. But it's nothing, compared to the contempt I feel for myself. I don't love you. . . . I wanted you from the first moment I saw you. I wanted you as one wants a whore—for the same reason and purpose. I spent two years damning myself, because I thought you were above a desire of this kind. You're not. You're as vile an animal as I am. . . . I had never broken my word. Now I've broken an oath [the marriage vows] I gave for life. I had never committed an act that had to be hidden. Now I am to lie, to sneak, to hide.[6]

Dagny simply doesn't share those feelings of guilt. There had been no conflict between her thoughts and actions, between her

---

[5] *Atlas Shrugged*, p. 156.
[6] *Atlas Shrugged*, pp. 242–243.

desire and the attainment thereof. She had nothing to apologize for. Her thinking reflects that of Ayn Rand:

> Did you call it depravity? I am much more depraved than you are: you hold it as your guilt, and I—as my pride. I'm more proud of it than anything I've done, more proud than of building the [John Galt Railroad] Line. If I'm asked to name my proudest attainment, I will say: I have slept with Hank Rearden. I had earned it.[7]

This story illustrates what Rand's philosophy had declared. Only a life lived in self-exaltation can bring success in love, and the person one sleeps with reflects to some degree one's own sense of self-worth. Sexual fulfillment cannot be found by consenting to the altruistic, self-sacrificial vision of love. The conflict that Rearden experienced was a result of his compromise with altruism. The devastation could be worse.

What would motivate James Taggart, the altruistic railroad executive, to marry Cheryl Brooks, a waitress from a local diner? Brooks is a diligent, industrious young woman who left her impoverished home in search of a more promising future. Her chance meeting one night with Taggart at the local diner where she worked changed the course of her life. Their courtship ultimately resulted in marriage; however, Taggart's motive was less than chivalrous or romantic. Socially, James considered Cheryl one of the dregs. His decision to marry a lowly waitress served only to verify his claim to be a devoted altruist, a man motivated by nothing but selfless charity. Naive and spellbound, Cheryl thought James, and not his sister Dagny, was the courageous individual who had guided Taggart Transcontinental through adversity and

---

[7] *Atlas Shrugged*, p. 244.

crisis. Unaware of the truth, Cheryl felt immensely honored by his attention and love.

After their wedding, Cheryl begins a program of self-improvement in order to repay James for his love and confidence. The *Pygmalion*-like transformation is remarkable as she becomes a wife befitting a railroad president: confident, knowledgeable, gracious, and elegant.[8] However, Taggart's response to her growth was perplexing and tormenting. James should have been pleased by her progress, but all Cheryl found was a husband who hated her for having become worthy of his love. But after all, James Taggart was seeking the worst. Was he not?

∞

Stories like these illustrate the devastating effect of altruism in the area of romantic love. After reading them, I could not help but wonder how the monstrosity of altruism came to be. Rand did not leave me in doubt as to its source. John Galt was quite explicit when he implicated Christianity. "What is the nature of the guilt that your teachers call his Original Sin? What are the evils man acquired when he fell from a state they consider perfection? . . . He was sentenced to experience desire—he acquired the capacity of sexual enjoyment."[9] Galt pictured Original Sin as describing a pivotal moment when man first experienced desire. Unfortunately, this sexual desire and enjoyment, which ought to have been celebrated, was regarded by Judaism and Christianity as arising from sin and failure. According to Rand, this negative view of sex has played a significant role in creating and fostering the repressive and dichotomous view of sex held and experienced by the majority of men and women. Rand's argument appeared persuasive to me, and I came to agree with her. If man is to be liberated, he must throw off the chains of this antilife philosophy of which Christianity is the chief representative.

---

[8] Ronald Merrill, *The Ideas of Ayn Rand*, p. 77.
[9] *Atlas Shrugged*, p. 951.

The Psychology of Romantic Love

Nathaniel Branden also shares in this view. In his best-selling book *The Psychology of Romantic Love*, he examines the Christian concept of love in detail. Even though Branden's book was published many years after he had left the Objectivist movement, his view of Christian love is consistent with his early writings in *The Objectivist* and the approach taken by Rand herself. Moreover, Branden's writings remain influential among Rand's admirers; consequently, it will be instructive to examine his view. For the sake of completeness, I have quoted him at length:

> The central thrust of this new religion [Christianity] was a profound asceticism, an intense hostility to human sexuality, and a fanatical scorn of earthly life. Hostility to pleasure—above all, to sexual pleasure—was not merely one tenet among many of this religion; it was central and basic. The Church's hostility to sex was rooted in its hostility to physical—earthly—existence and its view that physical enjoyment of life on earth necessarily meant spiritual evil. . . .
>
> Saint Paul elevated the Greek concept of the soul-body dichotomy to unprecedented importance in the Western world. . . . The body is only a prison in which the soul is trapped. It is the body that drags a person down to sin, to the quest for pleasure, to sexual lust.
>
> Christianity upheld to men and women an ideal of love that was consistently selfless and nonsexual. Love and sex were, in effect, proclaimed to stand at opposite poles: the source of love was God; the source of sex was, in effect, the devil. "It is good for a man not to touch a woman," taught Saint Paul; but if men lack the necessary self-control "let them marry: for it is better to marry than to burn [with lust]."[10]

According to Branden, Christianity also fostered the prevailing attitude of the medieval church against sex and against women:

---

[10] *The Psychology of Romantic Love*, pp. 18–19.

It was not a great sin, in the eyes of the medieval church, for a priest to fornicate with a whore. But for a priest to fall in love and marry, that is, for his sex life to be integrated as an expression of his total person, was a cardinal offense. . . .

The Church's essential antisexualism was paralleled by an essential antifeminism. With the rise of Christianity in medieval Europe, women lost virtually all the rights they had won under the Romans; they were regarded, in effect, as vassals of the male, to whom they were to be entirely subordinate; more precisely, they were regarded as domesticated animals. . . . On the one hand, woman was symbolized by Eve, the sexual temptress, the cause of man's spiritual downfall. On the other hand, she existed in the image of Mary, the Virgin mother, the symbol of purity who transforms and lifts man's soul upward. The whore and the virgin—or the whore and the mother—have dominated the concept of woman in Western culture ever since.

To state the dichotomy in modern terms: There is the woman one desires and the woman one admires; there is the woman one sleeps with and the woman one marries. . . . On the deepest level Christianity has always been a fierce opponent of romantic love.[11]

The quotation has been extensive, but we may summarize Branden's conclusions briefly.

- Christianity was hostile to physical existence, earthly life, and sexual pleasure.
- Christianity held a view of love that was nonsexual and selfless.
- The source of that selfless love was God; the source of sex was the devil.
- In Christianity, the woman was viewed as the temptress who brought about man's spiritual downfall.
- Christianity was antifeminine, and women became vassals under this system.

---

[11] *The Psychology of Romantic Love*, pp. 21–22.

- Christianity intensified the mind-body dichotomy: There is the woman one admires and the woman one desires.

Branden's analysis and conclusions seemed very plausible, especially to a person like myself, whose mind had already been prepared by Rand's fiction and philosophy. Christianity appeared as a system of beliefs that condemned man to a state of unfulfilled existence. Branden's writings merely fueled my antagonism toward it.

A Turning

However, that antagonism began to wane years later, when I began my own inquiry into the view of romantic love found in the Scriptures. The beautiful expressions of love I found in the Song of Solomon were unexpected. What the Shulammite bride said of her bridegroom, Solomon, intrigued me. "On my bed night after night I sought him whom my soul loves; . . . 'Have you seen him whom my soul loves?'"[12] A sense of quiet wonder filled me as I considered the reference to a *soulmate*. The idea of a soulmate was one that I had learned from Branden.[13] I had not expected to find it in the Bible.

A passage from the Book of Ephesians surprised me: "So husbands ought also to love their own wives as their own bodies. He who loves his own wife loves himself; for no one ever hated his own flesh, but nourishes and cherishes it just as Christ also does the church."[14] In the act of marriage, the husband and wife begin a process whereby they are transformed into one flesh.[15] You have to understand how revolutionary this seemed to me. The allusion to the *physical* by a religion that was supposed to be purely *spiritual* was puzzling enough, but the summons for a husband to nurture his wife in the context of love for his *own* body astounded me. Here was concern for another borne out of concern for oneself. Is that typical of altruism?

---

[12] The Song of Solomon 3:1, 3.
[13] *The Psychology of Romantic Love*, p. 102.
[14] Ephesians 5:28–29.
[15] Ephesians 5:31.

All of this suggested to me that Christianity deserved more consideration than I had given it. The issues raised by Branden's analysis served as a catalyst, and I probed further with these questions in mind. Was Christianity genuinely hostile to physical existence, earthly life, and sexual pleasure? Does physical enjoyment necessarily imply spiritual evil? What are we to make of Saint Paul's apparent injunction against women? Indeed, what was the Christian view of women?

Hostility toward Physical Existence and Life

This first question has already been addressed in the last two chapters. We considered the creation event in Genesis and discovered its profound implications for human worth and dignity. The Objectivist belief that Christianity is fundamentally hostile to physical existence, or earthly life, was shown to be mistaken, for "God saw all that He had made, and behold, it was very good."[16]

Christianity and Sexual Love

What about sexual love? Does Christianity exhibit hostility toward it? Both Rand and Branden imply that man's discovery of sexual enjoyment coincided with the dawning of Original Sin. Once again, we must turn to Genesis for a description of the events referenced by these two authors in order to judge the accuracy of their conclusions.

The man Adam was at first alone, but his Creator had other plans. "It is not good for man to be alone, I [the Lord God] will make him a helper suitable for him."[17] Then God created woman. Adam spoke prophetically when he said that husband and wife would be joined as one flesh.[18] They were intended to grow together spiritually, emotionally, and physically. And Scripture shows how God blessed the sexual capacities of the first couple. "Be fruitful

---

[16] Genesis 1:31.
[17] Genesis 2:18.
[18] Genesis 2:23–24.

and multiply," he said.[19] The timing of these events has to be emphasized. They took place *prior* to the Fall of man. Does anyone seriously wish to argue that man and woman did not have the anatomy and physiology for sexual enjoyment before the Fall? Or that procreation was intended as a pleasureless activity? No textual evidence exists for Rand's claim that sexual enjoyment originated with Original Sin.[20] Instead, sexual pleasure, love, and the marriage covenant all appear to have been well established prior to the Fall. The author of these gifts was the Creator God—not the devil.

Furthermore, man's disobedience resulting in Original Sin was not seen as the result of some sexual enticement from the woman. Perhaps Branden got that idea from medieval Roman Catholic theology, but it is not what biblical Christianity teaches. The temptation had to do with disobeying a specific commandment given by the Creator not to eat the fruit of a particular tree. However, even after Adam's failure, God had not changed his mind about the enjoyment and blessing that marriage and sexual love were to bring husband and wife. The Book of Proverbs, a book of wisdom for living in a fallen world, is quite candid about sexual love. Speaking to the husband, it says:

> Let your fountain be blessed, and rejoice in the wife of your youth. As a loving hind and a graceful doe, let her breasts satisfy you at all times; be exhilarated always with her love.[21]

The Song of Solomon expresses sexuality in a tasteful and beautiful way. Solomon says to his bride:

> How beautiful you are, my darling, . . . Your lips are like a scarlet thread, and your mouth is lovely. . . . Your two breasts are like two fawns, twins of a gazelle, which feed among the lilies.[22]

---

[19] Genesis 1:28.

[20] The word *desire* in Genesis 3:16 does not refer to sexual desire. It refers to a tendency after the Fall for the woman, who once worked in partnership with her husband, to want to rule over him.

[21] Proverbs 5:18–19.

[22] The Song of Solomon 4:1, 3, 5.

The bride was no less responsive and complimentary in her description of the bridegroom:

> My beloved is dazzling and ruddy, . . . His hands are rods of gold . . . His abdomen is carved ivory inlaid with sapphires. His legs are pillars of alabaster set on pedestals of pure gold; his appearance is like Lebanon, choice as the cedars. His mouth is full of sweetness. And he is wholly desirable. This is my beloved and this is my friend.[23]

And what can this next verse describe except what contemporary culture has come to know as French kissing?

> Your lips, my bride, drip honey; honey and milk are under your tongue.[24]

It is almost embarrassing how explicit Solomon is. Nevertheless, both he and his wife project a sense of passion, excitement, wonder, and love about each other. How then can anyone conclude that Christianity advocates a sexless, pleasureless marriage for man and woman? The Scriptures describe a sexual love between husband and wife that is as liberating and fulfilling an experience as one could hope for.

Perhaps we find it difficult to believe that the Bible might teach otherwise because a false picture of religion's puritanical stance against sexual love has been loudly trumpeted and impressed upon our minds by those who want to justify their own permissive code of sexual conduct. I discovered, and now we together have learned, that the Scriptures do not hold a prudish stance toward sexuality. But neither does it advocate permissiveness in such matters. Indeed, there are biblical injunctions against sexual activity prior to and outside of marriage. On the heels of a passage that celebrates the beauty of sexual love are specific warnings against adultery.

---

[23] The Song of Solomon 5:10, 14–16.
[24] The Song of Solomon 4:11.

Drink water from your own cistern, and fresh water from your own well. . . . For why should you, my son, be exhilarated with an adulteress, and embrace the bosom of a foreigner? For the ways of a man are before the eyes of the Lord, and He watches all his paths. His own iniquities will capture the wicked, and he will be held with the cords of his sin. He will die for lack of instruction.[25]

The picture of God watching over us might appear threatening to some; however, notice that it is the man's own iniquities that will destroy him. Moreover, to stand firmly against destructive sexual behavior cannot be equated with condemning sexual pleasure per se. What if a loving Creator understands not only what would bring us genuine fulfillment, but also what would destroy us? What if these principles are given not for the sake of minimizing our joy, but so that there might come the maximum fulfillment of our sexual lives and our whole lives? The Scriptures speak of a joy and preciousness of relationship that only comes with full devotion to one person for life and warns that adultery, however appealing it may appear at first, can lead only to disappointment and tragedy. Contemporary experience also bears witness to the practical wisdom of this view, since exclusive commitment to one person also reduces the scourge of disease, the possibility of violent retribution, and the disintegration of families. Perhaps the Creator knows what works.

What Did Paul Say?

But if Christianity sanctions sexual enjoyment within marriage, how do we explain the apostle Paul's apparent antisexual stance? Branden writes:

"It is good for a man not to touch a woman," taught Saint Paul; but if men lack the necessary self-control "let them marry: for it is better to marry than to burn [with lust]."[26]

---

[25] Proverbs 5:15, 20–23.
[26] *The Psychology of Romantic Love*, p. 19.

(I have quoted Branden verbatim.) When I first read this passage, I assumed that the reference to the scripture was accurate. It did not occur to me to check it, because the verse seemed to confirm Branden's position and affirm what I wanted to hear. Subsequently, I realized that serious scholarship was lacking. First, notice that Branden failed to cite the passage he quoted. In addition, an examination of the relevant passage in 1 Corinthians, chapter 7 shows that Branden quoted only verses 1 and 9 and ignored the intervening material. The entire text of 1 Corinthians 7:1–9 appears below.

> [1]Now concerning the things about which you wrote, it is good for a man not to touch a woman.
> [2]But because of immoralities, let each man have his own wife, and let each woman have her own husband.
> [3]Let the husband fulfill his duty to his wife, and likewise also the wife to her husband.
> [4]The wife does not have authority over her own body, but the husband does; and likewise also the husband does not have authority over his own body, but the wife does.
> [5]Stop depriving one another, except by agreement for a time that you may devote yourselves to prayer, and come together again lest Satan tempt you because of your lack of self-control.
> [6]But this I say by way of concession, not of command.
> [7]Yet I wish that all men were even as I myself am. However, each man has his own gift from God, one in this manner, and another in that.
> [8]But I say to the unmarried and to widows that it is good for them if they remain even as I.
> [9]But if they do not have self-control, let them marry; for it is better to marry than to burn.

With the entire text available for examination, it became obvious to me that Branden had taken Paul's words out of context. His summary of Paul's teaching was neither complete nor accurate. The missing verses along with other passages provide valuable clues as to what Paul meant.

Paul begins by reaffirming sex as a privilege of marriage (vv. 1–2). However, marriage, while approved by God, may not be desirable given the difficult historical context at Corinth. Later in the same letter, Paul informs us that much effort is required to promote a healthy marriage. For this reason, a life of singleness will enable some people to more effectively fulfill God's purpose in their lives.[27] However, the gift of singleness has not been granted to everyone (vv. 7–9). Therefore, neither the single nor the married person should regard their marital status with an attitude of superiority. Nevertheless, we might conclude from the Scriptures that marriage is the norm. The person who cannot control his or her passion and commit to a life of singleness should marry (v. 9).

Within marriage, husband and wife are as one flesh and have authority over each other (vv. 3–5).[28] Sexual intercourse is made mutually and lovingly available. It is not something to be withheld or demanded by either party. The concession spoken of in verse 6 allows for marriage partners to abstain from sexual intercourse for a limited and agreed-upon period of time. However, the concession is not, as some have supposed, a reluctant allowance for occasional sexual union, as if it were some plague to be avoided. Quite the contrary, Paul believes that husband and wife are to have regular sexual communication. Loving passion for one's spouse is not sinful, but natural and scriptural. Thus, when the medieval church equated the desire of the husband and the wife for each other with sin, they were simply wrong. They will find no scriptural basis for that belief.

---

[27] 1 Corinthians 7:28–35.

[28] If what verse 4 says about the husband and wife mutually possessing and having authority over each other's bodies seems distasteful to some, consider what Rand wrote in *Atlas Shrugged*. Dagny spoke of the pride of once owning Francisco's body (*Atlas Shrugged*, p. 119). Rand speaks of Galt acting as if Dagny's body were his possession (*Atlas Shrugged*, p. 888). Rand also writes, "I cannot conceive of a rational woman who does not want to be precisely *an instrument of her husband's selfish enjoyment*" ("Of Living Death (II)," *The Objectivist*, October 1968, p. 532). Therefore, Objectivists can voice no objection to this terminology since they themselves use it.

Moreover, it seems to me that Branden's repeated reference to the medieval church confuses the issue. It is well known that the medieval Roman Catholic Church committed atrocities. But it is also well known that the medieval church had more regard for its own religious traditions than what was taught in the Scriptures. A review of the history of the Reformation era indicates that it was precisely the arrogance of religious institutions in exalting themselves above the truth of God's Word that had brought about the dark ages. It was the rediscovery of truth that set men free and brought about a genuine renaissance of life in the sixteenth and seventeenth centuries.

For these reasons, Branden's charge of asceticism against Christianity also misses the mark. The medieval church's asceticism and antisexualism did not originate with Paul or the Bible. The challenge of asceticism to Christianity, as I discovered, occurred long before the medieval period. And Paul had prepared an answer for them:

> "Do not handle, do not taste, do not touch!" . . . These are matters which have, to be sure, the appearance of wisdom in self-made religion and self-abasement and severe treatment of the body, but are of no value against fleshly indulgence.[29]

When Paul spoke of fleshly indulgence, he was not speaking of orgies. Asceticism had taught and encouraged the willful mistreatment of the body and abstinence from things given by God for our enjoyment. As Gordon Clark explains in *Colossians*, the ascetics told men to do things that either were not required by God or went beyond what God had commanded. Paul argued that this sort of "conceited humility" did not contribute to the life that God desired for his people.[30]

Paul, of course, was not saying that one can handle, taste, and touch whatever one wishes. He abhors that variation of the soul-body dichotomy as well. The Corinthians, for example, had

---

[29] Colossians 2:21, 23.
[30] *Colossians*, pp. 102–108.

the peculiar notion that because their spirits were saved, they could do whatever they wished with their bodies, *e.g.*, they thought they were free to indulge in prostitution. The medievalist appears to have fallen into the same trap. As Branden reports, "It was not a great sin, in the eyes of the medieval church, for a priest to fornicate with a whore. But for a priest to fall in love and marry, that is, for his sex life to be integrated as an expression of his total person, was a cardinal offense." Apparently the medieval church had forgotten Paul's instructions to the Corinthian church to glorify God in all that they did.[31] Loving and desiring one's spouse does glorify the Creator; indulging in fornication does not. Far from advocating a soul-body dichotomy, Paul argues for full-integration in sexual love and its ultimate fulfillment within the confines of marriage.

Woman: Domesticated Animal or Fellow Heir of Life?

Branden's criticism of the medieval church continues unabated as he charges Christianity with regarding women as domesticated animals. First, a caveat and reminder: Just because the medieval church or any sector of the church held such a distorted view does not mean that biblical Christianity teaches it. As in nearly every issue, Genesis, the book of beginnings, sheds much light on how women are to be treated; it serves as the touchstone of truth.

In Genesis 2:18 the Creator declares, "It is not good for the man to be alone; I will make him a helper suitable for him." The New King James Version translates it as "a helper comparable to him." The King James Version translates the phrase as "a help meet for him." The word *meet* means "precisely adapted to a particular situation, need, or circumstance" (*Webster's Ninth New Collegiate Dictionary*). The word for *helper* in Hebrew is *ezer* and can mean a partner in either a military or strategic sense.[32] This brief analysis

---

[31] 1 Corinthians 6:19–20.

[32] Harris, R. Laird, Archer, Gleason L., and Bruce K. Waltke (editors), *Theological Wordbook of the Old Testament* (Chicago, IL: Moody Press, 1980), Volume II, p. 660.

of the key words suggests something very precious about the woman. First, she is comparable to the man because both have received the divine rational image.[33] The woman could not possibly be regarded as a domesticated animal, because animals do not possess the divine image. (Of note, it was Aristotle who regarded women as misbegotten males.) Second, the Creator removed something from man's side to fashion woman. An essential part of man has been given to the woman. For this reason, they are precisely adapted to one another. The text suggests that man was previously complete but alone. Now he and the woman are to be partners, joint heirs, if you will, participating in the grace of life.[34] It is difficult to see how one could arrive at a view of women as subordinate and domesticated animals from this starting point.

Next, Branden charges Christianity with demeaning women by fostering the view that "Eve, the sexual temptress, [was] the cause of man's spiritual downfall." We have already noted that Adam's failure resulted from his violation of God's command, not as a result of sexual temptation from Eve. Moreover, the Scriptures never assign full responsibility for the man's downfall to the woman. In fact, man is singled out as the one who failed. Paul, that supposed misogynist, lays the responsibility squarely upon the man. "Therefore, just as through one man sin entered into the world, and death through sin, and so death spread to all men. . . ."[35] One man, not one woman. The woman may have been deceived into taking the fruit first, but the man consciously disobeyed and thus incurred primary responsibility for the fall of the human race.[36]

But suppose Adam had acted differently. What if, as one writer imagines, Adam had not disobeyed, but acted in a responsible and redemptive way to restore the woman whom he loved, perhaps by offering to suffer the penalty in her place?[37] Perhaps the original creative order could have been restored. But Adam failed

---

[33] Genesis 1:27.

[34] 1 Peter 3:7.

[35] Romans 5:12; see also Romans 5:15 and 5:17.

[36] 1 Timothy 2:14.

[37] Jack W. Hayford, *A Man's Starting Place* (Nashville, TN: Thomas Nelson, 1995), pp. 71–78.

in this respect, and the responsibility fell to the Second Adam from heaven, Jesus the Messiah, who did come to earth and die on behalf of those whom he calls his Bride, his Church. Hence, the preciousness of womanhood emerges from the pages of the Bible where men are encouraged to nurture and honor their wives. Male leadership in the home does not consist merely in setting the course for the family, but it is a call and a privilege to serve in the redemptive purposes of God. It is not a position for the abuse of power.

While there exist controversial passages in the Bible about women that cannot be fully dealt with here, a serious consideration of the Scriptures as a whole will reveal the importance of women. In the Old Testament, God commands Abraham to listen to Sarah.[38] Why listen to women if they are to be regarded as animals? Esther was a key figure in the salvation of the Jews from genocide.[39] And regarding the abilities of women, the model woman described in Proverbs 31 would pose a challenge even to the Dagny Taggarts of this world.

In the New Testament era, the good news of Christianity teaches that women are worthy and that they too can know their Creator and have a personal relationship with him. Mary had the privilege of sitting at the feet of Jesus and listening to him.[40] Against tradition, Christ spoke to a woman at the well in Samaria.[41] On Pentecost, the Spirit of God was poured out upon both men and women.[42] Furthermore, we find the apostle Paul commending women and teaching *mutual* love and honor between husband and wife.[43]

The truth of the gospel, as I came to realize, sets both men and women free. Christianity has elevated the position of women everywhere it has gone. As but one example, it was Christian missionaries, convinced of the Bible's regard for the worth of women, who brought about an end to *suttee*, the Indian practice of burning

---

[38] Genesis 21:12.
[39] Esther.
[40] Luke 10:38–42.
[41] John 4:7–27.
[42] Acts 2:17.
[43] Ephesians 5:22–33.

widows on the funeral pyres of their deceased husbands, and the widespread infanticide of baby girls in India and China.[44]

Full Integration and the Unity of Love

It should now be obvious that Rand and Branden misunderstood and misrepresented the Christian view of romantic love. After considering the evidence, can we continue to regard the altruistic villains of *Atlas Shrugged* as the equivalent of Christian believers? Do we see them loving others by securing their good? Were Lillian Rearden's oral attacks on her husband and her subsequent affair with James Taggart acts of love and honor? In marrying Cheryl Brooks, was James Taggart attempting to secure her good or was he seeking to display his sacrificial nature and false humility before men? Envy, deceit, and pride are really quite alive and well in these fictional characters who are supposed to abound in love and self-sacrifice. They are the products of bad epistemology, but it isn't Christianity that they believed in or practiced.

Why then do so many people accept Rand's misrepresentation of Christianity? For one thing, Rand's masterful portrayal of love and romance lends enormous credibility to her own theory of love. She knew how to capitalize on the longing for intimacy that dwells in each one of us. Moreover, Rand spoke to a generation that knew very little about Christianity. So when she equates Christianity with the unbiblical teachings of some churches and portrays it as a system that leads to the negation of love, readers, already captivated by her fiction, are inclined to go along with her. They reject the Christian view without ever having considered it. To them, Rand's explanation seems accurate enough. I, too, was vulnerable to her powers of persuasion, but eventually I came to understand differently.

What Christianity offers between husband and wife is a love that embraces the whole person: spirit and body. In the final analysis, love is a choice, an unreserved commitment that sustains and complements an emotional response. I find the totality of that love

---

[44] D. James Kennedy and Jerry Newcombe, *What If Jesus Had Never Been Born?* pp. 14–17.

most beautifully expressed in the marriage vows found in England's *Book of Common Prayer*. The man concludes the exchange of vows by expressing this promise to the woman: "With this ring I thee wed: with my body I thee worship: and with all my worldly goods I thee endow."[45] The God of Christianity intends for husband and wife to experience fulfillment in the whole of their lives, both physical and spiritual. Perhaps we may conclude by stating the synthesis in these terms: There is the woman one admires and the woman one desires; there is the woman one marries and the woman one sleeps with. They are one and the same. On the deepest level, Christianity has always been the most passionate and ardent proponent of romantic love.

---

[45] *The Book of Common Prayer 1559: The Elizabethan Prayer Book*, edited by John E. Booty (Charlottesville, VA: University Press of Virginia, 1976), p. 293.

6

In Pursuit of Objectivist Love

[Wanted by the Inquisitors, Francisco d'Anconia's ancestor Sebastián d'Anconia] left behind him his fortune, his estate, his marble palace and the girl he loved—and he sailed to a new world. . . . Fifteen years after he left Spain, Sebastián d'Anconia sent for the girl he loved; she had waited for him.

Atlas Shrugged

You recently celebrated your fiftieth wedding anniversary to the same man.

Phil Donahue addressing Ayn Rand
Donahue, May 1979

[Dagny] never wondered whether [Francisco] was true to her or not; she knew he was. She knew even though she was too young to know the reason, that indiscriminate desire and unselective indulgence were possible only to those who regarded sex and themselves as evil.

Atlas Shrugged

If [Nathaniel Branden] feels for me what he says he feels, and sees in me what he says he sees—he'd be willing to be part of a harem. Doesn't he know that the great proof of my love for him is that I chose him *despite* a happy marriage and the difference in our ages? Doesn't he know that an exclusive commitment for life is impossible?

Ayn Rand, as quoted by Barbara Branden
The Passion of Ayn Rand

Sebastián d'Anconia waited fifteen years for the woman he loved. There is something of the heroic inherent in that story. It hearkens back to the chivalry of a bygone era. Whatever your temperament may be, I believe a hidden part of all of us longs for that kind of nobility in love. The fact that Ayn Rand included the story of Sebastián d'Anconia's patience and fidelity in *Atlas Shrugged* suggests that she thought his passion and purity worthy of being emulated. But is that kind of love consistent with the rest of Rand's philosophy? What Francisco d'Anconia says bears repetition:

> Tell me what a man finds sexually attractive and I will tell you his entire philosophy of life. Show me the woman he sleeps with and I will tell you his valuation of himself.[1]

He also declares:

> The man who is proudly certain of his own value, will want the *highest type of woman he can find*, the woman he admires, the strongest, the hardest to conquer—because only the possession of a heroine will give him the sense of an achievement, not the possession of a brainless slut.[2] (Emphasis added.)

Rand believes that a man's sense of self-worth is crucial to his ultimate sexual and romantic fulfillment. However, her philosophy goes beyond advocating self-confidence in love. It seems to require that a person *verify* that self-confidence by the choice of the *highest type* of companion he can find. That is, a person's valuation of himself may be determined by looking at whether the woman he chooses is a heroine. Let us designate this principle as the *pursuit of the highest type*, or "the Dagny principle." In the remainder of this chapter, we will explore the pursuit of love using

[1] *Atlas Shrugged*, p. 460.
[2] *Atlas Shrugged*, p. 460.

this Objectivist principle. Did the heroes of *Atlas Shrugged* live by it? If so, did they succeed? What are the consequences of living this way? In order to answer these questions, we must first examine the romantic history of Dagny Taggart.

The Romantic Life of Dagny Taggart

Dagny's first lover was Francisco d'Anconia. It happened during her seventeenth summer. Because she and Francisco had been close companions since childhood, it seemed inevitable that a romantic relationship would develop between them. He was dashing and intelligent, "the climax of the d'Anconias." She was a woman of beauty, vitality, and strength. Their life together was destined to be passionate and powerful.

But the secret strike initiated by John Galt changed everything. Francisco's role in the strike required that he keep the truth even from Dagny, and he ends their affair without explanation. Dagny is confused and devastated by the inexplicable conclusion to their love; moreover, she is unable to fathom the life of depravity that Francisco now leads as a worthless playboy. Years later, she reaches for the man she admires most, Henry Rearden. Even though Rearden is a man bound by many contradictions, he is the highest type of man Dagny could find. And so they begin a fulfilling affair.

Later, Dagny's aerial pursuit of John Galt ends in a crash landing in Atlantis.

> When [Dagny] opened her eyes, she saw sunlight, green leaves and a man's face. She thought: I know what this is. This was the world as she had expected to see it at sixteen—and now she had reached it—and it seemed so simple, so unastonishing, that the thing she felt was like a blessing pronounced upon the universe by means of three words: But of course. She was looking up at the face of a man who knelt by her side, and she knew that in all the years behind her, *this* was what she would have given her life to see: a face that bore no mark of pain or fear or guilt.[3]

---

[3] *Atlas Shrugged*, p. 652.

That face belonged to John Galt, and it was the face of the perfect man that Dagny had always dreamed of. First, there was a recognition; then, an attraction. But the situation becomes complicated. While in Atlantis, Dagny discovers that Francisco had remained faithful to her for twelve years. He had remained single and celibate and only pretended to be a playboy. Like his ancestor Sebastián d'Anconia before him, Francisco too had counted the cost and waited for his girl. Would this knowledge now bring Dagny back to Francisco in preference to Galt or Rearden? Could she deny her feelings for John Galt?

Galt also has to weigh his desire for Dagny against the pain that his friend Francisco might experience in losing Dagny after such a long wait. Life can seem so cruel. At one point, Francisco asks Dagny to be his houseguest for the remainder of her stay in Atlantis. (She had been staying with Galt and working as his housekeeper to pay for her expenses.) Dagny defers the decision to Galt under the pretense of being in his debt and employment. However, her real intention was to learn of Galt's feelings for her. Without hesitation, Galt denies Dagny permission to move to Francisco's home. He later confronts her, "You had to put me to the test in order to learn whether I'd fall to the lowest possible stage of altruism?" Dagny then ponders what altruism would have meant for the three of them:

Galt, giving up the woman he wanted, for the sake of his friend, faking his greatest feeling out of existence and himself out of her life, no matter what the cost to him and to her, then dragging the rest of his years through the waste of the unreached and unfulfilled—she, turning for consolation to a second choice, faking a love she did not feel, being willing to fake, since her will to self-deceit was the essential required for Galt's self-sacrifice, then living out her years in hopeless longing, accepting, as relief for an unhealing wound, some moments of weary affection, plus the tenet that love is futile and happiness is not to be found on earth—Francisco, struggling in the elusive fog of a counterfeit reality, his life a fraud staged by the two who were dearest to him and most trusted, struggling to grasp what was missing from his happiness, struggling down the brittle scaffold of a lie over the abyss of the discovery that he was not the man she loved, but only a resented substitute, half-charity-patient, half-crutch, . . . the three of them, who had had all the gifts of existence spread out before them, ending up as embittered hulks, who cry in despair that life is frustration—the frustration of not being able to make unreality real.[4]

In the end, of course, none of them faked reality. John Galt and Dagny knew they were meant for each other. And when Francisco discovers their love for each other, he calmly acknowledges, "It is as it had—and ought—to be. . . . [I]t wasn't chance."[5]

Sobering Thoughts

A review of the details of Dagny's history was necessary because the pattern of her love life is crucial to understanding the Objectivist theory of love. Dagny's relationships may convey an initial sense of excitement, romance, and eventual fulfillment; however, once the veneer of drama has been stripped away we are left with two very sobering thoughts. First, Rand sanctions sexual intimacy before marriage. Second, Rand justifies a change in romantic partners so long as rational self-interest is served. Marriage is not a prohibition against having affairs, and divorce proceedings may be undertaken should it become necessary for the fulfillment of new romantic desires.

These are conclusions that may be deduced from a consideration of the stories in *Atlas Shrugged* alone, but Rand said as much in an interview with *Playboy* magazine. *The Ayn Rand Lexicon* records the portion of the interview relevant to the subject of love.[6]

---

[4] *Atlas Shrugged*, p. 741.

[5] *Atlas Shrugged*, p. 753. This love triangle, or love tetrahedron if one includes Rearden, stirs up interesting emotions in the reader. One sympathizes with Rearden's loss. A hope is expressed that Francisco, often considered by readers as more dashing and chivalrous than Galt, might yet regain Dagny's affection. But logic triumphs: The highest man and the highest woman had to be together in the end.

[6] "*Playboy's* Interview with Ayn Rand," pamphlet, p. 8 as quoted in *The Ayn Rand Lexicon*, edited by Harry Binswanger, p. 459.

Rand begins by affirming the importance of sex in man's life. Because Rand has a high regard for sex, she feels it necessary to condemn promiscuity as immoral. However, her position on promiscuity is a curious one. *Promiscuity* means "not restricted to one sexual partner" (*Webster's Ninth New Collegiate Dictionary*). And yet, Dagny had three sexual partners: Francisco, Rearden, and John Galt. By strict dictionary criterion, Dagny was promiscuous.

Rand then says that sexual involvement should be limited to "very serious relationship[s]," but she leaves *serious* undefined. Clearly, by *serious* she did not mean marriage, because she goes on to say, "Whether that relationship should or should not become a marriage is a question which depends on the circumstances and the context of the two persons' lives." Obviously, Rand did not intend to limit sexual intimacy to a relationship based on a lifelong commitment. But then her restriction of sex to a "very serious relationship" hardly represents a restriction at all. Practically speaking, Rand's restriction may reduce the number of sexual partners an Objectivist has over a lifetime. However, in principle, there is no difference between the Objectivist and the playboy, for each person has his own idea of what *serious* means. A secondary appeal to rational self-interest is not much more promising, for each person has his own idea of what constitutes rational self-interest.[7] At least Christianity defines a serious relationship as marriage, a lifelong commitment made before God and witnesses.

Now Rand does acknowledge the importance of marriage as an institution, but she does not and perhaps could not explain why it is important. Indeed, her language is rather vague. According to her, marriage may be desirable if a man and a woman are certain that they want to spend the rest of their lives together.

> But this does *not* mean that any relationship based on less than total certainty is improper. I think the question of an affair or a marriage depends on the knowledge and the position of the two

---

[7] See chapter 9 on morality and government.

persons involved and should be left up to them. Either is moral, provided only that both parties take the relationship seriously and that it is based on values.[8]

Here, *affair* seems to mean a serious sexual relationship prior to marriage. However, common usage of the word would include extramarital sexual liaisons. Nevertheless, Rand is here talking about whether a serious sexual relationship should become marriage. She views marriage as both possible and proper. However, it is unlikely that we can regard marriage as a permanent institution in the Objectivist scheme of things, since total certainty can never be attained given the Dagny principle. Consider Dagny's earlier musings about the love triangle between Francisco, Galt, and herself. If Francisco and Dagny had been married before Dagny fell in love with Galt, would Rand have insisted that Galt and Dagny deny their feelings for each other and continue the charade for Francisco's benefit? Obviously not. Moreover, Rand sanctioned Rearden's affair with Dagny while he was married to Lillian. Since faking reality is not an Objectivist virtue, we may conclude that marriage does not serve as an injunction against extramarital affairs and, consequently, has few advantages other than to satisfy legal and cultural requirements.

The Pursuit of the Highest Type

However, let us examine Rand's position more carefully. When she said that romantic relationships are based on values, what precisely did she mean? Apparently, it means that a person acts in rational self-interest and in accordance with the Dagny principle. Remember, love is a person's response to his highest values found in the person of another. And those values depend on a person's basic philosophy of life and view of self. Therefore, a rational person who desires a romantic relationship should want to find someone who shares in his basic life values and who is the highest type

---

[8] *"Playboy's* Interview with Ayn Rand," pamphlet, p. 8 as quoted in *The Ayn Rand Lexicon*, p. 459.

of person that he can find. But love is probably more complicated than this view initially suggests. In *Atlas Shrugged*, Galt, Ragnar, Francisco, and the other men in the valley presumably all have the same basic philosophical values, yet Dagny chooses John Galt above all others. How do we explain her choice? In *The Ideas of Ayn Rand*, Ronald Merrill comments:

> [Dagny was not portrayed] as being sexually attracted to all the strikers equally, though presumably they all share the philosophical values of John Galt. It would seem obvious that there must be something more than philosophical premises determining romantic choices.[9]

Merrill then suggests that Rand would have clarified her statements about love had she not been limited by considerations of form and length that are inherent in writing a novel. Perhaps intelligence, profession, physical attractiveness, personality, and sense of life are qualities that explain why different men and women choose each other. Given the opportunity to expand on her novel, Merrill believes Rand would have provided additional details that account for her characters' specific romantic choices.

Whatever the reason for Dagny and Galt's mutual attraction, a more important question requires our attention. In light of the Dagny principle, can we expect Dagny and Galt's choice of each other to remain final? (Remember what this principle says: A man of self-esteem will want the highest type of woman he can find.) The relationship between Dagny and Galt as depicted in *Atlas Shrugged* appears permanent only because it occurs at the end of the story and because Rand had created no other characters of such high nobility and achievement. Obviously there is no woman who supersedes Dagny as the consummate heroine, nor is there another man who matches the intellect and will of John Galt.

But what if the story had not ended when it did? What if on returning to the world Galt discovers someone more desirable than Dagny? Would he not be justified in pursuing a romantic relation-

---

[9] *The Ideas of Ayn Rand*, p. 83.

ship with his new love interest? Inconceivable, you say? Then consider this more realistic scenario. I would suggest that it should have been possible for any of the secondary heroines in *Atlas Shrugged* to have desired John Galt because he was the "highest" type to them. Why does Kay Ludlow not choose John Galt instead of Ragnar Danneskjöld? Ludlow is a beautiful and intelligent actress. Surely, she is worthy of Galt. Of course, Ragnar is also a wonderful man by Objectivist standards, but did he invent the motor? Was he smart enough to recognize the problem with altruism and initiate the strike? Why is it implausible for Ludlow to leave Ragnar for Galt just as Dagny ultimately rejected Rearden and Francisco in favor of Galt? Why could Ludlow not name as her proudest attainment that she had slept with John Galt?

The objection might be raised that Ludlow and Ragnar were already married. However, as I mentioned before, Dagny's thoughts about the love triangle between Francisco, Galt, and herself clearly show that Objectivism abhors the faking of reality in relationships. Does one think that an inconvenience like marriage should stand in the way of happiness and rational self-fulfillment?

Perhaps the problem lies with Galt. Since Galt had already set his hopes on Dagny, he simply was not interested in Ludlow. But this merely leads to other questions. How could Galt be sure that he would eventually win over Dagny? How could Francisco be certain that he would get Dagny back? Why do they both remain celibate with hopes of one day possessing her?

Since leaving the Objectivist movement, Nathaniel Branden has commented on that point.[10] He criticizes Rand for having imposed celibacy on Francisco d'Anconia. According to Branden, it is not only psychologically unrealistic, but a violation of rational self-interest. Francisco remains faithful to Dagny even while playing the part of a playboy. John Galt presumably remains a virgin until he is in his midthirties, when he makes love to Dagny in the underground tunnels of Taggart Transcontinental. Why the two remain celibate is unclear. Perhaps Branden is suggesting that if he

---

[10] "Break Free! An Interview with Nathaniel Branden," *Reason*, October 1971, pp. 4–19.

had written *Atlas Shrugged* he would have included sexual relationships between the two heroes and other women. I wonder if Branden is concerned that Rand's portrayal of Galt and Francisco as celibates might make sexual abstinence out to be a virtue. I doubt that was Rand's intent.

Merrill defends Rand on this issue, and his analysis is very revealing.[11] He claims that the incidents in *Atlas Shrugged* are not meant to be taken "as literal prescriptions for human behavior." They are merely symbolic. Moreover, Merrill explains that practical limitations and considerations inherent in the writing of a novel mean that Rand never could have developed a character to everyone's full satisfaction. Every writer has to make difficult choices. Some details are included while others are excluded. After all, that is the selective nature of art. It is too much to expect perfection. I agree. Rand is a superb novelist, and *Atlas Shrugged* remains a masterpiece of Romantic literature. But what is Merrill really saying? Is he implying that, given enough room in *Atlas Shrugged*, Rand *would have* written about sexual relationships between Galt and other women prior to his romantic union with Dagny?

This discussion merely underscores the point I made earlier. Despite Rand's condemnation of promiscuity and unselective indulgence, it would not have been immoral by Objectivist standards for Galt to have had an affair with another woman, even if he were ultimately interested in Dagny. Reason would have shown him that the probability of a relationship with Dagny was small. To wait patiently for years was an act of faith; it was an act of self-immolation and sacrifice. Galt should have pursued the highest woman available to him while reserving the option to pursue Dagny at a later date.

Indeed, is there not a contradiction here? Rand seems to have held Francisco and Galt to a different standard than Dagny. Before ending their relationship, Francisco advises Dagny to act on her own judgment with regard to his apparent depravity. He would not ask her to wait for him and take him on faith.[12] Dagny did not

---

[11] *The Ideas of Ayn Rand*, pp. 79, 83–84.
[12] *Atlas Shrugged*, p. 114.

wait for Francisco, and she did not take him on faith. Moreover, it is clear from Dagny's waking thoughts after the crash in Atlantis that she had long held a vision of her perfect man. Neither Francisco's nor Rearden's face matched the quality of the one in Dagny's vision. Nevertheless, she pursued relationships with both men. Do we fault her for not preserving her virginity and waiting for her ideal man?

This line of analysis using the Dagny principle may be expanded and applied to the secondary heroes and heroines of *Atlas Shrugged*. Imagine that each man and woman in Atlantis has an order of preference for members of the opposite sex. They each have a mental rank list of men and women who meet some minimum standard that they have set for a serious romantic relationship. Thus we can readily see that the possible number and combinations of romantic partners increase exponentially as we move away from the ideal of a John Galt or Dagny Taggart. For example, there may be only one person who meets John Galt's minimum criteria. But for the rest of us, there are many options, and the number of highest types also increases as our circle of acquaintances expands and our experience accumulates. Whether it is philosophical values, intelligence, beauty, personality, or sense of life that we judge by, it makes little difference. Some combination of these factors will always leave us with a preference list of some sort. This poses an important dilemma. Of these many possible candidates, whom do we choose? However we arrive at this decision, the more important question is: How do we deal with the pursuit of the highest type after we have settled on one partner? Should a person end his search at this point, or should he remain open to future options? If a person takes the Dagny principle seriously, he cannot terminate his search. He should pursue the highest person available now and remain open to the possibility of finding someone higher in the future. And if that higher prospect appears responsive to his romantic overtures, he is obligated to pursue her. Surely, the failure to do so would reflect bad epistemology and poor self-image.

Whatever Rand meant by the highest type, the fact remains that marriage is not permanent for her. That is the core of the issue. Seeking the highest type of person as a continuing principle for romantic love is doomed to failure. There is always the possibility of someone coming along who appears to be better, and we can always rationalize why the new person is better than the old. The previous partner may have been wonderful but just not wonderful enough. And that reduces the Objectivist view of love to the whim-worship and hedonism that Rand condemns. After all, the whim-worshiper also eschews permanence and expresses a preference for whomever he happens to like at the moment. One suspects that the difference between the Objectivist and the whim-worshiper may be one of degree rather than one of principle.[13]

Objectivists in Pursuit of Objectivist Love

If the preceding discussion seems too abstract, then a look at the attempt by Objectivists to pursue Objectivist love may prove helpful and instructive. Barbara Branden candidly acknowledged the difficulties and dangers inherent in Rand's theory of love. In *The Passion of Ayn Rand* she writes:

> Few things in life are so complex and so little understood as that which motivates our passionate sexual response; to require, as proof of psychological health, that this motivation lead only to the choice of a "hero," is to inflict, on oneself and others, inestimable damage.[14]

Indeed, we can imagine the immense psychological burden shouldered by a man who has to choose a heroine as his lover in order to verify his own worth and value. In fact, some admirers of Rand face difficulties when they are unable to find a John Galt or Dagny Taggart in real life.

In the passage quoted above, Barbara Branden is also recounting her own unhappy marriage to Nathaniel Branden. The two first met because of their mutual interest in Rand's writings. They

---

[13] We will discuss this question in greater detail in chapter 9 on morality and government.
[14] *The Passion of Ayn Rand*, p. 249.

became close friends of Rand and eventually established the Objectivist movement with her. Early on, Rand sensed that Barbara and Nathaniel were destined for greatness, and it seemed inevitable that two young, intelligent, and attractive persons sharing the same philosophical values would be drawn to each other romantically. Even though Barbara initially had reservations about Nathaniel, eventually the logic of Rand's theory overcame her reticence. "Nathaniel appeared to embody the values I cherished," Barbara recalls. To choose him would verify her own philosophical values and psychological vibrancy. Even though she did not feel a genuine sense of affection and love for him, she married him. She expressed this hope: "[T]he day would come when I would respond to Nathaniel as I should and wanted to respond. The road would be cleared and I would be free to live my life rationally. It was all perfectly simple—and perfectly impossible of achievement."[15]

The story becomes increasingly complicated and ugly.[16] By the time of the Brandens' marriage, Rand had been married for over twenty years to Frank O'Connor, by all accounts a mild-mannered, gentle, and nurturing man. However, it seems their relationship never lived up to the passion and excitement found in the relationships Rand described in her fiction. Into this void in Rand's life came Nathaniel Branden, an attractive and intellectually gifted young man. For Rand, her fictional characters seem to come alive in him. For Branden, the admiration and affection of so great a personality as Ayn Rand stirred in him a desire for romantic fulfillment with her that was unfettered by a previous commitment to his wife, Barbara. Moreover, their affair took place *with* the consent of their spouses. But how could they not consent? While "indiscriminate desire and unselective indulgence"[17] were not possible to the Objectivists, apparently discriminate desire and selective indulgence were. The Dagny principle legitimized the affair.

---

[15] *The Passion of Ayn Rand*, p. 249.
[16] *The Passion of Ayn Rand*, pp. 253–264.
[17] *Atlas Shrugged*, p. 108.

Years later, while continuing both the affair with Rand and his marriage with Barbara, Nathaniel Branden became attracted to a third woman, Patrecia Gullison. Intellectually, she could not compete with either Ayn Rand or Barbara Branden. She was not the highest type in that sense. Whatever it was about Patrecia that made her attractive to him, Nathaniel Branden knew only that she made him feel alive. In Barbara Branden's words:

> With Patrecia, Nathaniel could be young again, he could be carefree and open and unafraid; he need not guard every word and every thought; he could be *himself*, and know that who he was satisfied Patrecia utterly. Her love was unconditional. It contradicted everything he had learned about the nature of love, everything he had taught others; and he discovered that he needed it as a drowning man needs air and breath and solidity beneath his feet.[18]

However, Branden was unable to justify his latest romantic choice based on the Objectivist theory of love; therefore, he hid this new relationship from Rand. When Rand finally discovered the truth, she confronted him and ultimately ousted him from the Objectivist movement.[19]

Before the final revelation of Branden's relationship with Patrecia, while Rand was still contemplating the change in his behavior toward her, she remarked:

> If [Nathaniel Branden] feels for me what he says he feels, and sees in me what he says he sees—he'd be willing to be part of a harem. Doesn't he know that the great proof of my love for him is that I chose him *despite* a happy marriage and the difference in our ages? Doesn't he know that an exclusive commitment for life is impossible?[20]

If this is the opinion of the founder of Objectivism, then we may conclude that whatever sense of awe and wonder Dagny and

---

[18] *The Passion of Ayn Rand*, p. 332.
[19] *The Passion of Ayn Rand*, pp. 331–358.
[20] *The Passion of Ayn Rand*, p. 337.

Galt's love may have aroused in us, it was not meant to be either permanent or secure. The Dagny principle, taken to its logical conclusion, leads to the never-ending pursuit of self-fulfillment. Its disastrous consequences can be seen in the lives of Rand and her followers.

Personal Cost

The personal cost of such behavior is immense. The pain that results from the breakup of a relationship is bound to be worse when couples have been intimate sexually than when no such involvement has taken place. Dagny experienced that feeling of bewilderment and agony when Francisco ended their relationship.[21] Moreover, aside from the devastation that results from a broken relationship, intimacy may never have been fully realized during the relationship. Imagine a person entering a relationship not having committed himself to his partner. Instead, he has an eye out for a higher person who may come along. Without cutting off all the bridges, how can he possess the resolve and perseverance necessary to overcome the conflicts and obstacles that inevitably come with marriage and life? Remember, Rand treats the realm of relationships and economics alike. "A trader is a man who earns what he gets and does not give or take the undeserved. A trader does not ask to be paid for his failures, nor does he ask to be loved for his flaws."[22] But such a view makes traitors of us all, for profound intimacy and security is possible only where there is full commitment.

Earlier I mentioned that in principle there is ultimately no difference between the Objectivist and the playboy. However, I believe there is a difference in temperament, but it rests on a contradiction in Rand's philosophy. A playboy who regards sex with the casual attitude of a predator on the prowl will experience little of the emotional devastation I have spoken of. During the first of his many one-night stands, he probably will harden himself against any feelings of guilt or pain. However, I suggest that this is not the

---

[21] *Atlas Shrugged*, pp. 114–115.
[22] *Atlas Shrugged*, p. 948.

case with most of Rand's admirers. I believe they care very much
about love and values. It is the nobility of Sebastián d'Anconia's
love and Rand's exalted view of sex that drew them in the first
place. Sincere though they may be, they are unfortunately caught
in a contradiction. Rand's literary devices encourage her admirers to strive for the ideal of exclusive commitment and nobility
in love, but her theory makes it impossible for them to achieve
it. It has not been my purpose to criticize anyone for desiring
genuine love, but to show that Objectivist principles cannot help
him attain it. Perhaps now the Christian alternative of committing to and loving a person for a lifetime is not as foolish as it
once appeared.

Further Consequences

The deficiency in the Objectivist theory of love also becomes
clear in situations where a person is called upon to sacrifice or
even risk his own life for his wife. Rand writes:

> Concern for the welfare of those one loves is a rational part of
> one's selfish interests. If a man who is passionately in love with
> his wife spends a fortune to cure her of a dangerous illness, it
> would be absurd to claim that he does it as a "sacrifice" for *her*
> sake, not his own, and that it makes no difference to *him*, per-
> sonally and selfishly, whether she lives or dies.[23]

Since love is a response to our highest values, and since the
woman that a man loves is presumably his highest value outside of
himself, it stands to reason that a man would want to protect and
save his wife. But Rand continues with another example:

> The proper method of judging when or whether one should help
> another person is by reference to one's own rational self-interest
> and one's own hierarchy of values: the time, money or effort one
> gives or the risk one takes should be proportionate to the value
> of the person in relation to one's own happiness.

---

[23] "The Ethics of Emergencies," *The Virtue of Selfishness*, pp. 44–45.

To illustrate this on the altruists' favorite example: the issue of saving a drowning person. If the person to be saved is a stranger, it is morally proper to save him only when the danger to one's own life is minimal; when the danger is great, it would be immoral to attempt it: only a lack of self-esteem could permit one to value one's life no higher than that of any random stranger. . . . If the person to be saved is not a stranger, then the risk one should be willing to take is greater in proportion to the greatness of that person's value to oneself. If it is the man or woman one loves, then one can be willing to give one's own life to save him or her—for the selfish reason that life without the loved person could be unbearable.

Conversely, if a man is able to swim and to save his drowning wife, but becomes panicky, gives in to an unjustified, irrational fear and lets her drown, then spends his life in loneliness and misery—one would not call him "selfish"; one would condemn him morally for his treason to himself and to his own values, that is: his failure to fight for the preservation of a value crucial to his own happiness.[24]

However, setting aside the case of a person who either cannot swim or cannot swim well enough to attempt a rescue, a question arises: When is it ever justifiable by Objectivist standards for a person to risk his own life in order to save another? To say that one should judge the proportional risk based on the relative importance of the drowning person to oneself is nebulous at best. All rescue involves risk. No matter how well a person swims, there are no guarantees. In addition, it is often the victim's panicky movements, as well as the specific conditions of the environment in which the rescue takes place, that threaten the rescuer's safety. And such an assessment of risk cannot be made beforehand. Moreover, since our earlier discussion shows that an exclusive commitment to one person for life cannot be secured by Objectivist standards, how can we expect a person to risk his life to save a woman who is *replaceable*?

---

[24] "The Ethics of Emergencies," *The Virtue of Selfishness*, pp. 45–46.

If a man's wife was drowning and the man was guided by Objectivist standards, he would be completely justified and rational in thinking in the following way: There are likely to be many women out there who possess qualities similar to or superior to those he admired in his wife. Undoubtedly, the man had shared many unique and irreplaceable moments with his current wife. But if he died while attempting to rescue her, there would be no future to share with her or anyone else. How much better it would be to live and enjoy more special moments with a new wife. I wonder if anything beyond rescuing someone drowning in four feet of water in a swimming pool would constitute a reasonable risk.

In *Atlas Shrugged*, John Galt threatens to commit suicide if Dagny is tortured by the looters' government. That is an unreasonable choice. If Dagny had been killed, Galt would still have a life to live and values to pursue. To be sure, Galt may have preferred Dagny as his partner. But if Galt committed suicide, there would be no Galt to enjoy life and no possibility of finding another lover.[25]

The principle of rational self-interest is not helpful in nonemergency situations either. A shocking but astute observation made by an orthopedic surgeon at Harvard best illustrated the problem for me. During a career counseling session that I attended years ago along with several other medical students, the surgeon told us about the decision he made many years ago to cut back on his busy practice. He wanted to spend more time with his children. He said, "Your kids are all you have. When I grow older, I want my kids to remember me and the time I spent with them." He sounded like a noble family man until he added, "If your busy practice causes you to lose your wife, you can always find another one. But your kids are all you have." By his reasoning, he could have replaced his children as well.

Ultimately, Rand must have regarded any relationship as expendable. She said, "If [men] place such things as friendship and family ties above their own productive work . . . then they are im-

---

[25] We will consider this question in greater detail in chapter 9 on morality and government.

moral. Friendship, family life and human relationships are not primary in a man's life."[26] But if it is immoral to place family above productive work—and risking one's life to save one's wife does indeed put one's productive work at risk—then risking one's life to save one's wife is immoral.

Redeeming Love

"Art is the indispensable medium for the communication of a moral ideal," Rand once said.[27] But not all that is communicated through art is ideally moral. What Rand has communicated through her novels to a generation of admirers is a disastrous concept of love. The ethics of rational self-interest and the Dagny principle has left the high hopes of Objectivist love unfulfilled.

What are we to do? Is everything lost? Perhaps not. Let us consider again Rand's views on the legitimacy of saving strangers. We may yet discover something of hope and love, arrived at by a different pathway.

Rand had said it would be irrational for a man of self-esteem to put his life at great risk in order to save a stranger. A person should risk his life only to save someone of high value to him. This being the case, perhaps we may conclude that a great man who chooses to risk his life and save a person has by that act demonstrated the worth and value of the victim to himself. What then does this imply about Christ's willingness to save the person who calls to him? What does it say about the value of that person to Messiah? The conclusion to be drawn is too wonderful. God, who is infinitely great in his majesty and glory, has bestowed immense value and honor on us by his willingness to lay down his life and rescue us. For "God so loved the world, that He gave His only begotten Son, that whoever believes in Him should not perish, but have eternal life."[28] He says, "I will call those who were not My people, 'My people,' and her who was not beloved, 'beloved.' . . . [T]hey shall

---

[26] *"Playboy's* Interview with Ayn Rand," pamphlet, p. 7 as quoted in William O'Neill, *With Charity toward None*, footnote number 177, p. 193.
[27] *The Romantic Manifesto*, p. 21.
[28] John 3:16.

be called the sons of the living God."[29] Furthermore, Christ's actions testify to his courage, steadfastness, and rationality. Jesus did not shrink back in cowardice or panic in irrational fear when confronted with death on the cross. Instead, he endured, despising the shame, so that he might win eternal life for many. How ardently he must love us. And how worthy he is of our love.

Christ's sacrifice on the cross tells of his love for those who believe in him, yet it also speaks to the issue of romantic love. It is no coincidence that Christian believers are called the Bride of Christ and that the husband is called upon to love his wife even as Christ gave himself up and died for the Church.[30] In contrast to the Objectivist view, which ultimately calls for the satisfaction of one's own desires and the verification of one's self-worth through the never-ending pursuit of the highest type, Christian love represents a decision and calls for commitment. It does not deny the legitimacy of physical appeal, shared sense of life, or any other reasons why two people might be attracted to each other, but it demands the one thing that will outlast all other considerations and make genuine love and intimacy possible: commitment of the kind that Christ showed. That commitment extends to situations beyond the infrequent occasions of possible drowning or severe sickness, when a man is supposed to lay down his life for his wife. It is the daily plague of self-centeredness with the concomitant tendency to neglect, to fantasize, and to criticize that needs to be laid down in favor of a love that accepts, edifies, encourages, and protects. And should we pursue Christ's model of love, we will finally discover the genuine love and intimacy that we have always longed for.

Unshakable, immovable, faithful and true
Full of wisdom, strength and beauty
These things are true of You

---

[29] Romans 9:25–26.
[30] Ephesians 5:25–26.

Fearless, courageous
Righteousness shines through in all You do
Yet You're so humble, You laid down Your life
These things are true of You

And as I turn my face to You
Oh Lord, I ask and pray
By the power of Your love and grace
Make these things true of me too
Make these things true of me too

Tommy Walker

PART TWO

THE PHILOSOPHY

7

A SURVEY OF OBJECTIVISM

As a human being, you have no choice about the fact that you need a philosophy. Your only choice is whether you define your philosophy by a conscious, rational, disciplined process of thought and scrupulously logical deliberation—or let your subconscious accumulate a junk heap of unwarranted conclusions, false generalizations, undefined contradictions, undigested slogans, unidentified wishes, doubts and fears thrown together by chance. . . .

Ayn Rand, *Philosophy: Who Needs It*

S he has been called "The Voice of Reason." With great admiration, Nathaniel Branden once referred to her as "Mrs. Logic."[1] Barbara Branden recalled how she was struck by the perceptive, intense, and haunting quality of Ayn Rand's eyes on meeting her for the first time.[2] If the eyes are the window to the soul, then Rand's eyes apparently radiated the intensity of her intellect.

In an age that was characterized by a dearth of philosophical systems that spoke coherently about reality and the certainty of knowledge, Ayn Rand's philosophy of Objectivism attracted the attention of thousands because she seemed to have produced one. Objectivism, she claimed, was a philosophical system built on and deduced from fundamental axioms or principles. Just as geometric theorems are valid only if they are deduced from fundamental axioms, so also are philosophical truths. And if the axioms are wrong, then the subsequent propositions and conclusions cannot be correct.

But where does one begin the study of philosophy? The task may seem overwhelming. Like mathematics, which has many subdisciplines, philosophy also has different branches of interest and study. Every system of philosophy has these divisions. However, the diversity of fields should not distract from the possible unity of the subject, for the issues are all interrelated. One question leads to another. For example, the question of price controls in the field of economics depends on another question: What is the function of government? This question, in turn, is determined by a person's view of the relationship between individual men and society. Is society an entity, or is it merely a collection of individuals? Are individuals to be subordinated to the purpose of society, or does society exist in order to protect individual rights? What kind of behavior or morality is appropriate to indi-

---

[1] Barbara Branden, *The Passion of Ayn Rand*, p. 233.
[2] *The Passion of Ayn Rand*, p. x.

viduals anyway? And how do we know which morality is correct? Furthermore, that judgment depends on our prior understanding of the nature of man and his relation to other men. So we must ask: What is the nature of man? What is the nature of reality? How do we discover the answers to these questions? And how do we know anything anyway? Thus it may be seen that all questions about life and philosophy are hierarchical and interdependent.

So what are the branches of philosophy? Most philosophers would agree that metaphysics (the study of the nature of reality), epistemology (the study of the nature and limits of knowledge), ethics (the study of morality), and politics (the study of government) form the primary disciplines of philosophy. Once, a book salesman asked Ayn Rand to present the essentials of her philosophy while standing on one foot. She summarized her philosophy of Objectivism as follows:

1. Metaphysics: Objective Reality
2. Epistemology: Reason
3. Ethics: Self-Interest
4. Politics: Capitalism[3]

There is a reason for the order in which Rand chose to present the main branches of her philosophy. Ethics and politics, the practical disciplines of philosophy, are dependent upon epistemology and metaphysics, the more fundamental areas of study. Together, they ought to form a cohesive whole. Like a skyscraper, the foundations must be sound if the integrity of the highest floors is to be preserved. In the chapters that follow, we will examine in considerable detail Rand's philosophy with respect to these four branches of study. However, for the sake of any who are not familiar with her beliefs, it will be helpful to summarize the essentials of her philosophy here.

---

[3] "Introducing Objectivism," *The Objectivist Newsletter*, August 1962, p. 35.

Metaphysics

Rand believed in the primacy of existence. In metaphysics, she taught that reality exists independently of any consciousness that perceives it. The world out there exists, and we do not alter it by our thoughts or feelings. Quoting Francis Bacon, Rand said, "Nature, to be commanded, must be obeyed," and in her own vernacular, "Wishing won't make it so."[4]

Rand knew there were philosophers who taught that reality depends on our thinking of it. They seem to believe either that reality is entirely a creation of our imagination and has the potential of vanishing when we stop thinking about it, or that the mind alters the sensory information presented to it so as to yield an unfaithful representation of the world out there. Either way, that view of reality seems to make it impossible to possess knowledge. Practically, it tends toward skepticism, subjectivism, or both. In addition, philosophies that make reality dependent on consciousness seem to have a tendency to discount the importance of physical existence and therefore undermine the right of man to achieve happiness on earth. Consequently, Rand repeatedly asserted the proposition "existence exists" in an effort to emphasize the existence of an objective material reality.[5] Indeed, "existence exists" became one of the famous axioms of her philosophical system; it resonated as a battle cry for the Objectivist revolution. Moreover, like Aristotle who defined the law of identity, *A is A*, Rand asserted that there is no contradiction in reality. A thing is itself, and not another.

Epistemology

Naturally, the question then arises: How do we know? If a person makes certain claims about the nature of this reality, be it the mechanistic and atomic theories of the nineteenth century or the quantum mechanical and statistical theories of the twentieth century, the question remains: How does one know?

---

[4] "Introducing Objectivism," *The Objectivist Newsletter*, August 1962, p. 35.
[5] *Atlas Shrugged*, p. 942.

For Rand, the method is reason. What Rand meant by reason was sensation plus abstraction. "Reason is the faculty that perceives, identifies and integrates the material provided by [man's] senses."[6] This approach to knowledge is fundamentally an Aristotelian one. It is also a form of empiricism. According to Rand, the senses are the sole pathways through which information about reality is conveyed to the mind for further processing. That processing involves abstraction by the identification of similarities or differences among the materials provided by the senses, and results in the formation of percepts (a group of sensations) and, eventually, concepts. Therefore, consciousness, the faculty that perceives reality, is ultimately based on sensation.

However, in order to avoid what we earlier noted as the distressing view of some philosophers, namely that our minds and sensory apparatus distort the data obtained from reality, Rand insisted, after Aristotle, on a *tabula rasa* mind. *Tabula rasa* means that the mind is a blank slate at birth. It possesses no preconceived ideas, Platonic forms, or Kantian categories that can be imposed on sensory experience to produce knowledge. The reason for this formulation is to promote objectivity, so that knowledge is not dependent on the preformed categories and modes of thinking inherent in the mind, which Rand claimed were subjective and arbitrary.

Concepts and categories of thought, including logic, then are derived from perceptions that in turn are based on our sensory experience of a reality that is objective and independent of our thinking. This method renders irrelevant the attitude and method of faith, which Rand defined as the acceptance of beliefs without evidence. Faith is in fact "a short-circuit destroying the mind. . . ."[7] For Rand, truth is based on reality, which is objective; and that which can be validly derived from reality by a process of sensation and abstraction is truth.

---

[6] *Atlas Shrugged*, p. 942.
[7] *Atlas Shrugged*, p. 945.

Ethics

Having asserted an objective reality and a consciousness capable of apprehending that reality, Rand's next task was to develop her ethical system. Rand was well known for her staunch support of the morality of rational self-interest; however, her thinking was more profound than it first appears. Her approach to the problem of ethics begins with a basic question. "The first question is not: What particular code of values should man accept? The first question is: Does man need values at all—and why?"[8]

Is a code of ethics arbitrary? Is it unsupported by the facts of reality, or is it an objective requirement of man's nature? For Rand, ethics is indeed grounded in objective reality. She reasoned as follows: Only living beings face an alternative—existence or nonexistence. Matter changes from one form to another, but only living things can cease to exist. It is this alternative confronting living things that makes a code of values and a code of survival possible. Among living things, plants and animals possess automatic codes of survival, but man does not.[9] Man's mind is superior to the animals because it exhibits rationality and logic, but man is also distinguished from the animals in that he has to *choose* to think. In other words, man is a being of *volitional* consciousness. And because man can also choose *not* to think, he "is the only living species that has the power to act as his own destroyer. . . ."[10] Consequently, for man, "the question 'to be or not to be' is the question 'to think or not to think.'"[11] Therefore, it is the goal of survival and man's possession of volitional consciousness that distinguishes him from other living things and makes the development of a moral code both possible and necessary.

Like Aristotle, Rand believed that what a living being *is* implies what it *ought* to do. In the case of human beings, what man *is* implies what he *ought* to do. Therefore, the standard of Objectivist

---

[8] "The Objectivist Ethics," *The Virtue of Selfishness*, p. 13.
[9] "The Objectivist Ethics," *The Virtue of Selfishness*, pp. 15–19.
[10] "The Objectivist Ethics," *The Virtue of Selfishness*, p. 22.
[11] *Atlas Shrugged*, p. 939.

ethics is man's life *as* man, or "man's survival *qua* man" as Rand liked to phrase it. And what is man? He is a sovereign, rational being who, according to Rand, has to be man by choice. Consequently, the purpose of ethics is to teach him how to live like a man, like a rational human being. Therefore, Rand declared, "The Objectivist ethics holds man's life as the *standard* of value—and *his own life* as the ethical *purpose* of every individual man."[12]

The standard of value, according to Objectivism, is the quality of life suitable to a man *qua* man. And what does the life of a rational man consist of? It is characterized by the values of reason, purpose, and self-esteem and the virtues of rationality, productiveness, and pride. Furthermore, because each man is an end in himself—his life is his purpose—he has to live for his own sake. He can neither sacrifice himself to others, nor ask that others be sacrificed to him. This means that for every individual "*the achievement of his own happiness is man's highest moral purpose.*"[13] Hence, the Objectivist code of ethics consists of rational self-interest. However, this code of ethics is not subjective. It is absolute, objective, and grounded in reality and reason. "Morality is a code of black and white," Rand wrote. "There may be 'gray' men, but there can be no 'gray' moral principles."[14]

Politics

"Every political system is based on some code of ethics," Rand observed.[15] This is no less true of Objectivism. Indeed, what implications does Rand's ethics of rational self-interest have for her theory of government? Since each man's happiness is the moral purpose of his life, Rand argued that each man is also an end in himself. Therefore, no person should be sacrificed for the benefit of another. Instead, men ought always to deal with each other as traders, giving value for value. Whether the areas of concern are

---

[12] "The Objectivist Ethics," *The Virtue of Selfishness*, p. 25.
[13] "The Objectivist Ethics," *The Virtue of Selfishness*, p. 27.
[14] "The Cult of Moral Grayness," *The Virtue of Selfishness*, p. 79.
[15] "Man's Rights," *Capitalism: The Unknown Ideal*, p. 320.

human relationships or economic exchange, rational beings deal with each other by trade. Hence, the conditions in society that permit men to deal with each other as traders need to be thought out and systematized into a political structure. For Rand, the basic principle of such a political system is freedom, and in Objectivist politics it is summarized in what the Libertarians have come to refer to as the *nonaggression axiom*: "[N]o man may *initiate* the use of physical force against others," said Rand.[16] Force may be used only in response to the initiation of force. Hence, the moral purpose of government is to protect man's rights. These rights include the "right to his own life, to his own liberty, to his *own property*, and to the pursuit of his own happiness."[17]

According to Rand, the only system that accomplishes this is the original American ideal, *laissez-faire* capitalism. Only in *laissez-faire* capitalism, where there is a complete separation of state and economics, do men have the opportunity to live as man *qua* man. Under capitalism, they are accorded the freedom to think, to gain knowledge, to associate, and to trade. Freedom also encourages rationality, productivity, and generosity. Freedom is what makes the life of a rational human being possible. Therefore, capitalism is the only system compatible with the nature of man and the morality of rational self-interest.

Under this system, government powers are severely restricted. Government serves only as a protector of individual rights and is limited to the functions of police, law courts, and national defense. Economic intervention by the government is considered the initiation of physical force upon the free choice and market decisions made by individuals; such meddling would be outlawed. Examples of government interference that are prohibited by Objectivism span the spectrum from minimum wage regulation to antitrust legislation, from price supports to censorship.

Rand believed that the economic disasters of the past have been the result of fallacious intervention by governments that failed to recognize the fundamental nature of man. Man is a rational being

16 "The Objectivist Ethics," *The Virtue of Selfishness*, p. 32.
17 "The Objectivist Ethics," *The Virtue of Selfishness*, p. 33.

who requires freedom in order to think, to trade, and to pursue his own happiness. That failure to identify and understand the nature of man has led to the abandonment of *laissez-faire* principles and the adoption of an alien political system. That political system is socialism, and it has been spawned by the destructive morality of altruism. Altruism "holds that man has no right to exist for his own sake, that service to others is the only justification of his existence, and that self-sacrifice is his highest moral duty, virtue and value."[18] Consequently, Rand saw the imminent collapse of civilization as rooted in the philosophy of altruism. Hence, her defense of *laissez-faire* capitalism is based on moral principles and not merely on issues of productivity and efficiency. While Rand was best known as an advocate of egoism and capitalism, she saw herself primarily as a champion of reason, for she recognized that it was the validity of her views on the fundamental issues of philosophy that would make her defense of egoism and capitalism viable. So it is with Rand's theory of knowledge and view of reality that we begin our detailed analysis in the next chapter.

---

[18] "The Objectivist Ethics," *The Virtue of Selfishness*, p. 34.

8

REASON AND REALITY

In philosophy, the fundamentals are metaphysics and epistemology. On the basis of a knowable universe and of a rational
faculty's competence to grasp it, you can define man's proper ethics, politics and esthetics. . . . But what will you accomplish if you
advocate honesty in ethics, while telling men that there is no such
thing as truth, fact or reality? What will you do if you advocate
political freedom on the grounds that you *feel* it is good, and find
yourself confronting an ambitious thug who declares that he feels
quite differently.

Ayn Rand, *Philosophy: Who Needs It*

A theory which explained everything else in the whole universe but which made it impossible to believe that our thinking
was valid, would be utterly out of court.

C. S. Lewis, *Miracles*

I n the climactic radio address in *Atlas Shrugged*, John Galt proclaims the basic principles of Objectivism:

> Existence exists—and the act of grasping that statement implies two corollary axioms: that something exists which one perceives and that one exists possessing consciousness, consciousness being the faculty of perceiving that which exists.
>
> If nothing exists, there can be no consciousness: a consciousness with nothing to be conscious of is a contradiction in terms. . . .
>
> To exist is to be something, as distinguished from the nothing of non-existence, it is to be an entity of a specific nature made of specific attributes. . . . *A is A*. A thing is itself. You have never grasped the meaning of [Aristotle's] statement. I am here to complete it: Existence is Identity, Consciousness is Identification.[1]

In the span of a few paragraphs, Rand has laid out the fundamentals of her philosophy. First, Rand stresses the existence of an external world that is independent of our perception of it. Existence exists. Moreover, existence is logical. Each thing that exists has an identity. It cannot be otherwise, and she considers it meaningless to question why a thing is itself and not another. Next, consciousness is the faculty by which we perceive reality. Reason is the method of cognition, and it works by a process of sensation and abstraction. The laws of logic are themselves developed in this process. These features of her philosophy make it a form of Aristotelianism.[2]

---

[1] *Atlas Shrugged*, p. 942.

[2] While Rand disagreed with many of Aristotle's ideas, she openly acknowledged her indebtedness to Aristotle for his contributions to her philosophy. She paid tribute to his accomplishments in philosophy, especially in logic, by naming the three parts of *Atlas Shrugged* after his laws: "Non-contradiction," "Either-or," and "A is A." See "About the Author," *Atlas Shrugged*.

At first, Rand's claims seem self-evident. For example, the chair that I see in front of me exists whether I think about it or not. The chair has unique chemical and physical characteristics that make up its identity. These characteristics do not contradict each other. If they were contradictory, how could the chair exist? Moreover, who in their right mind would deny this common-sense view of reality? Who would be so obtuse as to deny existence or the laws of logic? Rand's answer is: most philosophers. "In philosophy, we are taught that man's mind is impotent, that reality is unknowable, that knowledge is an illusion, and reason a superstition."[3] It seems that those who have been entrusted with the task of helping us think through these issues have betrayed our trust and perverted the search for truth. Rand argues that it was the philosophers' rebellion against Aristotelian logic, reason, and reality that has led civilization to its current state of corruption and impending collapse. Without the confidence and certainty that radiated from Aristotle's philosophy, imperfect though it may be, today's intellectuals find themselves mired in the stagnating swamp of skepticism. Rand proposed to correct that trend by completing and clarifying Aristotle's ideas and thereby providing an antidote to the deadly philosophies espoused by the alleged guardians of man's mind.

There are several reasons why Rand's philosophical views appeal to many readers. First, the existence of an external world and the idea that knowledge comes to us through the senses seem so obvious that we are inclined to trust a philosophy that supports these views. Second, Rand's fiction presents her philosophy effectively. Her stories illustrate how the right philosophy—her philosophy of Objectivism—leads to triumphant living while the wrong philosophies result in wretched and unfulfilled existence. Finally, her confident exposition of the subject, accompanied by her literary eloquence, contrasts with the muddled thinking of her antagonists, at least the way she portrayed them as thinking. Commenting on the Scottish philosopher David Hume, Rand writes: "When Hume declared that the apparent existence of an object did not guarantee

---

[3] *For the New Intellectual*, pp. 10–11.

that it would not vanish spontaneously next moment, . . . what men were hearing was the manifesto of a philosophical movement that can be designated only as *Attila-ism*."[4] Probably few admirers of Rand actually gave David Hume a fair hearing before accepting Rand's conclusions about him. Nevertheless, Rand set the alternatives before us. Choose the possibility of John Galt and the philosophy of Objectivism, or choose James Taggart and the philosophy of David Hume, Immanuel Kant, and Attila the Hun. Given that choice, what is a sane man to do?

Axioms: A Preliminary Consideration

At the age of fourteen, when I discovered Rand's writings, I was impressed by Rand's claim that her philosophy was systematically deduced from fundamental axioms. As a freshman in high school and just becoming acquainted with the logical consistency of geometry, I was drawn by the suggestion that philosophy could be as rigorous as mathematics. In geometry, we begin with a few basic propositions known as *axioms*. (Axioms are the rock-bottom ideas of any system of thought. There is nothing more basic. Axioms are not proven; they are chosen and assumed to be true. If they had to be proven, there would be something still more basic. Then those more basic statements would be the axioms.) Next, axioms are used to derive other truths by a process of deductive logic; the resultant truths are known as *theorems*. Hence, a few axioms may be used to derive many theorems. The situation is similar in philosophy. A few basic principles may be used to derive hundreds of theorems in epistemology, metaphysics, ethics, and politics. Different systems of philosophy begin with different presuppositions or axioms. And it seemed to me that Rand's system had succeeded where others had failed. Not only did her axioms appear valid, but her conclusions seemed consistent with what common sense revealed about the world.

Several years later, in college, I became better acquainted with set theory and axiomatic systems. This exposure helped me to gain

---

[4] *For the New Intellectual*, p. 29.

a better understanding of Objectivism. But it also raised some questions. If Objectivism were an axiomatic system, then it seemed to me that the same criticisms that applied to mathematical systems based on axioms were also applicable to Rand's philosophy. Of great interest to me was the *incompleteness theorem* formulated by the Austrian mathematician Kurt Gödel.

In *Gödel Escher Bach*, Douglas Hofstadter gives one of the more easily understood definitions of this theorem. "All consistent axiomatic formulations of number theory include undecidable propositions."[5] Basically, Gödel found that for any particular axiomatic system, there will be some ideas or propositions whose truth or falsehood simply cannot be decided upon by an appeal to the axioms of that system. A proposition may be true even if it cannot be deduced from the axioms.

Gödel's incompleteness theorem, as I understood it, means that even if Rand had deduced her philosophy from her axioms (and we have yet to verify this), there would still be propositions whose truth or falsehood could not be determined within the context of her axioms. Practically, this means that Objectivism should not claim to know more than it can prove. Nor can Objectivists deny the truth of a proposition in question that they oppose simply by saying there was insufficient evidence for it. Unless the proposition can be proven false (a universal negative), it may still be true. This gave me pause to think. Does the Objectivist belief in material existence automatically rule out immaterial realities like God?[6] Or, does belief in the validity of the senses exclude the validity of nonsensory pathways to knowledge, like revelation? The propositions in question may in fact be true; however, from the standpoint of Objectivist axioms, they are undecidable.

Subsequently, I discovered a number of writers who also thought Rand's axioms were of limited utility; however, they reached this conclusion without invoking Gödel's incompleteness theorem. For example, in *The Philosophic Thought of Ayn Rand*, Wallace Matson

---

[5] *Gödel Escher Bach*, p. 17.
[6] See chapter 11 on the logical indefensibility of the antitheistic assertion of a universal negative: "There is no God."

comments that even philosophers who disagree with Rand are
unlikely to deny her axioms. "The subjectivists are not so obliging
as to deny existence outright."[7] Perhaps that is because Rand's
axiom of existence is not as useful as she would like us to believe.
Matson continues, "It is not generally conceded to be sufficient to
enunciate an 'axiom' to the effect that 'Existence exists' and 'to
sweep one's arm around [as Rand does] and say: "I mean *this*.""[8]

Moreover, in *Without a Prayer*, John Robbins points out that an
attribute like existence that can be used to describe everything is
essentially meaningless.[9] To say that A exists, B exists, C exists,
etc., makes the word *exists* meaningless, just as saying A is white,
B is white, C is white, etc., makes *white* meaningless. Existence
would then be indistinguishable from nonexistence, just as white-
ness would be indistinguishable from blackness.

Furthermore, Rand's claim that her philosophy is the only one
worthy of the Aristotelian tradition has been disputed. As Robert
Hollinger points out, other philosophers, including Quine and
Wittgenstein, may have just as much right to claim the heritage
and blessing of Aristotle as Rand did.[10] Again the problem has to
do with fundamentals, and Hollinger concludes:

> Unless Rand's philosophy can be supported by more than the
> four axioms [Hollinger includes two of Rand's other basic ideas
> in his list] cited above, or until it can be shown that these axi-
> oms support only her philosophy, it will be difficult to take her
> views seriously. That is, she must show that her remarks are not
> merely the banalities they seem to be.[11]

Hollinger's words may seem harsh, but they ought to be given due
consideration. Too many readers ignore these issues because they

---

[7] Wallace Matson, "Rand on Concepts," in *The Philosophic Thought of Ayn Rand*,
edited by Douglas Den Uyl and Douglas Rasmussen, p. 27.
[8] Wallace Matson, "Rand on Concepts," *The Philosophic Thought of Ayn Rand*,
p. 27; *Introduction to Objectivist Epistemology*, p. 53.
[9] *Without a Prayer*, p. 87.
[10] Robert Hollinger, "Ayn Rand's Epistemology," *The Philosophic Thought of Ayn
Rand*, pp. 55–56.
[11] Robert Hollinger, "Ayn Rand's Epistemology," *The Philosophic Thought of Ayn
Rand*, p. 40.

find Rand's fiction and her support of individualism appealing. Her basic ideas have to be verified. Indeed, it was my initial doubt and reservations concerning Rand's axioms that eventually helped to break the hold that Rand's philosophy had on me and opened my eyes to the possibility of truth elsewhere. Subsequently, John Robbins's insightful analysis of Rand's philosophy in *Answer to Ayn Rand* (now republished as *Without a Prayer*) helped me to better understand where Objectivist epistemology falls short in the task of establishing truth and knowing reality.

In the remainder of this chapter, I will attempt to reconstruct the basic elements of Rand's epistemology and metaphysics and discuss them critically. Some problems common to all empirical theories, including those of Aristotle and of Hume will be considered in the process. The seminal works of John Robbins and philosopher Gordon Clark, among others, will be brought to bear on the subject. Finally, a positive construction will be offered to the reader for consideration. We begin with some preliminary questions about the nature of existence and consciousness.

Preliminary Questions about Existence and Consciousness

In order for knowledge to be possible, truth must exist. Truth is universal: unchanging and applicable for all time and space. Rand shared in the belief that knowledge and truth have to exist. She recognized the self-defeating nature of skepticism. In *Atlas Shrugged*, the young metallurgist working for Rearden, just out of college and affectionately known as the Wet Nurse, represents the product of modern universities that brainwash their students into believing that there are no absolutes. Did it ever occur to them that those who say "There are no absolutes!" are at the same time uttering an absolute? Hence, skepticism refutes itself. However, a belief in the existence of truth and the self-refutation of skepticism does not constitute a default proof for the Objectivist philosophy. It remains to be seen if Objectivism can provide a workable theory of knowledge that explains and arrives at truth.

Let us return to Rand's basic axioms: Existence exists, and consciousness is the faculty that perceives existence. These statements leave open two questions: What is the nature of consciousness as a faculty of perception, and what is the nature of the existence that is perceived? Antiskeptical beliefs about the nature of thought, logic, truth, and existence do not automatically lead us to the conclusion that existence consists of a physical realm external to our consciousness that is known by means of the senses. Of course, if nothing—matter, energy, mind, or other realms—existed at all, then consciousness would not exist either. Rand is correct in saying that a "consciousness with nothing to be conscious of is a contradiction in terms"; however, that truism does not automatically guarantee the presence of an external world. As Robbins points out, all that a consciousness requires in order to be conscious are the contents of consciousness.[12] The contents of consciousness exist, but we cannot assume that the nature of these existents are external objects. The conscious awareness of qualities like green, hard, sweet, or loud, and entities like persons, places, or things cannot guarantee that they are not just events taking place in my mind. Let me illustrate with a diagram.

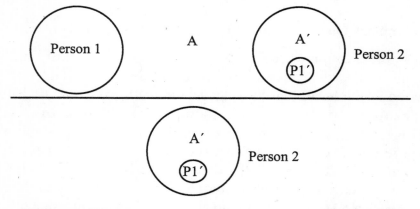

Figure 8.1. The object A as well as person 1 (P1) are recognized as images A´ and P1´ in the mind of person 2. But person 2 never has any reason to suppose that an external A or P1 actually exists. As far as person 2 is concerned, the situation represented in the top half of this figure may be equivalent to the situation depicted in the bottom half of this figure without the external referents A and P1.

---

[12] *Without a Prayer*, pp. 87–88.

The common-sense view of the world is depicted in the top half of figure 8.1. The large circles represent the minds of persons 1 and 2. An external object A is presumed to exist with a corresponding image A´ in the mind of person 2. Person 1 (P1) is transformed into an image P1´ in the mind of person 2. While the world may *appear* to operate in this way, this view cannot be defended. We do not have any reason to suppose this is the way the world is actually structured. As far as person 2 is concerned, all that he can be sure of are the images A´ and P1´ in his mind. The real state of affairs may be as depicted in the bottom half of the diagram, without any independently existing external object A or person 1.

However, Rand believed in the existence of external objects. And the view depicted in the bottom half of figure 8.1 was anathema to her, for it suggests the "prior certainty of consciousness."[13,14] Rand did not want reality to depend on thoughts whether they were yours, mine, or God's; therefore, she insisted upon the existence of an independent, external world of matter. For her, matter was more basic than consciousness. But what evidence did she have for this external world of matter? Whatever we perceive or experience takes place within our consciousness. We begin with the contents of our consciousness. And from that vantage point, the assertion that an external reality exists consisting of indestructible matter merely begs the question. Ultimately, any assertions we make about the nature of reality depend on a prior question: How do you know? If a person cannot defend his theory of knowledge, he cannot claim to know what reality consists of. Therefore, epistemology, rather than metaphysics, has to be the more basic area of inquiry. At times, Rand appeared to understand the proper order of philosophic investigation, even though much of her writing suggests that she believed metaphysics to be the starting place of philosophical inquiry. She did, however, say, "Philosophy is the

---

[13] Book Review on *Aristotle* (by John Herman Randall), *The Objectivist Newsletter*, May 1963, p. 18.
[14] *For the New Intellectual*, p. 28.

foundation of science; epistemology is the foundation of philosophy."[15] Moreover, she writes:

> Two questions are involved in [man's] every conclusion, conviction, decision, choice or claim: *What* do I know?—and: *How* do I know it? It is the task of epistemology to provide the answer to the "How?"—which then enables the special sciences to provide the answers to the "What?"[16]

However, as Robbins points out, "[M]etaphysics is a 'special science' in the sense used here, for it answers the question 'What?'"[17] Thus Rand's own words show that metaphysics cannot be the beginning point of philosophical inquiry; epistemology is.

Objectivist Epistemology

Rand describes herself as *the* champion of reason, and she defines *reason* as follows:

> Reason is the faculty that perceives, identifies and integrates the material provided by [man's] senses.[18]

> Reason . . . is man's only means of perceiving reality, his only source of knowledge, his only guide to action, and his basic means of survival.[19]

Thus we may conclude that Rand's version of reason is sensation plus abstraction. The process of thought is governed by logic, and "logic is the art of *non-contradictory identification*."[20] Whatever reason is, it is neither emotions nor feelings. Nor is it *faith*, which Nathaniel Branden, Rand's former associate, defines as

> the acceptance of ideas or allegations without sensory evidence or rational demonstration. "Faith in reason" is a contradiction

---

[15] *Introduction to Objectivist Epistemology*, p. 99.
[16] *Introduction to Objectivist Epistemology*, p. 105.
[17] *Without a Prayer*, p. 21.
[18] *Atlas Shrugged*, p. 942.
[19] "Introducing Objectivism," *The Objectivist Newsletter*, August 1962, p. 35.
[20] *Atlas Shrugged*, p. 943.

in terms. "Faith" is a concept that possesses meaning only *in contradistinction* to reason. The concept of "faith" cannot *antecede* reason, it cannot provide the grounds for the acceptance of reason—it is the revolt *against* reason.[21]

Branden also writes, "Faith is the equation of *feeling* with *knowledge*."[22] Moreover, Rand defines faith as "a short-circuit destroying the mind. . . ."[23] She draws a sharp distinction between faith and reason and even goes so far as to characterize the advocates of faith as champions of force and brutal tyranny, while claiming the aura of freedom for the advocates of reason.[24] Thus reason and faith appear to stand as polar opposites that cannot be reconciled.

Apparently, one of the reasons for Rand's emphasis on the antithesis of reason and faith was this: She hoped to defeat opposing philosophies, such as those of Kant and Hegel, by portraying them as advocates of faith, force, and feelings and by denying them the blessing of *reason*. We should be careful, however, with Rand's definition of reason as sensation plus abstraction. As Robbins points out, different philosophers define reason differently.[25] Reason can mean sensory experience (Hume), pure logic (Hegel), or a combination of both (Aquinas). It would be a mistake to conclude that Rand had exclusive claims to the meaning of *reason*.

Mimi Gladstein, for example, commits this error in her book *The Ayn Rand Companion*.[26] In her review of *Answer to Ayn Rand*, by John Robbins, Gladstein operates under the assumption that faith is feelings and that revelation is an *unreasonable* and unworkable theory of knowledge. Ironically, Gladstein congratulates William O'Neill, the author of *With Charity toward None*, for his evenhanded criticism of Rand. Yet even O'Neill lists revelation,

[21] Nathaniel Branden, "The Stolen Concept," *The Objectivist Newsletter*, January 1963, p. 4.
[22] Nathaniel Branden, "Mental Health versus Mysticism and Self-Sacrifice," *The Virtue of Selfishness*, p. 37.
[23] *Atlas Shrugged*, p. 945.
[24] "Faith and Force," *Philosophy: Who Needs It*, p. 80.
[25] *Without a Prayer*, pp. 12–13.
[26] *The Ayn Rand Companion*, p. 91.

albeit not specifically the kind Robbins had in mind, as an alternative theory of knowledge.[27] Part of the reason for Gladstein's and most people's misunderstanding of revelation comes from Objectivism's mistaken characterization of faith as feelings. Now, an irrationalist like Sören Kierkegaard may indeed have emphasized infinite passion as the essence of religion,[28] but that is hardly the meaning of Christian revelation. We shall have more to say about the meaning of faith and reason in Christianity at the conclusion of this chapter; but for now, the crux of the matter is this: Nearly every philosopher claims to be on the side of *reason*. Therefore, we would do well to recognize that Rand does not have exclusive claims to *reason*. Moreover, we should be hesitant to accept Rand's characterization of other philosophers as irrational until we have made an effort to understand their position. Nevertheless, in Rand's case, she has staked her particular theory of knowledge on sensation and abstraction, and that is where we shall begin.

The Validity of the Senses

Rand asserts that our information about reality and our grasp of truth proceeds from the senses. Since Rand gives the senses such a prominent place in her theory of knowledge, should we not expect her to demonstrate the validity of sensation? Unfortunately such a demonstration does not exist. In the *Introduction to Objectivist Epistemology*, she writes:

> . . . I do not include here a discussion of the validity of man's senses—since the arguments of those who attack the senses are merely variants of the fallacy of the "stolen concept." For the purpose of this series, the validity of the senses must be taken for granted. . . .[29]

---

[27] *With Charity toward None*, p. 84; *The Ayn Rand Companion*, p. 90.
[28] *Concluding Unscientific Postscript*, translated by D.F. Swensen and Walter Lowrie (Princeton, NJ: Princeton University Press, 1941), p. 182; see also Gordon Clark, *Three Types of Religious Philosophy*, pp. 95–108.
[29] *Introduction to Objectivist Epistemology*, p. 4.

Indeed, the proof for the validity of the senses is not to be found in the *Introduction to Objectivist Epistemology* or in any of Rand's other writings.[30] Instead, we are asked to take the validity of the senses for granted without proof.

The only argument that Rand produces in support of her theory of sensation is a negative one. According to Rand, arguments against the senses invariably commit what she calls the fallacy of the "stolen concept." What precisely is the fallacy of the stolen concept, and how does its violation assure the validity of sensation as the means to knowledge? Nathaniel Branden defines the fallacy as "the act of using a concept while ignoring, contradicting or denying the validity of the concepts on which it logically and genetically depends."[31] For the sake of clarity, his argument can be divided into two parts.

First, he writes:

> It is rational to ask: "*How* does man achieve knowledge?" It is not rational to ask: "*Can* man achieve knowledge?"—because the ability to ask the question presupposes a knowledge of man and of the nature of knowledge.[32]

Second,

> It is rational to ask: "*How* do the senses enable man to perceive reality?" It is not rational to ask: "*Do* the senses enable man to perceive reality?"—because if they do not, by what means did the speaker acquire his knowledge of the senses, of perception, of man and of reality?[33]

---

[30] See *Without a Prayer* for John Robbins's critical examination of Leonard Peikoff's (*Objectivism: The Philosophy of Ayn Rand*) and David Kelly's (*The Evidence of the Senses*) attempts to establish the validity of the senses.

[31] Nathaniel Branden, "The Stolen Concept," *The Objectivist Newsletter*, January 1963, p. 4.

[32] Nathaniel Branden, "The Stolen Concept," *The Objectivist Newsletter*, January 1963, p. 2.

[33] Nathaniel Branden, "The Stolen Concept," *The Objectivist Newsletter*, January 1963, p. 4.

Part one of Branden's argument is simply a refutation of skepticism. Augustine formulated this argument long ago in anticipation of Descartes's famous *cogito ergo sum*, or "I think; therefore, I am." For if I claim that I know nothing, I am in fact claiming that I know something. If I know something, then I know at least that I exist.[34, 35] Consequently, skepticism refutes itself, and knowledge is possible. However, part two of Branden's argument is fallacious. Just because knowledge is possible, we cannot conclude that sensation is *one of many* valid pathways, much less the *only* pathway to knowledge as Branden claims. The validity of sensation is what needs to be demonstrated and proven.

As Robbins observes, Branden simply begs the question in his argument for the validity of the senses:

> Questioning the "validity" of the senses ("accuracy" or "cognitive reliability" might be better terms) presupposes only awareness of the ideas of the senses, of perception, of man, and of reality. Such questioning does not "logically or genetically" presuppose that knowledge can be gained only through the senses— nor has Rand or Branden ever shown that such questioning makes this latter presupposition. Just as talking about unicorns, dreams, minds, square roots, or justice does not presuppose that our knowledge of them came through the senses, so speaking of reality and the senses does not presuppose our knowledge of them came through the senses.[36]

Moreover, Robbins is not alone in exposing the problems associated with Rand and Branden's appeal to the fallacy of the stolen concept. In reference to a separate issue, Wallace Matson generalizes the problem. In *The Philosophic Thought of Ayn Rand*, he writes:

> The argument based on the stolen concept is transcendental: His argument against *p* depends crucially on concept *C*. But it is impossible that he should have concept *C* unless *p* were true.

---

[34] *City of God*, Book XI, chapter 26; see also W. T. Jones, *A History of Western Philosophy*, Volume II, pp. 87–88.

[35] Wilhelm Windelband, *A History of Philosophy*, Volume I, p. 277.

[36] *Without a Prayer*, p. 35.

Therefore, etc. If such an argument is to go through, it must be established beyond doubt that the second premise is true, i.e., that there is no possible route to the possession of concept *C* other than via *p*. This amounts to proof of a universal negative, a task of formidable difficulty.[37]

If we substitute "the validity of the senses as the means of apprehending reality and gaining knowledge" for *p* and "the ability to speak about reality, the senses, and knowledge" for *C* in the paragraph above, we see that Matson arrives at the same conclusion as Robbins. In other words, if Rand wanted to claim that the senses are the only way to knowledge without proving it, she would have had to establish the impossibility of obtaining knowledge by any other means. This she did not do.

The upshot of this discussion is threefold. The refutation of skepticism is not a theory of knowledge. Nor can such a refutation constitute a validation of sensory epistemology as advocated by empiricism or Objectivism. Finally, it does not satisfactorily argue against other theories of knowledge that are either independent of the senses or only partially dependent on them as a means to knowledge. As a young admirer of Ayn Rand, I was impressed by her refutation of skepticism but failed to realize that it did not constitute a proof for the Objectivist theory of knowledge. I naively used the fallacy of the stolen concept to justify claims for the validity of the senses. Unfortunately, this fancy sounding fallacy becomes a dangerous tool when wielded uncritically. Now that the issue has been clarified, we can no longer take the validity of the senses for granted lest we be accused of taking Rand on faith. However, to get any further in Rand's theory of knowledge, we will have to proceed with a suspension of disbelief regarding the validity of the senses.

The Stages of Consciousness

The reader will recall from the last chapter that Objectivism believes man's mind is blank, or *tabula rasa*, at birth. As we mentioned

---

[37] Walter Matson, "Rand on Concepts," *The Philosophic Thought of Ayn Rand*, p. 27.

before, the *tabula rasa* requirement for consciousness comes from a need to avoid preexistent ideas, categories, or forms in the mind that can distort the material provided by the senses. Quite obviously, it is also necessary because, for Rand, all knowledge came through the senses. Thus, Rand presented her theory within the context of a blank mind. She writes:

> [M]an's consciousness develops in three stages: the stage of sensations, the perceptual, the conceptual—epistemologically, the base of all of man's knowledge is the *perceptual* stage.
>
> Sensations, as such, are not retained in man's memory, nor is man able to experience a pure isolated sensation. As far as can be ascertained, an infant's sensory experience is an undifferentiated chaos. Discriminated awareness begins on the level of percepts.
>
> A percept is a group of sensations automatically retained and integrated by the brain of a living organism. . . . The knowledge of sensations as components of percepts is not direct, it is acquired by man much later: it is a scientific, *conceptual* discovery.[38]
>
> A *concept* is a mental integration of two or more units which are isolated according to a specific characteristic(s) and united by a specific definition.[39]

To summarize, the development of man's consciousness takes place in three stages: sensation, perception, and conception. But notice how quickly Rand skips from sensations to perceptions as the building blocks of man's knowledge. For a philosophy that is built on sensation, this is an interesting position to take. Read her statements again. Presumably, Rand had to resort to the perceptual stage to validate her theory of knowledge because she could not validate sensations. Moreover, sensations cannot be experienced in a pure form. Sensation is "undifferentiated chaos." Yet Rand would have us believe that this sensory chaos is transformed by

---

[38] *Introduction to Objectivist Epistemology*, pp. 5–6.
[39] *Introduction to Objectivist Epistemology*, p. 11.

the brain into percepts and the result of that transformation is correct. How does this take place? Somehow. First, we are asked to take the validity of senses for granted. Then we are told that undifferentiated sensory chaos is transformed into percepts in a mysterious but reliable manner by a blank mind. Are these not the very assertions in need of demonstration? Again, the fact that knowledge is possible and skepticism refutes itself does not imply that the theory of sensation is valid. The reader should never confuse the two. Since Rand could not get us beyond the sensory stage of consciousness, we might conclude, as Robbins did, that "[Rand's] theory of knowledge collapses on page one."[40]

Concept Formation

Yet the difficulties do not end with Rand's theory of sensation and perception; they continue in her discussion of concept formation. Rand writes:

> The issue of concepts (known as "the problem of universals") is philosophy's central issue. Since man's knowledge is gained and held in conceptual form, the validity of man's knowledge depends on the validity of concepts. But concepts are abstractions or universals, and everything that man perceives is particular, concrete. What is the relationship between abstractions and concretes? To what precisely do concepts refer in reality? Do they refer to something real, something that exists—or are they merely inventions of man's mind, arbitrary constructs or loose approximations that cannot claim to represent knowledge?[41]

Perhaps a note of explanation is in order here. The *concretes* are individuals. They are you, me, this chair, and this car. They are individual objects. In contrast, *concepts* are universals or abstractions. They include the species *man* and *furniture* and *car*. They represent generalities or classes of objects. How the individuals and concepts/universals are related to each other is one of the main questions in philosophy.

---

[40] *Without a Prayer*, p. 40.
[41] *Introduction to Objectivist Epistemology*, p. 1.

Now Rand, like Aristotle, believed that the mind identifies individual things by sensing them and then proceeds by a process of mental differentiation and integration to form concepts. But as we have seen, Rand does not have a theory of sensation to stand on any longer. How then does she propose to validate the identification of individuals when she cannot even validate the method of sensation? Nevertheless, let us consider what she has to say about concept formation. (I have segregated and numbered the passages below for the sake of clarity; the emphasis and items set off in parenthesis are Rand's own.)

1. The building-block of man's knowledge is the concept of an "*existent*"—of something that exists, be it a thing, an attribute or an action. Since it is a concept, man cannot grasp it *explicitly* until he has reached the conceptual stage. But it is implicit in every percept . . . and man grasps it *implicitly* on the perceptual level. . . . It is this implicit knowledge that permits his consciousness to develop further. (It may be supposed that the concept "existent" is implicit even on the level of sensations. . . . A sensation is a sensation of *something*, as distinguished from the *nothing* of the preceding and succeeding moments. A sensation does not tell man *what* exists, but only *that* it exists.)[42]

2. The (implicit) concept "existent" undergoes three stages of development in man's mind. The first stage is a child's awareness of objects, of things—which represents the (implicit) concept "*entity*." The second and closely allied stage is the awareness of specific, particular things which he can recognize and distinguish from the rest of his perceptual field—which represents the (implicit) concept "*identity*." The third stage consists of grasping relationships among these entities by grasping the similarities and differences of their identities. This requires the transformation of the (implicit) concept "entity" into the (implicit) concept "*unit*."[43]

---

[42] *Introduction to Objectivist Epistemology*, p. 6.
[43] *Introduction to Objectivist Epistemology*, pp. 6–7.

3. A *concept* is a mental integration of two or more units which are isolated according to a specific characteristic(s) and united by a specific definition.[44]

Recall that Rand has already told us that consciousness develops in three stages: sensual, perceptual, and conceptual. But given Rand's definition of a concept as the third stage of consciousness that results from integrating the products of the previous level of consciousness, namely perception, the question arises: How can a concept be present *prior to* the formation of concepts? Yet this is what Rand claims actually happens. Look at paragraphs 1 and 2 again. A *concept* "existent" is present *implicitly* even at the sensory or perceptual level. It seems to me a concept either exists or does not exist. By using the word *implicit* did Rand wish to say that a nonverbalized *concept* is present at the level of perception and sensation? If that is indeed what she meant, then we would have to ask whether the absence of verbalization of a concept makes the concept any less of a concept? This seems implausible to me. Elsewhere Rand writes, "Words transform concepts into (mental) entities. . . ."[45] What can this mean except that concepts are present in the mind even if they are not verbalized or symbolized? And if concepts are present in the mind, are they not mental entities already? And if concepts are not mental entities, what could Rand possibly have meant when she defined a concept as a "mental integration."

As Robbins demonstrates, Rand did in fact believe that concepts are present in the mind before a verbal designation is given.[46] Rand's account of how a child's consciousness develops confirms this:

When a child observes that two objects (which he will later learn to designate as "tables") resemble each other, but are different from four other objects ("chairs"), his mind is focusing on a particular attribute of the objects (their shape), then isolating

---

[44] *Introduction to Objectivist Epistemology*, p. 11.
[45] *Introduction to Objectivist Epistemology*, p. 12.
[46] *Without a Prayer*, p. 59.

them according to their differences, and integrating them as units into separate groups according to their similarities.[47]

Note the phrase "which he will later learn to designate as 'tables.'" This clearly shows that concepts are present in the mind of the child before he learns to formulate words like *tables* or *chairs* to represent those concepts. Therefore, by Rand's own admission, the *implicit* in "implicit concepts" is meaningless. To summarize, concepts, which are supposed to be formed after sensation and perception, are already present at those initial stages of consciousness. Apparently, Rand wanted her concepts to be both concepts and not concepts. Was she trying to have her cake and eat it too?

Once the meaningless term *implicit* is removed, the reader can readily see that the concepts *existent*, *entity*, and *identity* (see paragraphs 1 and 2 above) are present at the sensory and perceptual stages of consciousness of a child learning to identify objects. Is this not tantamount to a confession by Rand that the child had to have the concept *existent* in mind before he could recognize an existent and the concept *table* in mind before he could recognize table? As Robbins emphasizes, "Not to recognize a table *as a table* is not to recognize it at all."[48] To identify something as a unit, is to have the concept *unit* already in mind. Rand could not escape the necessity of having universals in the mind to allow for the identification of the individual.[49] Yet she was trying to prove just the opposite. The concept/universal was supposed to be derived and

---

[47] *Introduction to Objectivist Epistemology*, p. 7.

[48] *Without a Prayer*, p. 47. Brand Blanshard has written: "We have found that generality is already present in the earliest free ideas, and very obviously so in the first intentional use of words. To call something a dog is to classify it, to grasp it as a kind or type, to recognize it as an instance of a character or a set of characters that may go beyond it and be exemplified elsewhere. . . . Thus in the use of a common noun we are already grasping a universal, that is, a character that may not be exhausted in this instance, but has, or may have, other embodiments. But this is not the first appearance of the universal. It will be recalled that even to perceive anything is to perceive it *as* something. And to perceive it as something is once again to use a universal" (*The Nature of Thought*, Volume I, pp. 567–568).

[49] *Without a Prayer*, p. 62.

abstracted from the individual/concrete, not the other way around. Therefore, we must conclude that Rand contradicted herself.

In fact, Rand contradicts herself repeatedly. A couple more examples serve as confirmation. Rand describes her *axiomatic concepts*, those of existence, consciousness, and identity, in a number of ways:

- as "perceived or experienced directly, but grasped conceptually,"[50]
- as "irreducible primaries,"[51] and
- as "implicit in every state of awareness, from the first sensation to the first percept to the sum of all concepts."[52]

Once again, the reader will note that she contradicts herself by saying that axiomatic concepts are both *abstractions* (concepts) developed from percepts and *irreducible primaries* present at the stage of sensations. Again, Rand apparently wants her concepts to be both concepts and not concepts at the same time. Unfortunately, she cannot have it both ways. And she cannot extricate herself from this difficulty merely by using words like *implicit* and *axiomatic*.

If the foregoing argument has been correct and universals are necessary for the identification of individuals, then Rand's initial premise, that the mind is free of *a priori,* preexistent forms or categories, is also false. Universals are necessary for learning to begin, and the *tabula rasa* mind that Rand insists upon simply does not exist. Moreover, Robbins demonstrates the seriousness of this defect in Rand's theory.[53] The child's mind at birth, according to Rand, is *tabula rasa.* "He has the potential of awareness—the mechanism of a human consciousness—but no content. . . . He knows nothing of the external world."[54] However,

---

[50] *Introduction to Objectivist Epistemology*, p. 74.
[51] *Introduction to Objectivist Epistemology*, p. 73.
[52] *Introduction to Objectivist Epistemology*, p. 74.
[53] *Without a Prayer*, pp. 29–31.
[54] "The Comprachicos," *The New Left: The Anti-Industrial Revolution*, pp. 190–191.

if the child's consciousness has no content at birth, then what are
we to make of Rand's other statement: "[A] consciousness with
nothing to be conscious of is a contradiction in terms"?[55] Elsewhere, Rand also writes, "A content-less state of consciousness
is a contradiction in terms."[56] Since Rand advocated a *tabula rasa*
mind, and *tabula rasa* means "contentless," it would appear that
a *tabula rasa* mind is a contradiction in terms.

Truth, Contextual Absolutes, and Open-Ended Concepts

Truth, as we said earlier, has to be universal. It has to be unchanging and must hold for all time and space. Rand claimed that
her epistemology of sensation plus abstraction could arrive at truth.
"Truth is the product of the recognition (i.e., identification) of the
facts of reality. Man identifies and integrates the facts of reality by
means of concepts."[57] Yet, as we have seen, Rand could not validate sensation or her process of concept formation. Moreover, it is
apparent that her reliance on sensation and perception must entail
the use of induction. As we shall discuss in greater detail in chapter 10, induction is always a logical fallacy, and it cannot lead us to
unchanging, absolute truth. Why is that the case? The answer is
simple. Induction is based on observation, and no amount of observation of individual events can ever lead to the formulation of a
universal, unchanging principle. (A scientist who only observes
black crows never has sufficient reason to say that "All crows are
black," simply because he has never observed all crows, past,
present, and future.) As if those difficulties were not enough, Rand
further undermines her claims to truth and knowledge by stating
that concepts are developed contextually.

To use Rand's example, when a child first observes man, animals, and cars, he defines man as "a thing that moves and makes
sounds."[58] After further observation, the child learns to distinguish
man from other things that move and make sounds. At this point,

---

[55] *Atlas Shrugged*, p. 942.
[56] *Introduction to Objectivist Epistemology*, p. 38.
[57] *Introduction to Objectivist Epistemology*, p. 63.
[58] *Introduction to Objectivist Epistemology*, p. 56.

he replaces his previous definition of man with a new one. Man is "a living thing that walks on two legs and has no fur." According to Rand, the previous definition of man as "a thing that moves and makes sounds" remains implicit and in no way contradicts the more current definition. When the child becomes more mature, he defines man as "a rational animal." In this schema, the child's definition and concept of man at every stage is contextual. It is determined within the framework and scope of his understanding and experience. That is why, when comparing a layman's knowledge to the knowledge of a specialist, Rand felt she could say:

> If his grasp is non-contradictory, then even if the scope of his knowledge is modest and the content of his concepts is primitive, *it will not contradict the content of the same concepts in the mind of the most advanced scientists.*[59]

Returning to the example of the child, Rand claims that the most advanced definition of man ("rational animal") includes the prior definitions of man as "a thing that moves and makes sounds" and "a living thing that walks on two feet and has no fur." However, as Robbins explains, there are some major problems with this assertion. How does the definition of man as a "rational animal" *include* the definition of man as "a thing that moves and makes sounds"?[60]

Let me illustrate this diagrammatically. The successively larger circles in figure 8.2 (next page) show the situation as it really is. "Rational animal" is a subset of "a living thing that walks on two feet and has no fur," which, in turn, is a subset of "a thing that moves and makes sounds." However, it does not follow that the definition of man as "a rational animal" *includes* the definition of man as "a living thing that walks on two feet and has no fur" or as "a thing that moves and make sounds." A definition is not merely a description.[61] "A definition," according to Rand, "is a statement that identifies the nature of the units subsumed under a concept. . . . The purpose of a definition is to distinguish a concept from all other

---

[59] *Introduction to Objectivist Epistemology,* p. 56.
[60] *Introduction to Objectivist Epistemology,* pp. 58–59; *Without a Prayer,* p. 75.
[61] *Introduction to Objectivist Epistemology,* p. 54.

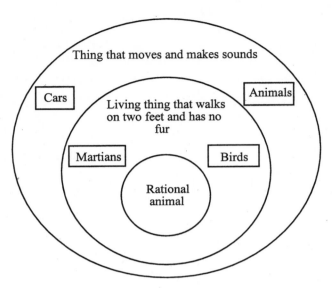

Figure 8.2. The definition of man as "a rational animal" does not *include* the definition of man as "a thing that moves and makes sounds." Nor can this latter definition help the child distinguish man from cars and animals.

concepts and thus to keep its units differentiated from all other existents."[62] In other words, the definition of man uniquely identifies the nature of man and distinguishes man from all other concepts.

Now does the phrase "a thing that moves and makes sounds" uniquely identify man? Of course not. Man, cars, and animals all fit that description. Does the phrase "a living thing that walks on two feet and has no fur" uniquely identify man? It also does not. Martians and birds both fit that description. To be sure, these two phrases are *descriptions* of man; however, they are not the *definition* of man. Therefore, those descriptions of man are incorrect definitions of man, and they could not possibly have served as a unique identifier of man in the mind of the child in Rand's example. The child would not have been able to recognize man as distinct from cars, animals, Martians, or birds by using those earlier, incorrect definitions.

In reality, a child does recognize man as distinct from other entities, but he does not accomplish this feat in the manner that Rand

---

[62] *Introduction to Objectivist Epistemology*, p. 52.

described. The child's recognition of man as a distinct entity takes place at the beginning, not the end, of the learning process. Robbins explains, "Unless one knows *prior* to developing any concept or articulating a defining statement which existents are men, how does one proceed to develop these 'open-ended' concepts at all?"[63] Rand apparently understood the process of learning backward.

In addition, Rand's acknowledgment that her concepts are open-ended and contextually absolute lands her in a quagmire of difficulties.[64] The phrase *contextually absolute* is a contradiction. Nothing can be both tentative and absolute. If concepts are contextual, then they are subject to change. And if they are subject to change, then they cannot claim to be absolute and unchanging truth. Thus we see that Rand advocated yet another contradiction. Again, as Robbins explains:

> The fatal flaw is that in [Rand's] theory, prior concepts, or prior contextual definitions of concepts—such as those of the infant, the child, and the youngster—are verified only by later concepts (or definitions). The implications of this theory should be obvious to all: Any contextual definition cannot be verified or "validated" without using another contextual definition developed later. Therefore, one cannot possibly know that the definition one currently holds is "correct" until it has been replaced by a new definition.[65]

The process of generating contextual definitions may be repeated *ad infinitum,* but it can only result in a series of tentative definitions that never arrive at the truth.

In addition, one suspects that Rand was trying to escape this skeptical conclusion by abolishing the difference between a concept and its referents. Rand writes, "[C]oncepts represent condensations of knowledge. . . ."[66] For example, out of all the attributes that characterize man, we select "rational animal" as the definition of

---

[63] *Without a Prayer*, p. 75.
[64] *Introduction to Objectivist Epistemology*, pp. 56, 62.
[65] *Without a Prayer*, p. 75.
[66] *Introduction to Objectivist Epistemology*, p. 87.

man. Our concept of man using the definition "rational animal" is an abstraction from all of the available information we have about man. The concept represents a condensation, an abstraction, of that information. However, Rand then makes this astounding claim: "Concepts stand for specific kinds of existents, including *all* the characteristics of these existents, observed and not-yet-observed, known and unknown."[67] She also writes, "[A] concept subsumes *all* the characteristics of its referents, including the yet-to-be-discovered."[68] This is tantamount to saying that a concept *is* its referents. What Rand means is this: The concept of a man includes all that has been discovered about man—man is a living thing that utilizes logic, moves, walks on two legs, possesses 1.2 million neurons in each of his optic nerves, etc.—but it also includes other characteristics yet to be discovered. That is, the concept of man is identical to the existent man.

There are several problems with Rand's claim. First, if the *concept* of man is identical with the *real existent* man and all of his characteristics, then the concept cannot represent a condensation of knowledge as Rand had said. It would no longer be an abstraction. A second point is rather obvious. If a concept is a *mental* integration of units, how can it be equivalent to the *extramental* entity man?[69] Moreover, the characteristics yet to be discovered about the extramental entity man simply are not as yet present in the mind. Period. Therefore, the concept we have in mind is incomplete, contextual, and subject to change. As Robbins points out, "[Rand] also seemed to believe that if one realizes aforetime that concepts may change, that is, are open-ended, then concepts really do not change. This is tantamount to saying that concepts subsume unknown existents and qualities yet to be discovered (how could Rand know this?)."[70] Indeed, what evidence did Rand have for these yet-to-be discovered qualities? None whatsoever. And, since Rand's concepts do in fact

[67] *Introduction to Objectivist Epistemology*, p. 87.
[68] *Introduction to Objectivist Epistemology*, p. 88.
[69] *Introduction to Objectivist Epistemology*, p. 88.
[70] *Without a Prayer*, pp. 94–95.

change, she could not claim to have developed an epistemology that discovers unchanging, absolute truth.

We may conclude from our discussion up to this point that Rand failed to demonstrate the validity of the senses, she failed to give a valid account of concept formation, and she failed to demonstrate how her contextually absolute and open-ended concepts could reach truth. Can Rand's version of empiricism be rehabilitated, or does the problem lie within empiricism itself? A consideration of Aristotle and Hume will hopefully demonstrate that the failure of empiricism is not unique to Rand.

The Problem of Individuation

Over two thousand years ago Aristotle tried to build a theory of knowledge based on sensation. He encountered an immediate difficulty. As Robbins and Clark have explained, in any form of empiricism, the identification of individual sense objects is a necessary first step in the process of learning. Abstraction and concept formation cannot take place without the mind first identifying the individuals that are to be mentally integrated and categorized. Rand did not address this question directly. However, as I have mentioned already, her surreptitious use of universals, what she called *implicit concepts*, to help identify individual sense objects, is tantamount to a confession of her philosophy's failure with regard to this problem. Therefore, we will turn our attention to Aristotle instead and see if he succeeds where Rand falls short.

The universe according to Aristotle consists of an aggregate of individual things. Only these individual things are real. Aristotle refers to these individual objects as *primary substances* or primary realities. Rand calls them *entities*. We will call them *individuals*. But how do we go about identifying these individuals? Aristotle begins, as Rand does, by asserting the *tabula rasa* nature of the human mind. The mind is blank at birth and has no *a priori* equipment for learning. With these initial conditions, will it be possible to identify individuals?

In *An Introduction to Christian Philosophy*, Gordon Clark develops the following example. Should we regard a mountain like Mt.

Blanca in Colorado as an individual? If Mt. Blanca is an individual, then what status should be accorded the rocks that constitute Mt. Blanca? Is a single rock now merely a fraction of an individual, itself not an individual, and consequently unreal? Or, consider the Sangre de Cristo mountain range, of which Mt. Blanca is a part. If the mountain range is an individual, then Mt. Blanca, which we formerly thought of as an individual, is now only part of an individual and, consequently, also unreal. Clark asks, "Which then is the individual: rock, mountain, or range? The question is embarrassing, for the identification of individuals cannot be made on the empirical basis Aristotle adopts."[71],[72] The embarrassment extends to Rand's theory. As we saw, despite a valiant attempt, she could not avoid using universals during the initial stages of sensation and perception. This is tantamount to a confession that a blank mind cannot learn. To return to Clark's example, most assuredly we know and identify rock, mountain, and range, but we do not come to that knowledge by the empiricism of Rand or Aristotle.

Clark goes on to demonstrate how Aristotle also failed to justify and derive his categories of thought from experience.[73] How indeed can universal categories be derived from particular instances of observation? Moreover, the laws of logic themselves cannot be validated empirically. Clark comments, "To suppose that logic is adequate to reality requires a knowledge of reality prior to and independent of the law. But the law itself denies that there is any knowledge independent of it."[74] Indeed, logical propositions (for example, the proposition "A is not *not-A*") have to be present already in the mind before we can even begin to apprehend reality. However, both Rand and Aristotle, despite their apparent esteem for logic, made logic untenable by their insistence on a blank mind. Aristotle, like Rand, fell short in his attempt to derive all knowledge from experience.

---

[71] *An Introduction to Christian Philosophy*, pp. 30–31. By contrast, the theory of *infima species* appears much more plausible. See Gordon Clark, *The Trinity*, pp. 101–109, and *Clark Speaks from the Grave*, pp. 67–74.

[72] *Without a Prayer*, pp. 44–45.

[73] *An Introduction to Christian Philosophy*, pp. 32–34.

[74] *An Introduction to Christian Philosophy*, p. 35.

Hume

Rand may have admired Aristotle, but she detested the philosopher David Hume. She often used Hume as an example when describing the characteristics of Attila, one of her philosophical archetypes of evil. In *For the New Intellectual*, she writes:

> When Hume declared that he saw objects moving about, but never saw such a thing as "causality"—it was the voice of Attila that men were hearing. It was Attila's soul that spoke when Hume declared that he experienced a flow of fleeting states inside his skull, such as sensations, feelings or memories, but had never caught the experience of such a thing as *consciousness* or *self*. When Hume declared that the apparent existence of an object did not guarantee that it would not vanish spontaneously next moment, and the sunrise of today did not prove that the sun would rise tomorrow; when he declared that philosophical speculation was a game, like chess or hunting, of no significance whatever to the practical course of human existence, since reason proved that existence was unintelligible and only the ignorant maintained the illusion of knowledge . . . what men were hearing was the manifesto of a philosophical movement that can be designated only as *Attila-ism*.[75]

However, literary embellishment and caricatures cannot replace detailed examination and rebuttal of another philosopher's views. Hume was skeptical, but, like Rand, he was also an empiricist. Hume was merely pointing out the logical consequences of empiricism, of which Objectivism is a variant. As W. T. Jones indicates in *A History of Western Philosophy*:

> Hume did not deny or even doubt, that there is a world outside man and his experience. He was merely concerned to show that neither he nor anyone else can produce any evidence to justify this belief: The arguments by which philosophers have sought to prove that an external world exists are all invalid. Hume's case against the philosophers consists merely in pressing home the consequences of the representative theory of perception.[76]

---

[75] *For the New Intellectual*, p. 29.
[76] *A History of Western Philosophy*, Volume III, p. 311.

The problem of the representative theory of perception plagues all empirical philosophies. Hume believed, as Rand did, that the senses convey an impression or an image of the world to the mind. (Didn't Rand say that consciousness is an active process? According to her theory, are perceptions not produced from sensations by the brain? Are concepts not mental integrations produced by man's consciousness from perceptions? In all of this, did Rand offer us anything other than a representative theory of perception? And as we saw earlier, Rand's claim that a concept is equivalent to its extramental referents is contradictory. Thus her attempt to avoid the representative theory of perception was not successful, and Objectivist epistemology remains vulnerable to Hume's criticism.) But if all we have in our minds are sense impressions and images, how do we know that they are derived from an external world? Even if we knew an external world actually existed, how could we know that our images conveyed an accurate impression of it? Hume doubted that we could overcome this objection:

> [N]othing can ever be present to the mind but an image or perception, and that the senses are only the inlets, through which these images are conveyed, without being able to produce any immediate intercourse between the mind and the object.[77]

Hume continues:

> By what argument can it be proved, that the perceptions of the mind must be caused by external objects, entirely different from them, though resembling them (if that be possible) and could not arise either from the energy of the mind itself, or from the suggestion of some invisible and unknown spirit, or from some other cause still more unknown to us?[78]

Hume merely emphasizes what I pointed out earlier in the chapter, and illustrated in figure 8.1. Beginning with the premises of empiricism, a person can only be certain of the contents of his

---

[77] "Of the Academical or Sceptical Philosophy," *Enquiries Concerning Human Understanding and Concerning the Principles of Morals*, XII, Part I, p. 118.
[78] "Of the Academical or Sceptical Philosophy," *Enquiries Concerning Human Understanding and Concerning the Principles of Morals*, XII, Part I, p. 119.

own consciousness and the experiences therein. He never has any reason to believe that they are caused by external persons or objects. Again, Hume writes:

> Let us fix our attention out of ourselves as much as possible; let us chase our imagination to the heavens, or to the utmost limits of the universe; we never really advance a step beyond ourselves, nor can conceive any kind of existence but those perceptions, which have appeared in that narrow compass. This is the universe of the imagination, nor have we any idea but what is there produced.[79]

Therefore, empiricism results in *solipsism*, where a person can know neither external objects nor other minds. He becomes trapped within the confines of his own consciousness.

If this discussion seems too abstract, perhaps a few diagrams will help. Let us suppose an object A exists in the external world, and there is a consciousness present to perceive it (see figure 8.3).

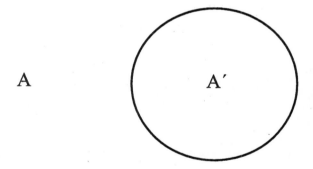

Figure 8.3. A is the external object. The circle represents the consciousness of a person. A´ represents the image of the external object after mental processing.

Suppose the person apprehends object A by means of sensation and abstraction. This results in an image or representation A´ in his mind. Now, how can the person check to see if the image A´ is

---

[79] "Of the Idea of Existence, and of External Existence," *A Treatise of Human Nature*, Volume I, Book I, Part II, Section VI, pp. 71–72.

an accurate representation of A? In order to compare A and A´, he would have to know A by a means other than the empirical method by which he came to know A´. Thus we see that direct knowledge of the object A cannot be obtained on an empirical basis. With empiricism, the person is left with an image A´ that may not faithfully represent the external object A. Furthermore, this basic fallacy of representationalism isolates each person and traps him within his experiences. Not only do we not have any reason to believe that A´ is an accurate image of A, we also do not have any reason to believe that A exists as an actual external object. (Recall figure 8.1).

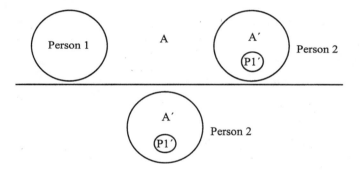

Figure 8.1. The object A as well as person 1 (P1) are recognized as images A´ and P1´ in the mind of person 2. But person 2 never has any reason to suppose that an external A or P1 actually exists. As far as person 2 is concerned, the situation represented in the top half of this figure may be equivalent to the situation depicted in the bottom half of this figure without the external referents A and P1.

All we can be sure of is the experience of image A´. But then it is not illogical to suppose that some process within consciousness itself is responsible for A´ and that A does not exist as an independent, external object. Moreover, in figure 8.1, person 2 knows only his image of person 1. Person 2 has no reason to suppose that person 1 actually exists or possesses consciousness. The result, as Clark points out, is that "there is no one to communicate with."[80]

---

[80] *Three Types of Religious Philosophy*, p. 121.

If the existence of external objects or persons cannot be validated, we are left once again with solipsism, where a person can know nothing but the modifications of his own mind.[81]

Even if we assumed that external objects and other persons actually exist, the empirical theory would still fail to account for communication and the possibility of truth. If the object A is transformed into images in the minds of persons 1 and 2 as A´ and A´´, respectively, how could we ascertain that the two persons had the same image or thought? (See figure 8.4.)

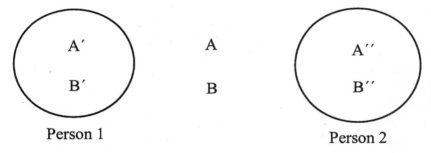

Person 1   Person 2

Figure 8.4. The external object A is imaged as A´ and A´´. A word (B) spoken and heard by two persons becomes neural impulses B´and B´´. There is no way to know if A´and A´´ or B´and B´´ are equivalent or accurate representations of A and B. Thus empiricism renders communication and truth impossible.

---

[81] Gordon Clark has shown that Hume's philosophy is even more skeptical than Hume thought. Any image that we have of the alleged external object is necessarily a combination of several sensations. An apple possesses a certain shape associated with a color and taste. Yet there are other sounds and colors presented simultaneously to our minds. On a purely empirical basis, without universals, how do we determine which combination represents the apple? "Yet it is at the beginning that a knowledge of togetherness is needed. . . . [T]he initial sensations must be recognized as occurring together before the mind combines them into things; though the empirical theory makes this idea of togetherness the result of comparing things subsequent to the act of combining. . . . Empiricism therefore fails at the beginning: it surreptitiously furnishes its unfurnished mind with the use of time and space, while it professes to manufacture these ideas at a later stage of the learning process. Insist on a blank mind, and learning never begins" (*Thales to Dewey*, p. 394).

According to the empirical-material-behavioral theory, images and thoughts are the result of neurological impulses in the brain. However, no two physical motions, much less two neurological impulses, can ever be exactly the same. Each physical event in the mind represents a unique, subjective experience. Therefore, no individual can ever have the same thought twice. Furthermore, no two persons, much less two billion persons, can ever have the same image or thought in their minds. If thoughts are not universal, then truth, as absolute and unchanging, does not exist and communication between two persons becomes impossible.[82]

Rand recognized that Hume's position led to skepticism, but somehow she failed to see that her epistemology meets the same fate. Here, we have to be careful. Just because Rand claimed that her empirical philosophy was different from Hume's does not make it so. She was unable to demonstrate the validity of the senses. Her account of concept formation, as a mental integration of the material provided by the senses, is in essence a mental transformation of a real A into an image A´. This lands her in the same quagmire of representationalism and solipsism.[83] An alternative epistemology is needed. Immanuel Kant attempted to formulate one, but despite positing the categories, he too failed to rebut Hume. Consequently, a gap between the world of appearances (the phenomenal world) and the world of things in themselves (the noumenal world) remains. A chasm remains between the image that we have of an object (its appearance) and the real object itself. At the conclusion of this chapter, we will see how Christian theism remedies this difficulty. But let us pause now to consider Rand's metaphysics.

Metaphysics

If the discussion thus far has been correct, then Rand has failed to establish a workable theory of knowledge. And if her epistemology cannot tell us how we know, how can we trust what she says

---

[82] *Three Types of Religious Philosophy*, p. 121.
[83] Wallace Matson, "Rand on Concepts," *The Philosophic Thought of Ayn Rand*, pp. 23, 27–29.

about reality? Nevertheless, we press on. What does Rand believe about existence?

> There is only one fundamental alternative in the universe: existence or non-existence—and it pertains to a single class of entities: to living organisms. The existence of inanimate matter is unconditional, the existence of life is not: it depends on a specific course of action. Matter is indestructible, it changes its forms, but it cannot cease to exist.[84]

Thus existence consists of indestructible, eternal, and unconscious matter. Unconscious matter gives rise to living organisms that possess consciousness. Therefore, matter is prior to consciousness. Rand apparently had a nineteenth-century, materialistic and mechanistic view of matter as consisting of hard solid atoms that behave according to Newtonian laws. However, twentieth-century physics has essentially dispelled that view of ultimate reality. Physicists Paul Davies and John Gribbin explain in *The Matter Myth*:

> The founders of quantum mechanics, notably Niels Bohr and Werner Heisenberg, argued that when we talk of atoms, electrons, and so on, we must not fall into the trap of imagining them as little "things," existing independently in their own right. Quantum mechanics enables us to relate different *observations* made on, say, an atom. The theory is to be regarded as a procedure for connecting these observations into some sort of consistent logical scheme—a mathematical algorithm. Use of the word "atom" is just an informal way of talking about that algorithm. . . . [B]ut that does not mean that the atom is actually *there* as a well-defined entity with a complete set of physical attributes of its own, such as a definite location in space and a definite velocity through space.[85]

They add, "Quantum physics undermines materialism because it reveals that matter has far less 'substance' than we might believe."[86]

---

[84] *Atlas Shrugged*, p. 939.
[85] *The Matter Myth*, p. 27.
[86] *The Matter Myth*, p. 14.

Ironically, Davies and Gribbin conclude their book by suggesting the possibility that there is no such thing as matter. Perhaps only consciousness exists after all.[87]

Similarly, Robbins points out how Rand later in life voiced doubts concerning her earlier view of reality. During a series of workshops on Objectivist epistemology, she comments:

> How can we make conclusions about the ultimate constituents of the universe? For instance, we couldn't say: everything is material, if by "material" we mean that of which the physical objects on the perceptual level are made. . . . If this is what we mean by "material," then we do not have the knowledge to say that ultimately everything is subatomic particles which in certain aggregates are matter. . . . The only thing of which we can be sure, philosophically, is that the ultimate stuff, if it's ever found, will have identity. . . .[88]

Is Rand's optimism well founded? Her tentative view on the ultimate nature of matter is reminiscent of Aristotle's.

Aristotle had characterized things as possessing both matter and form. Together, these two elements constitute the basic category that he called *substance*. Aristotle's substance is the equivalent of Rand's *existence*. Aristotle further divides substance into two classes: primary and secondary. Primary substances, as we saw earlier, are individuals, or concretes, like *this man* or *this horse*. Secondary substances are the universals, or concepts, such as the species *man* or *horse*. Aristotle also says that the individual man is actually the matter onto which the form *man* is impressed. *Matter* is therefore the primary substance, and *form* is the secondary substance.

When Aristotle applies this theory to the task of distinguishing between two men, he attributes the difference between the two men to a difference in the *matter* that constitutes each man.[89] Therefore, what distinguishes John Galt from Francisco d'Anconia is the

---

[87] *The Matter Myth*, pp. 307–309.

[88] *Without a Prayer*, pp. 122–123; *Introduction to Objectivist Epistemology*, pp. 290–291 (second expanded edition).

[89] *Metaphysics*, 1058, a38–b9; see also *Clark Speaks from the Grave*, pp. 65–66.

matter that underlies each man. The form is a secondary substance that makes both Galt and d'Anconia of the same species *man*. Therefore, the form cannot distinguish between them. Only the matter that makes up each individual man is capable of distinguishing Galt from d'Anconia. But what is that matter? What is the stuff that makes an individual man himself? Aristotle says, "By matter I mean that which in itself is neither a particular thing nor of a certain quantity nor assigned to any other of the categories by which being is determined."[90]

However, this view of matter, according to Clark, is vague. "To prevent this tenuous non-reality from being a Parmenidean nothing, Aristotle calls it potentiality. . . . [T]he matter of substantial becoming is entirely potential and is in no way actual."[91]

Here I have to back up a little and explain what is meant by pure potentiality. The concepts of actuality and potentiality are basic to Aristotelian philosophy, but one gets the impression that they are really indefinable concepts. Aristotle's definitions often seem circular. For example, in his definition of motion, Aristotle writes, "It is the fulfillment of what is potential when it is already fully real and operates not as *itself* but as *movable*, that is motion."[92] Motion is thus defined by "movable."

When the ideas of actuality and potentiality are applied to physical objects, one suspects that any object can be thought of as a potential in the process of becoming another object, the actual. Every object is both potential and actual. For example, if a piece of marble being shaped by a sculptor possesses human form, then it is an actual piece of marble with the potential of becoming a statue of a Greek goddess.

But let us return to our main line of thought. If matter is purely potential, then it has no actuality and no form. This makes matter unknowable. Now recall that an individual man consists of matter (pure potentiality) plus the form *man*. It is the matter

---

[90] *Metaphysics*, 1029, a20–21; see also *Clark Speaks from the Grave*, pp. 65–66.
[91] *Thales to Dewey*, p. 142.
[92] *Physics*, 201, a28–29; see also *Thales to Dewey*, p. 125.

that makes the individual man himself, but this matter is already said to be pure potentiality and thus unknowable. Since we cannot know the matter, the stuff that makes this man himself, we cannot know the individual. Clark summarizes, "[S]ince matter is a virtual non-being and is unknowable, the primary realities, the independent and basic things of the universe are beyond our understanding."[93]

If the discussion seems too abstract, consider C. E. M. Joad's simplified explanation of this difficulty.[94] Let us examine a marble statue from the point of view that everything consists of matter and form. If we strip a marble statue of a Greek goddess of its form, we are left with a marble statue of a person. If we strip away the form of a person, we are left with a marble block. If we continue this process *ad infinitum*, what we end up with is a featureless matter that is strictly inconceivable. Again, notice how similar this featureless matter described by Joad is to Rand's concept of a nebulous "ultimate stuff." Joad concludes that Aristotle's "pure Matter" is "a creation of thought, which is not to be found in the realm of actual existence."[95]

Thus both Joad and Clark come to the same conclusion. Matter (Aristotle's *primary substance* and Rand's *existence*) is unknowable. It simply does not exist. Of note, Aristotle had written, "[E]verything except primary substances is either predicated of primary substances, or is present in them, and if these last [primary substances] did not exist, it would be impossible for anything else to exist."[96] To summarize, if primary substances (matter) did not exist, nothing else could exist. Since we have demonstrated that primary substances do not exist, we may properly conclude that nothing else can exist. Thus Aristotle's explanations for matter end in nothingness, an "ultimate stuff" that neither he nor Rand could define.

---

[93] *Thales to Dewey*, p. 143.
[94] *Guide to Philosophy*, p. 163.
[95] *Guide to Philosophy*, p. 164.
[96] *Categoriae*, 2, b4–6.

Materialist Implications for Volitional Consciousness

Rand's materialistic account of existence has other disturbing implications. Rand asserted the primacy of existence as opposed to the primacy of consciousness. That is, she believed consciousness is derived from matter. This view is consistent with Rand's assertion that man is a product of nature. However, if this were the case, then Rand's account of man as a being of volitional consciousness becomes rather contradictory. Positing man as a product of nature, she nevertheless claimed that man is above nature. Rand loved to quote Francis Bacon. "Nature to be commanded must be obeyed." However, this simply will not do. If one accepts the primacy of matter, then consciousness can only be explained as a derivative of matter, as the result of neurons firing in the brain. And the firing of neurons ultimately find their explanation in the physical motion of electrons and quarks. Thus consciousness is an epiphenomenon of matter. Placing man within the context of mechanistic causation, Rand would nevertheless have us believe that man is a being of volitional consciousness who can choose to think or not to think. But how is it possible for consciousness, which arises from unconscious matter, to be free from the laws that govern unconscious matter? How is free will possible?

Figure 8.5 shows schematically what a materialistic theory of consciousness has to entail. Consciousness arising from unconscious matter may be a complicated form of unconscious matter, but it can never escape from the realm of unconscious matter. And if consciousness cannot escape from the realm of unconscious matter, how can it fail to obey the laws that govern the material universe?

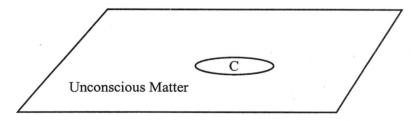

Figure 8.5. Consciousness (C) arising from unconscious, indestructible matter.

If Objectivism insists on volitional consciousness, the idea that consciousness is really free from physical, materialistic laws, then it has to posit consciousness as independent of and superior to matter. Consciousness may even combine with matter in a dualistic sense to form man, but in either case what is being advocated is the existence of an immaterial mind that is not subject to the laws governing the physical universe (see figure 8.6). Is Rand willing to admit to the presence of a spiritual dimension?

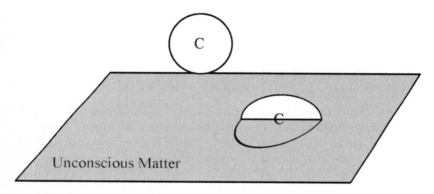

Figure 8.6. Consciousness (C) is superior to and independent of unconscious matter or in combination with it.

Rand did in fact consider man a spiritual being. The most obvious reference comes from the book jacket advertisement for *Atlas Shrugged*, which speaks of the rebirth of man's spirit. (In this regard, Christianity also speaks of the rebirth of the human spirit in contrast to the birth of the human body.[97]) However, the question is not whether Rand talks about man as a spiritual being. Obviously, she does. The question is whether Rand has any right to that concept given her materialistic first principles. The preceding discussion shows that she does not.

Years ago, while I was in basic agreement with Rand's philosophy, I came across an interesting series of articles in *The Objectivist* written by the physician-scientist Robert Efron. Efron argued *against*

---

[97] John 3:3–8.

the reductionist point of view in biology.[98] The reductionist point of view asserts that everything a living being does can ultimately be reduced to neural activity, molecular interaction, chemical reactions, and physical motion. Even though I was seeking a career as a physician and had been involved in biomedical research, I had not given the issue much thought until I read Efron's articles. As much as I wanted to agree with the Objectivist position on this issue, I never found Efron's arguments convincing. It seemed to me that if man is a product of nature, he cannot help but act in accordance with what nature has made him. Whatever he chooses, he chooses. Rand contradicted herself by giving man free will, as if a man could fail to behave as the inevitable firing of his neurons and the laws of physics dictate. The Objectivist theory of knowledge quickly degenerates into behaviorism.

Leonard Peikoff unfortunately could do no better than Efron. In chastising the materialist view of life and consciousness as inanimate mechanism while defending the Objectivist view, Peikoff writes:

> Whatever the ultimate explanation of biological phenomena— whether life derives from some as yet unknown (but nonmystical) element combining with matter as we now understand it, or from some special combination of known material ingredients—in either case, it will not alter the existence *or the identity* of a living organism; just as an explanation of consciousness, should such be forthcoming, would not alter *its* existence or identity.[99]

First, what does Peikoff mean by an "unknown but nonmystical" element combining with matter? If the element is unknown, how can Peikoff be certain it is not mystical? *Mystical* is apparently to be understood in antithesis to the *material*. But that would simply make the *non*mystical but unknown element another form of

---

[98] Robert Efron, "Biology without Consciousness—and Its Consequences," *The Objectivist*, February through May 1968, pp. 405–414, 423–427, 441–447, 457–461.

[99] *Objectivism*, p. 192.

matter, and nothing is gained by this analysis. For Peikoff's argument to make any sense, the nonmystical element has to be nonmaterial. But if it is nonmaterial, then what is it? Is it a mind or a thought or energy?

The reader should be reminded that energy and matter are ultimately interchangeable according to physics. Furthermore, there are physical laws governing energy as well as matter; therefore, *nonmaterial* in this case cannot refer to energy as described in physics. Nor can it mean mind or thought—if by such words we mean spiritual or supernatural elements that lie beyond the physical universe—because Peikoff and Rand refuse to accept the mystical and the supernatural. Yet this is precisely what Objectivism needs. It needs a nonphysical, nonmaterial element that will free its view of consciousness from the materialist-reductionist-behaviorist trap.

However, a nonphysical element is inconsistent with the materialist first principles of Objectivism. Remember, Objectivism believes in the primacy of existence. It does not believe in the supernatural or the primacy of consciousness. Yet, as figure 8.6 shows, this is precisely what Peikoff's nonmaterial element must be. It must be a spiritual element that is not subject to physical, material laws. (We shall consider an alternative view later in this chapter where a Divine Omnipotent Mind directs the course of both men and things, imparting consciousness to men but not to things. However, the primacy of consciousness is being asserted in that scenario, and Objectivism has no right to that concept.)

Let us continue with our examination of Peikoff's assertions. Even if we accept Peikoff's second alternative, that a special combination of known material ingredients somehow creates consciousness, I do not see how he can escape the materialist dilemma. Even if consciousness consists of a special combination of known material elements, and even if the laws governing that combination have yet to be discovered, does Peikoff really wish to claim that these not-yet-discovered laws do not govern cause and effect? Isn't that what laws are supposed to do—govern cause-and-effect relationships? If these laws govern cause and effect, we are back to square one, and there is no free will. If these yet-to-be-discovered laws do not govern cause and effect, how does Peikoff know that they will not?

If anyone needs further evidence for the insolubility of this problem, he has only to look at the contradictory accounts of free will in the Objectivist literature. Nathaniel Branden, for example, defines free will as the doctrine that "man is capable of performing actions that are not determined by forces outside his control; that man has the power of making choices which are, causally, *primaries*—i.e., not necessitated by antecedent factors."[100] In other words, man has free will. But Branden also concedes that a man's choices may be the consequence of a complex chain of mental operations that he is unconscious of. In these cases, "the choice to perform an action is not and cannot be an irreducible, causal primary."[101] In other words, man does not have free will. Which is it? Does man possess free will or not? This confusion is the inevitable result of positing the contradiction of volitional consciousness. Thus it is clear that the attempt by Objectivism to escape the materialist dilemma by positing the autonomy of volitional consciousness and reason while maintaining the primacy of indestructible matter has failed.[102]

Materialist Implications for Truth

We have seen that Rand's belief in the primacy of indestructible matter leads to the behaviorism that she despised. If our thoughts are simply the result of the motion of atoms in the brain, then those thoughts are illusions. Furthermore, your beliefs, which arise from the particular motion of atoms in your brain, would be as valid as my opposing beliefs, which arise from the particular motion of atoms in my brain. This view of consciousness makes truth impossible. Moreover, if we accept the materialistic account

---

[100] Nathaniel Branden, "The Intellectual Ammunition Department," *The Objectivist Newsletter*, January 1964, p. 3.

[101] Nathaniel Branden, "The Intellectual Ammunition Department," *The Objectivist Newsletter*, January 1964, p. 3.

[102] Rand's view of volitional consciousness and its role in morality is actually very similar to the view of Immanuel Kant.

of consciousness, then we are compelled to adopt the evolutionary hypothesis as the most likely explanation of man's origins. And if man evolved from inorganic molecules over billions of years, we are left with a disturbing conclusion. Logic and truth may not be the same for all men and all times. Men may have evolved at different times and places and from slightly or extremely different ancestors. In fact, he may still be evolving. Hence, there is no reason to expect that the mind works the same for all men. As Clark says:

> Evolution can hardly assert the unity of the human race, for several individuals of sub-human species may have more or less simultaneously produced the same variation. This nontheistic, naturalistic view is difficult to accept because it implies that the mind too, as well as the body, is an evolutionary product rather than a divine image. Instead of using eternal principles of logic, the mind operates with the practical results of biological adaptation. Concepts and propositions neither reach the truth nor even aim at it. Our equipment has evolved through a struggle to survive. Reason is simply the human method of handling things. It is a simplifying and therefore falsifying device. There is no evidence that our categories correspond to reality. Even if they did, a most unlikely accident, no one could know it; for to know that the laws of logic are adequate to the existent real, it is requisite to observe the real prior to using the laws. If the intellect is naturally produced, different types of intellect could equally well be produced by slightly different evolutionary processes. . . . If now this be the case, our traditional logic is but a passing evolutionary moment, our theories, dependent on this logic, are temporary reactions, parochial social habits, and Freudian rationalizations; and therefore the evolutionary theory, produced by these biological urges, cannot be true.[103]

It was in pondering this notion of the mind as an epiphenomenon of matter that C. S. Lewis, the eminent Oxford scholar, began to

---

[103] *In Defense of Theology*, pp. 115–116.

turn away from his materialism and atheism. In *Surprised by Joy*, he describes part of his journey:

> [W]e accepted as rock-bottom reality the universe revealed by the senses. But at the same time we continued to make for certain phenomena of consciousness all the claims that really went with a theistic or idealistic view. We maintained that abstract thought (if obedient to logical rules) gave indisputable truth, that our moral judgment was "valid," and our aesthetic experience not merely pleasing but "valuable." . . . Barfield [Lewis's friend] convinced me that it was inconsistent. If thought were a purely subjective event [the result of neural impulses in an individual's brain], these claims for it would have to be abandoned.[104]

Lewis and Clark both recognize what many do not. A materialistic account of consciousness cannot lead to truth. If it were true, then one philosophy is as good as another, and Objectivism is no more valid than the views it attacks.

Reconsidering Axioms

We have come a long way in this chapter toward understanding Rand's philosophy. To recapitulate, we found numerous difficulties with her epistemology. Not only did Rand fail to validate the senses and provide a coherent account of concept formation, but her empiricism and materialism stumbled over the question of how communication and truth are possible. Is there an alternative theory that succeeds where Objectivism has failed?

Earlier I mentioned that it was doubts about the completeness and usefulness of Rand's axioms that led me to consider the claims of Christianity. It seemed to me that Rand's two axioms failed to rule out the existence of God. Her axioms say two basic things:

1. Something exists.
2. Consciousness is the faculty that perceives existence.

---

[104] *Surprised by Joy*, p. 208. Note that thought is a subjective event because it takes place in an individual's brain, and no two neural impulses can ever be the same. See earlier discussion on Hume.

Both of these axioms make room for the God of Christianity.

First, if by *existence* Objectivism means external, material objects, there remains insufficient reason for denying the possible existence of immaterial realities such as spirit, mind, or even the Divine Mind. Indeed, even the Objectivist Leonard Peikoff acknowledges, "The concept [of existence] does not specify that a physical world exists."[105] By implication, existence may refer to something other than the physical universe. Moreover, one should realize that Christianity plainly asserts that God *exists*.[106] Christianity does not believe in a God that does not exist. It merely denies that God is corporeal and that the physical universe is all there is. Consequently, Rand's axiom of existence does very little to rule out God's reality.[107]

Second, with regard to Objectivism's definition of consciousness as the faculty that perceives existence, we have shown that Objectivism cannot justify its claim that sensation is the only way to knowledge. Even if we allowed that the senses gave some information, that belief does not exclude the possibility of a Divine Mind who reveals truth to men. Thus the truth of God's existence remains an undecidable proposition given the Objectivist axioms.

A Christian Construction

When Rand characterized Christianity as an emotional philosophy without rational foundation, she was perhaps hoping that her readers would be drawn to her philosophy of reason by default. Yet, given equal time, many Christians might respond that Christianity is *not* based on feelings. They consider it objective and reasonable. Wherein lies the conflict? Perhaps part of the conflict results from a confusion over definitions. What is faith, and what is reason? In *Religion, Reason and Revelation*, Gordon Clark

---

[105] *Objectivism*, p. 5.

[106] *Without a Prayer*, p. 87; see also *Three Types of Religious Philosophy*, pp. 43–44. Rand, of course, denied God's existence; she was an atheist. But the nonexistence of God is not contained in her axioms, nor is God's nonexistence immediately deducible from the axiom "existence exists."

[107] See chapter 11: Bridging the Chasm.

defines the Reformational view of these terms.[108] *Faith* is belief; it is an act of intellection. *Reason* is deductive logic.

Let us begin with faith. Nothing in the definition of faith as belief equates it with feelings, even though feelings may accompany or follow faith. Even Objectivism holds that happiness, a state of noncontradictory joy, results from *believing* in reason and acting rationally. Faith by itself is not the equivalent of feelings. Furthermore, it must be acknowledged by Objectivists that all philosophies begin with faith.[109] Rand herself admitted that all philosophies, explicitly or implicitly, begin with axioms. And axioms, by definition, are not proven; they are chosen. They are the rock-bottom ideas of any system of thought. Ayn Rand had her axioms just as Aristotle, Descartes, Hume, and Kant had theirs. If anyone attempts to think consistently at all, he also has to begin somewhere. Therefore, the choice of an axiom is based on unsubstantiated belief. It is based on faith. Ultimately, faith always precedes reason. As William O'Neill points out, Objectivism sets up an artificial opposition between faith and reason. "[T]here is no reason why faith *cannot* antecede reason, and, except where theories of innate knowledge or mystical revelation are utilized, there is no other way to ground reason except through faith. There are no 'logical reasons for being logical.'"[110] As Robbins explains, Rand may be an atheist in the sense of not believing in the God of Christianity, but she accepted the twin gods of indestructible matter and volitional consciousness.[111] Rand did indeed have faith. It isn't a question of having no faith. "The only question that remains is, Which faith—which axiom—shall reason serve?"[112] Thus, Christianity cannot be faulted for choosing revelation as its starting point and accepting the axiom: The Bible alone is the Word of God. For the moment, we have gained some breathing space for Christian theism.

---

[108] *Religion, Reason and Revelation*, pp. 87–110.
[109] *A Christian View of Men and Things*, pp. 14–16.
[110] *With Charity toward None*, pp. 100–101.
[111] *Without a Prayer*, pp. 108–143.
[112] *Without a Prayer*, p. 22.

Next, Clark defines reason as deductive logic. But doesn't Objectivism share in this view? Isn't logic what Rand meant by reason? The answer is yes and no. Recall that Rand's definition of reason begins with sensation and continues with abstraction. We saw the enormous difficulties she faced in defining and validating her version of empiricism. I will not repeat the analysis of it here. However, it should be recalled that Rand also denied innate knowledge, or intuition, in her preference for the *tabula rasa* mind. Hence, there are no categories in the mind and, therefore, no propositions of logic with which to organize experience. A blank mind cannot begin to learn. Moreover, sensation, observation, and induction—not deductive logic—constitute the basic method of cognition for Objectivism.

I will briefly outline the difficulties with this approach to knowledge and truth. First, sensation never provides stable, unchanging information. No two sensations are ever the same. In this world, errors, inaccuracies, and fluctuations abound. Second, the reliance on induction produces no universal judgments. Observation of individual events can never provide enough information for formulating a universal proposition. And truth, as we noted, has to be universal, absolute, and unchanging for all time and space. Thus, when Rand applied deductive logic to the information provided by sensation and induction, she was working with material that is acknowledged to be flawed. Deductions from nontruths can only yield truths by chance. Indeed, she ultimately had to acknowledge that her concepts were contextual and tentative.

In contrast, Christianity escapes this dilemma by refusing to accept induction. It accepts only deductive logic. And it begins with an axiom: the axiom of revelation. From this starting point, Christianity deduces a body of truth from the Scriptures. Truth is given by God in the form of understandable and communicable propositions. These propositions are universal and therefore do not depend on the fallacious method of induction. Moreover, logic, deductive logic, is exhibited in the Bible itself. God himself imparted the divine rational image to all men. Therefore, logic is universal and governs our approach to truth.

Our preliminary consideration of the meanings of faith and reason does much to deflate Rand's characterization of Christianity as an emotional, unpredictable, and unreasonable philosophy. Christianity depends on an axiom, and its method is sound, deductive logic. However, the astute reader will surely ask, "If axioms are accepted by faith, and not proven, how does one go about choosing which axiom to believe?" One method is to consider the system of philosophy that arises from a particular axiom. How much does the philosophy explain? And is it logically consistent? For example, John Robbins applied the procedure of *reductiones ad absurdum* to Rand's philosophy, and Gordon Clark has applied it to the basic method of numerous other non-Christian philosophies. In the process, they demonstrated important contradictions within these systems as well as the inability of these systems to provide answers to important philosophical questions. When these difficulties surface in a particular system, that philosophy must be considered false. Therefore, Christianity should not be dismissed out of hand merely because one does not like the idea of revelation. It ought to be examined to see if it succeeds where other philosophies fail.

We begin by giving attention to a problem that Rand's empiricism was unable to solve. Objectivist epistemology, as we saw, renders both communication and truth impossible. Truth, unchanging and universal, has to exist in order for communication to occur and for knowledge to be possible. Yet we saw how the Objectivist view could not fail to degenerate into a materialist, reductionist, and behaviorist epistemology. This approach made truth the equivalent of neural impulses and the motion of electrons in the brain. Since no two impulses can ever be the same in the brain of one person, much less in the brains of a million persons, it is impossible that unchanging truth should exist. Earlier, we saw how C. S. Lewis came to understand the inconsistency of his materialist viewpoint with the notion of universal truth that he held so dear. He also discovered something else:

> I was therefore compelled to give up realism. [Here, realism means independent, external objects.] I had been trying to defend it ever since I began reading philosophy. . . . [R]ealism satisfied an emotional need. I wanted Nature to be quite independent of our observation; something other, indifferent, self-existing. . . . But now

it seemed to me, I had to give that up. Unless I were to accept an unbelievable alternative, I must admit that mind was no late-come epiphenomenon; that the whole universe was, in the last resort, mental; that our logic was participation in a cosmic *Logos*.[113]

Truth, as Lewis discovered, cannot be explained by a physical motion in the brain. Truth has to be an immaterial thought, and its existence has to be both universal and mental. Existing always and everywhere, truth envelops all minds to some degree. That is how communication and truth are possible. Clark asks, "Is all this any more than the assertion that there is an eternal, immutable Mind, a Supreme Reason, a personal, Living God?"[114] It is participation with this Living Mind that allows us to communicate and know truth.

Let us see diagrammatically how Christian theism solves the problem where empiricism fails. Christian epistemology does not depend on the representative theory of perception and knowledge. It is a form of *realism* but not the materialistic realism that Lewis believed in when he was an atheist. Epistemological realism holds that the object presented to one's mind is the real object; it is not an image of the object "out there."[115] As Robbins explains, Christian philosophy holds that the "external object" is itself the object of knowledge. That is, both men and things are objects of knowledge, or thoughts, in the mind of God (see figure 8.7, next page).[116] Because the object A is a thought in the mind of God, there is no difficulty in God making it known to both persons 1 and 2, for persons 1 and 2 are also thoughts in the mind of God. Robbins writes:

> In distinction to some philosophies that hold a superficially similar position, Christian philosophy asserts that propositions, not concepts, are the objects of knowledge, for only propositions

[113] *Surprised by Joy*, p. 209.
[114] *A Christian View of Men and Things*, p. 215.
[115] *The Trinity*, p. 127.
[116] Genesis 1 explains that God spoke all things into existence. John 1:3 states that all things came into being through the Word, the logos or thought of God. Hebrews 1:3 says that Christ upholds all things by the word of his power.

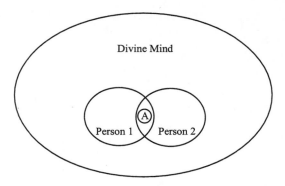

Figure 8.7. Persons 1 and 2 as well as object A are thoughts in the mind of God. Therefore, there is no difficulty in God making A known to both person 1 and person 2, or making persons 1 and 2 known to each other. Furthermore, there is no difficulty in God making truth known to all minds.

can be true or false.[117] Equally important, for this forms the uniqueness of Christian epistemology, these propositions are propositions in the mind of God. Christian epistemology avoids not only the problems of empiricism, it avoids the problems of idealism Plato enumerated in the *Parmenides*, particularly the problem of how the human mind and the objects of knowledge (the Ideas) are brought into conjunction. Since persons and truth are propositions in the mind of God, there is no gap between the phenomenal world and the noumenal world which must be bridged. We ourselves are in the mind of God. "In him we live and move and have our being" (Acts 17:28).[118]

Within the scope of this study, we cannot hope to discuss the Hegelian Absolute Mind and differentiate it from the Christian view. Suffice to say that the Hegelian Absolute is impersonal and not the personal, transcendent Creator of Christianity. Moreover, Hegelian logic and its dialectic method result in a Being that cannot be distinguished from non-Being. It does not obey the laws of Aristotelian logic. In the Absolute, *A* cannot be distinguished

---

[117] For example, "car" by itself is neither true nor false. But "the car is fast"— a proposition—can be true or false.
[118] *Without a Prayer*, pp. 223–224.

from *non-A*.[119] Furthermore, Hegel saw truth as unfolding in history. Hence, every stage of history along with the opinions expressed during that era is valid. But the truth of yesterday is false today, and the truth of today will be false tomorrow. Hegelianism collapses in relativism.[120]

In contrast, the Christian model holds a high view of logic. Logic is the way God thinks. And logic is itself contained in the axiom of revelation, for the Scriptures are written in propositional form and obey the laws of logic. The prologue to the Gospel of John states, "In the beginning was the Word, and the Word was with God, and the Word was God."[121] Inasmuch as the word *Word* in Greek was actually *Logos*, from which the terms *logic*, *wisdom*, and *thought* are derived, the verse may well be translated: "In the beginning was the Logic, and the Logic was with God, and the Logic was God."[122] "All things came into being by Him, and apart from Him [Christ the Logic] nothing came into being that has come into being. In Him was life, and the life was the light of men."[123] This light, the Logic of God, enlightens every man who comes into existence.[124] Thus there is no mystery why logic is the same for all men, because we all descend from the first created man. As Clark observes, God is rational and his creatures have been endowed with the rational image. Therefore, rational, propositional communication between God and man is possible. Furthermore, it is impossible to annihilate God in thought, for *Logos*, logic and truth, is inherent in the mind of even nonbelievers.[125]

Not only is truth possible, but beginning with the axiom of revelation Clark has also shown how necessary truths about epistemology, ethics, history, and government can all be deduced from the Scriptures. Clark's broad outline of a comprehensive Christian

---

[119] *For the New Intellectual*, p. 33; *Thales to Dewey*, p. 442.
[120] *Three Types of Religious Philosophy*, p. 98.
[121] John 1:1.
[122] Gordon Clark, *The Johannine Logos*, pp. 13–29.
[123] John 1:3–4.
[124] John 1:9; see also *The Johannine Logos*, p. 27.
[125] *Three Types of Religious Philosophy*, p. 39.

philosophy can be found in *A Christian View of Men and Things*. While revelation does not give us all truth—God reveals himself truly but not exhaustively[126]—Clark has shown that empiricism as a philosophy can produce no truths at all.[127] The situation is not dissimilar with other non-Christian philosophies. Thus Clark concludes his history of philosophy *Thales to Dewey* with this question: "[C]ould it be that a choice must be made between skeptical futility and a word from God?"[128] It is either nihilism or revelation. The reader is thus invited to consider the matter further and ponder the far-reaching consequences of this fundamental choice.[129] But for now, we have found in Christian theism a tower of refuge for truth that Objectivism could not sustain. It is a unique accomplishment that will continue to distinguish itself as we proceed to consider and examine the practical branches of the Objectivist philosophy.

---

[126] See *Francis A. Schaeffer Trilogy*, Book Three: *He Is There and He Is Not Silent*, p. 322. Indeed, revelation depends on what God wishes to communicate to men. "The secret things belong to God" (Deuteronomy 29:29). But God has provided substantial information in the Bible for epistemology, ethics, history, and government.

[127] *Thales to Dewey*, pp. 391–394; *A Christian View of Men and Things*, pp. 202–209.

[128] *Thales to Dewey*, p. 534.

[129] For anyone who wishes to consider further the failure of the secular philosophies to furnish truth, he may begin by examining the works of Gordon Clark or the writings of Francis Schaeffer.

9

MORALITY AND GOVERNMENT

To take ideas seriously means that you intend to live by, to *practice*, any idea you accept as true. Philosophy provides man with a comprehensive view of life. In order to evaluate it properly, ask yourself what a given theory, if accepted, would do to a human life, starting with your own.

Ayn Rand, *Philosophy: Who Needs It*

The Founding Fathers were America's first intellectuals and, so far, her last. It is their basic political line that the New Intellectuals have to continue.

Ayn Rand, *For the New Intellectual*

[A] philosopher's political views, to the extent that they contradict the essentials of his system, have little historical significance.

Leonard Peikoff, *The Ominous Parallels*

Ayn Rand's philosophy *begins with ethics* and merely terminates with a theory of truth and knowledge. Her epistemology and her metaphysical assumptions—indeed, the vast bulk of her philosophy—are essentially an *a posteriori* rationalization for a fervent *a priori* commitment to the ethics of laissez-faire capitalism. Her basic argument with the neo-mystics . . . has less to do with the *nature of metaphysical truth* than with the *nature of man as man*.

William F. O'Neill, *With Charity toward None*

A yn Rand claimed that her morality was grounded in objective reality and reason. She writes, "I am not *primarily* an advocate of capitalism, but of egoism; and I am not *primarily* an advocate of egoism, but of reason. If one recognizes the supremacy of reason and applies it consistently, all the rest follows."[1] In the last chapter, however, we encountered many difficulties and contradictions in Rand's theory of knowledge. If her morality of rational self-interest stands on shaky epistemological foundations, how can it be defended? If Rand's ethics was derived from an unworkable theory of knowledge, how can it be true? Furthermore, in part one of this book, we saw some of the practical problems that result from the Objectivist view of self-esteem, productive work, and romantic love. Perhaps such problems are not merely incidental, but superficial symptoms of profound contradictions in Rand's ethical philosophy. In the first section of this chapter, we will examine Rand's ethics in detail. Then we will consider the ramifications of her morality for a theory of government.

Moral Absolutes

The first thing that should be said about Rand is that she believed in moral absolutes. Rand was no advocate of moral relativism. For her, a rational code of ethics was an exact science that discovered moral truths in consonance with objective reality. Rand had no tolerance for the relativistic and skeptical persuasion of contemporary moral theorists. If someone had asked her, "Surely you don't think in terms of black-and-white, do you?" Rand would have replied, "You're damn right I do!"[2] Such confidence has an inherent appeal. But is it merely rhetoric, or is it substantiated by

---

[1] "Brief Summary," *The Objectivist*, September 1971, p. 1089.
[2] "The Cult of Moral Grayness," *The Virtue of Selfishness*, p. 79.

logical and defensible arguments? Can Rand make good her claim to have discovered absolutes in morality?

Failure of Materialism to Arrive at Truth

We saw in the last chapter that Rand was both a materialist and an empiricist. It would be worthwhile to review what implications these philosophical positions have for the possibility of truth. First, materialism leads logically to the abnegation of truth.[3] According to the physical-chemical-biological reductionist model of consciousness, thought consists of neural impulses in the brain. (Ultimately, neural impulses may be attributed to the antecedent motion of atoms.) However, no two sets of neural impulses can ever be the same in the brain of one person, much less in the brains of two or two billion persons. Therefore, thought cannot be universal, and absolute truths are not to be had. Moreover, the theory of evolution makes truth impossible, since men, evolving at different times and different places from different ancestors, may have developed different ways of adapting to reality. There is no reason to assume that logic is true for all men. Consequently, logic and truth are both relative. What is true for me may not be true for you. Thus materialism renders thought subjective and absolute truth impossible. Without absolutes, how can Objectivism advocate a system of absolute morality?

Failure of Empirical Ethics

The difficulties with Objectivist ethics do not end with the failure of its materialist epistemology to account for truth. Objectivism's method of cognition is itself fallacious. Its empirical epistemology based on sensation, observation, and induction is an inadequate theory of knowledge.[4] Induction, as we have seen, is always a logical fallacy. For the observation of individual events can never provide us with unchanging, universal principles for the simple reason that we can never observe all events past, present, and future. Thus,

---

[3] See chapter 8 on reason and reality.
[4] See chapter 8 on reason and reality.

when an empiricist devises a morality based on particular observations of men, he cannot generalize that recommendation to all
men and for all times. For example, the fact that most men and
most societies regard murder as evil and restrain themselves from
its practice does not prove that men ought not to commit murder.
After all, there are some men and some societies that believe murder and cannibalism to be good.[5, 6] And an observational and inductive theory of ethics has to take into account all observations.
(Moreover, as we shall see later, even if *all* men restrained themselves from committing murder, it would still not follow that murder is wrong.)

Even Aristotle, whose empiricism resembles that of Rand, acknowledged the tentative nature of his ethical theory. Yet Rand
writes critically of his work:

> The greatest of all philosophers, Aristotle, did not regard ethics
> as an exact science; he based his ethical system on observations
> of what the noble and wise men of his time chose to do, leaving
> unanswered the questions of: *why* they chose to do it and *why*
> he evaluated them as noble and wise.[7]

A word must be said in Aristotle's defense. Aristotle understood
the inconclusive nature of his empirical method. He did not deduce his code of ethics from first principles as in geometry; therefore, he acknowledged that his ethics failed to achieve final
certainty.[8] Did Rand's approach to ethics differ significantly from
Aristotle's? If Rand shared Aristotle's starting point in epistemology, how could she avoid the objections to empiricism that we
have enumerated? How could she fail to reach the same tentative
conclusion as Aristotle? Quite obviously, Rand thought she had
surmounted the difficulties that Aristotle and all empiricists en-

---

[5] Ravi Zacharias, *Can Man Live without God?* p. 182.
[6] Richard Leakey and Roger Lewin, *Origins*, p. 220.
[7] "The Objectivist Ethics," *The Virtue of Selfishness*, p. 14.
[8] *Nicomachean Ethics*, 1094, b12–28; W.T. Jones, *A History of Western Philosophy*, Volume I, pp. 259–261.

counter in the process of formulating a code of ethics. However, she would have succeeded in the task of providing a morality of absolutes only if her code of ethics were properly deduced from the basic axioms of Objectivism and if her system were otherwise free from major contradictions. It remains to be seen whether she was in fact successful.

The Objectivist Ethics: The Basic Choice

In *Atlas Shrugged*, John Galt declares, "My morality, the morality of reason, is contained in a single axiom: existence exists—and in a single choice: to live. The rest proceeds from these."[9] Previously, we noted that "existence exists" and "consciousness is identification" were the two fundamental axioms of Objectivism. Now the number of axioms has apparently been reduced to one, and out of nowhere appears the choice "to live." Notice, however, that "to live" is not an axiom of Objectivism. As John Robbins points out in *Without a Prayer*, it is a choice that lies beyond reason and ethics; it is a *metaethical* as well as an *amoral* choice.[10] The choice is metaethical because one cannot enter into Rand's system of morality without making this choice. It is amoral because, at this stage, we have not been given a system of morality that defines the choice "to live" as good or evil. Rand made her morality of reason subsequent to and dependent upon this primary choice "to live."

Rand claimed that the one fundamental alternative faced by living things is that of life and death.[11] However, she neglected to explain why human beings ought to choose life instead of death. Indeed, what deduction from the axioms of Objectivism requires this of us? To be sure, existence exists and consciousness is identification. However, these axioms do not require human beings who are alive to continue living. The fact that I *am* alive does not imply that I *ought* to continue living. (Nor is this problem solved by making "to live" an axiom of Objectivism. For then the execution of

---

[9] *Atlas Shrugged*, p. 944.
[10] *Without a Prayer*, pp. 154–155.
[11] *Atlas Shrugged*, p. 939.

criminals and John Galt's threat to commit suicide if Dagny Taggart were tortured would be unequivocally immoral.) Thus Rand's choice "to live" appears as an unsubstantiated one. This point should be kept clearly in mind as we follow the development of the Objectivist ethics, because the rest of Rand's theory is based on the unproven assumption that living things ought to continue living. The remainder of our discussion regarding Objectivist morality will follow the order of Rand's presentation in her essay "The Objectivist Ethics."

Life and Death: The Alternative

Rand writes:

> No philosopher has given a rational, objectively demonstrable, scientific answer to the question of *why* man needs a code of values. So long as that question remained unanswered, no rational, scientific, *objective* code of ethics could be discovered or defined.[12]

According to Rand, the first question to ask is not which system of morality men should accept, but why man needs a code of ethics at all?[13] If we could discover the conditions that make it incumbent upon men to develop a code of ethics, we might gain some insight into the kind of ethics they ought to accept. Indeed, Rand's formulation of the problem suggests that only one code of ethics can be objective, rational, and scientific.

First, some preliminary definitions are in order. *Ethics* "is a code of values to guide man's choices and actions—the choices and actions that determine the purpose and the course of his life. Ethics, as a science, deals with discovering and defining such a code."[14] But just what are values? Rand defines *value* as "that which one acts to gain and/or keep."[15] However, her definition

---

[12] "The Objectivist Ethics," *The Virtue of Selfishness*, p. 14.
[13] "The Objectivist Ethics," *The Virtue of Selfishness*, p. 13.
[14] "The Objectivist Ethics," *The Virtue of Selfishness*, p. 13.
[15] "The Objectivist Ethics," *The Virtue of Selfishness*, p. 15.

provides no restriction on what this value might be. The "goodness" or "badness" of values has not yet been specified. A value is simply something that a person desires, pursues, and maintains. However, as J. Charles King writes, that which is valued is not necessarily the valuable.[16] For example, the Nazis valued Aryan supremacy, world domination, and the destruction of the Jews. But the fact that the Nazis *valued* these things does not necessarily make them *valuable*. Indeed, Rand understood this: "'[V]alue' is not a primary; it presupposes an answer to the question: of value to *whom* and for *what*?"[17] This qualification of the idea of value, however, is a little confusing. As Robbins notes, the concept of value here presupposes value.[18] What is the presupposition involved here?

Rand explains. The concept of value "presupposes an entity capable of acting to achieve a goal in the face of an alternative. Where no alternative exists, no goals and no values are possible."[19] As John Galt indicates in *Atlas Shrugged:*

> There is only one fundamental alternative in the universe: existence or non-existence—and it pertains to a single class of entities: to living organisms. The existence of inanimate matter is unconditional, the existence of life is not: it depends on a specific course of action. Matter is indestructible, it changes its forms, but it cannot cease to exist. It is only a living organism that faces a constant alternative: the issue of life or death.[20]

Apparently, part of the answer to the question "Why do we need a code of values?" is to be found in the fundamental alternative facing living beings, for the alternative of life and death is what makes values possible. "Where no alternatives exist, . . . no values are possible."

[16] J. Charles King, "Life and the Theory of Value: The Randian Argument Reconsidered," in *The Philosophic Thought of Ayn Rand*, edited by Douglas Den Uyl and Douglas Rasmussen, p. 103.
[17] "The Objectivist Ethics," *The Virtue of Selfishness*, p. 15.
[18] *Without a Prayer*, p. 146.
[19] "The Objectivist Ethics," *The Virtue of Selfishness*, p. 15.
[20] *Atlas Shrugged*, p. 939.

But what is life, and what is death? According to Rand, "Life is a process of self-sustaining and self-generated action."[21] An organism seeks out those things that make the continuance of its life possible. As long as it is alive, it continues to be presented with alternatives and values. Death is the price of failure, and it is a state that offers no further values. Thus it would seem that values flow from the choice of life alone. Indeed, Rand concludes, "It is only the concept of 'Life' that makes the concept of 'Value' possible. It is only to a living entity that things can be good or evil."[22] Not only does Rand believe that the concept of "Life" antecedes the concept of "Value," she also believes that the life of an organism is the *ultimate value* for that particular organism. All other goals and values are to be evaluated with reference to this ultimate goal and value. As Rand said, "An organism's life is its *standard of value:* that which furthers its life is the *good,* that which threatens it is the *evil.*"[23]

Let us consider what Rand has asserted thus far. Is it really true that only the concept of "Life" makes the concept of "Value" possible? Value, as Rand says, presupposes an entity that faces the alternative of life and death. However, this definition of value makes the "Alternative of Life and Death" and not "Life" the presupposition of "Value." Why then did Rand feel it necessary to assert that "Life" made the concept of "Value" possible? If "Life" and "Death" are two parts of the fundamental alternative, we have to ask ourselves why the concept of "Death" could not have made the concept of "Value" possible? Philosophers Douglas Den Uyl and Douglas Rasmussen, in defending Rand's position, have suggested an answer to this question. According to them, life requires continuous maintenance whereas death requires only inactivity. "Death, a living thing not-being, does not require any actions for its maintenance."[24] Conse-

---

[21] "The Objectivist Ethics," *The Virtue of Selfishness,* p. 15.

[22] "The Objectivist Ethics," *The Virtue of Selfishness,* pp. 15–16.

[23] "The Objectivist Ethics," *The Virtue of Selfishness,* p. 17.

[24] Douglas Den Uyl and Douglas Rasmussen, "Nozick on the Randian Argument," *The Personalist,* April 1978, p. 191; also quoted in J. Charles King, "Life and the Theory of Value: The Randian Argument Reconsidered," *The Philosophic Thought of Ayn Rand,* p. 106.

quently, "Death" can neither be an ultimate value, nor can it make the concept "Value" intelligible.

Several points need to be addressed here. First, the fact that life requires continuous maintenance while death appears to be a terminal state that requires no further action does not imply that "Life" makes the concept "Value" possible. Values exist where there is an alternative. Where there are no alternatives, there are no values. But the absence of values only occurs when a person is actually dead (assuming there is no afterlife and no way of returning from the realm of death). While a person is still alive, he faces an alternative: that of life and death. Thus death represents a possible option and value. Let me emphasize this point: It matters not that a person who commits suicide has no further values once he is dead. While he is alive, the alternative of life and death is available to him, and he can choose death as a value.

Furthermore, it is simply not true that death requires no effort. Now it may be the case that the *state* of death, once achieved, requires no further actions. But the *goal* of death requires activity and effort. Altruists like James Taggart may very well value a slow, gradual death. Indeed, it requires a concerted and dedicated effort to evade reality every waking moment of one's life and to suppress what may well be natural tendencies toward self-preservation. Moreover, a person opting for a quicker form of death, such as by means of a single bullet to the brain, often has to exert extraordinary will power to pull the trigger and end his own life. Consequently, the goal of death requires effort and may serve as an *ultimate value*.

Den Uyl and Rasmussen also made the observation that the person who desires death, paradoxically, has to value life *first* in order to value death.[25] However, their argument, which purports to show that only "Life" makes "Value" possible, misses the mark. As Robbins points out, their argument merely demonstrates that life is a means to an end.[26] One has to be alive first in order to

---

[25] Douglas Den Uyl and Douglas Rasmussen, "Nozick on the Randian Argument," *The Personalist*, April 1978, p. 191.
[26] *Without a Prayer*, pp. 155–156.

commit suicide. Life, in this case, serves as an instrumental value, not the ultimate value. For the person committing suicide, death remains the ultimate goal and value.

All of this confusion about "Life" and "Value" result from a contradiction embedded within the Objectivist ethics. We will recall that Rand had already made the decision "to live" independent of the axioms she had chosen for her philosophy and prior to the formulation of her ethics. Thus Rand assumed that living things *ought* to go on living. Her entire code of ethics depends on this assumption. Her hierarchy of values and virtues are plausible only if one has decided "to live." But she gave no reason for this first ethical choice, this first *ought*. She gave no reason why a person ought to continue living. Consequently, neither Rand nor anyone else could fault a person for choosing the pathway of death.

Indeed, it is ironic that John Galt, the consummate Objectivist, threatens to commit suicide if Dagny Taggart is tortured by the looters' government. Since Rand had already informed us that evil is what threatens an organism's life, should we not conclude that John Galt is *evil* in threatening his own life? Or perhaps he is *amoral* because the initial choice to live or to die is a metaethical one. But he certainly cannot be good, not by Objectivist standards anyway.

These difficulties regarding the choice of life and death have profound consequences for Objectivist ethics. If Objectivism cannot help us decide on the fundamental issue of life and death, how can it hope to provide us with guidance on the myriad of other choices that confront us each day, the choices that confront us in each day of our lives on earth? As Robbins says, "The alternative of life and death is not one that is faced once and for all; it is faced every moment of every day; it is part of every choice one makes."[27] Consequently, if Objectivist morality cannot help us with the fundamental choice of life and death, it cannot help us make any decisions at all.

Life as Ultimate Value

We will now return to a question raised earlier, namely, What makes values possible? Rand had suggested that the alternative of

---

[27] *Without a Prayer*, p. 150.

life and death is what makes values possible. And she hoped to prove her assertion by using the example of an indestructible robot:

> [I]magine an immortal, indestructible robot, an entity which moves and acts, but which cannot be affected by anything, which cannot be changed in any respect, which cannot be damaged, injured or destroyed. Such an entity would not be able to have any values; it would have nothing to gain or to lose; it could not regard anything as *for* or *against* it, as serving or threatening its welfare, as fulfilling or frustrating its interests. It could have no interests and no goals.[28]

But King rightly points out that an entity that could not be affected by anything is simply an uninteresting and uninstructive example.[29] Indestructibility and impassability are not equivalent. Of course, a robot that could not be affected by anything at all, by definition, cannot respond to anything or take anything into account. A more enlightening example would be King's example of a man who became immortal as a result of exposure to some chemical. (A more familiar example is the comic-book hero Superman without the Achilles-heel vulnerability to Kryptonite.) This man would be immortal, but he remains a sentient being who can be affected intellectually and emotionally. He may wish to engage in productive work, eat delicious food (for the taste if not for survival), enjoy pleasant music, learn golf, read mystery novels, and fall in love. It is simply untrue to say that immortality and indestructibility remove the possibility of values. Therefore, we must conclude that Rand was mistaken. The alternative of life and death is not the only alternative that makes values possible.

Deriving the Ought from the Is

Next, Rand attempted to establish the connection between what an organism *is* and what it *ought* to do. In this respect, her ethics

---

[28] "The Objectivist Ethics," *The Virtue of Selfishness*, p. 16.

[29] J. Charles King, "Life and the Theory of Value: The Randian Argument Reconsidered," *The Philosophic Thought of Ayn Rand*, pp. 109–112.

resembles that of Aristotle. Aristotle believed that if we could determine what an organism *is* (what its function is), then we could specify what it *ought* to do (how it should behave). Rand writes confidently, "The fact that a living entity *is*, determines what it *ought* to do. So much for the issue of the relation between '*is*' and '*ought*.'"[30] Unfortunately, the problem is not as easy as Rand supposed. The philosopher David Hume had already shown that it is impossible to deduce what man *ought* to do from assertions about what man *is*.[31] In order to meet the criterion of logic, the terms in the conclusion of an argument have to appear in the premise of the same. The *ought* is in the conclusion, but where does it appear in the premise? (This is why, as we said earlier, even if all men restrained themselves from murder, it would still not follow that murder is wrong. The fact that man *is* a creature that has not been observed to commit murder does not imply that man *ought* not to commit murder.)[32] Moreover, even if we grant that Rand's argument was correct, one has to know what

---

[30] "The Objectivist Ethics," *The Virtue of Selfishness*, p. 17.

[31] *A Treatise of Human Nature* (Book III, Part I, Section I), in *The Philosophy of David Hume*, p. 247.

[32] Ronald Merrill believes there is no difference between descriptive (factual-"is") statements and normative (moral-"*ought*") statements. And he thinks he has surmounted the *is-ought* difficulty with the example of programming a computer (*The Ideas of Ayn Rand*, pp. 106–108). "You ought to format a new disk before attempting to write a file to it." This "ought" statement, Merrill believes, is both a descriptive and a normative statement. However, the computer example is not quite analogous to the human situation. For a human being I might say, "You ought to eat in order to stay healthy." Or, "You ought to think in order to come up with the answer to the problem." But these are not normative statements of moral necessity. They are descriptive statements. Let me rephrase them to make this plain. "A human being is an organism that needs nutrients in order to stay healthy." Or, "A human being is one that needs to think in order to solve problems." But the normative question is whether one *ought* to eat and stay healthy *and* whether one *ought* to solve problems. No amount of factual knowledge of how a human being functions tells us whether he ought to function in that way. Now, Merrill's example can also be rephrased. "A human being is an organism that has devised a computer to work by formatting a new disk before writing a file to it." But the question is whether one *ought* to use the computer and write a file. Merrill continues: "*So, if we can agree on what morality is to accomplish, we can develop moral rules as factual*

man *is* before one can say what he *ought* to do? Did Rand provide a coherent account of what man *is*?

What Is Man?

Rand's first step in her effort to provide a definition of man was to distinguish him from other living organisms. She began with an account of lower life forms.[33] Plants and animals, like all living beings, face the alternative of life and death. Therefore, plants and animals have values. Plants need sunlight and water; animals seek nourishment and shelter. Both kinds of organisms value the continuance of their biological lives and act automatically to achieve that goal. However, plants and animals cannot choose to act against their own interest. If a plant's cellular machinery for photosynthesis fails to function properly, it dies. If an antelope fails to elude its predator, it perishes. But neither the plant nor the antelope has a choice in what values to pursue. They function instinctively and automatically. It is a breakdown in these automatic mechanisms for survival that leads to death.

According to Rand, it is also their inability to choose that makes it impossible for plants and animals to have a code of morality. However, Rand says that they do have an automatic code of survival and an automatic code of values.[34] (Here we must wonder at the distinction between a code of morality, a code of values, and a code of survival.) Unfortunately, Rand had previously made the concept of good and evil (morality) contingent on the alternative of life and death—not choice. "An organism's life is its *standard of value:* that which furthers its life is the *good,* that which threatens it is the *evil.*"[35] Thus we are faced with a

---

statements. For normative statements are merely factual statements about means and ends. . . . Let us simply assert that 'ought' in the operational sense, and 'ought' in the normative sense, are after all equivalent, and challenge the critics to prove that they aren't!" (Emphasis added.) This is specious reasoning. Notice that Merrill presupposes the unproven assertion that agreement on means and ends exists and that we know what man *is* and *ought* to do.

[33] "The Objectivist Ethics," *The Virtue of Selfishness,* pp. 18–19.
[34] "The Objectivist Ethics," *The Virtue of Selfishness,* p. 19.
[35] "The Objectivist Ethics," *The Virtue of Selfishness,* p. 17.

dilemma: Are we to believe that animals and plants have a code of morality because they face the alternative of life and death? Or are we to believe they do not have a code of morality because they function automatically and exercise no choice? Rand's statements may be used to support either position or both. Presumably, she had intended to limit morality to human beings only. But why is it that only man requires morality? Apparently because

> Man has no automatic code of survival. . . . [H]is consciousness will not function *automatically*. . . . [M]an is the only living entity born without any guarantee of *remaining* conscious at all. Man's particular distinction from all other living species is the fact that *his* consciousness is *volitional*.[36]

In other words, only volitional consciousness, or free will ("the power of making choices which are, causally, *primaries*—i.e., not necessitated by antecedent factors") makes morality possible.[37] For Rand, man's free will extends even to his choice of personal identity: Man has to be man by choice. Moreover, this is not a choice that is made once and for all. In every waking hour, man has to choose to exercise his rational faculty, to deal with reality, and to ensure the propagation of his life.[38] If a man fails to think, he returns to a subhuman mode of consciousness and can no longer claim the status of man.

Thus Rand believes that a code of morality is possible to man only because he is free and his consciousness is volitional. If man did not possess free will, he would at best be an advanced animal that lived as well as its automatic code of survival allowed. But then none of his actions could be deemed evil because he exercised no free choice. Thus the Objectivist theory of morality presupposes the possibility of volitional consciousness. But is volitional consciousness possible?

---

[36] "The Objectivist Ethics," *The Virtue of Selfishness*, pp. 19–20.
[37] Nathaniel Branden, "Intellectual Ammunition Department," *The Objectivist Newsletter*, January 1964, p. 3.
[38] *Atlas Shrugged*, p. 944.

In the last chapter, we discussed Rand's belief in the primacy of the existence of indestructible matter. Consciousness is not a primary; instead, it is a secondary epiphenomenon of unconscious matter. However, this view of reality is incompatible with the concept of free will. Indeed, how can consciousness, which arises from unconscious matter, be free from the laws that govern unconscious matter? How is free will possible? We saw how Rand, Branden, Peikoff, and Efron all fell short in their attempts to justify the theory of volitional consciousness from their materialist premises. Since volitional consciousness is the attribute of man that makes morality possible, the Objectivist ethics collapses without it. Hence, we must conclude that Rand was unsuccessful in *this,* her first attempt to define what man actually *is.* Man is not a being of volitional consciousness. Therefore, her morality vanishes along with the myth of volitional consciousness.

Longevity or Quality of Life

Next, Rand attempted to answer the question she had raised earlier: Why does man need a code of ethics? The preceding discussion has prepared us for her solution: "Ethics is an *objective, metaphysical necessity of man's survival*—not by the grace of the supernatural nor of your neighbors nor of your whims, but by the grace of reality and the nature of life. . . . 'A code of values accepted by choice is a code of morality.'"[39] First, according to Rand, ethics is needed to ensure man's biological survival. Second, morality is made possible by the truth of volitional consciousness. However, Rand can substantiate neither of these claims. Remember, her code of ethics becomes viable only if one has chosen "to live." But she has never demonstrated that survival is obligatory. Moreover, in the preceding section, we showed that Rand had no right to the concept of volitional consciousness. However, for the sake of argument, we will overlook these difficulties and assume that Rand had already established man's biological survival as a

---

[39] "The Objectivist Ethics," *The Virtue of Selfishness,* p. 23.

standard of value in ethics. How does this help us define a code of ethics for man? Rand writes:

> The standard of value of the Objectivist ethics—the standard by which one judges what is good or evil—is *man's life*, or: that which is required for man's survival *qua* man. Since reason is man's basic means of survival, that which is proper to the life of a rational being is the good; that which negates, opposes or destroys it is the evil.[40]

But how did we get from biological survival to man's survival *qua* man? Up to now, Rand has been concerned with establishing the physical, biological survival of a man as the standard of value in ethics. Now she tells us that there is a quality of life man *qua* man that should serve as the standard. The transition is made almost imperceptibly. Rand seems to equate a *quality* of life with *longevity* of life. However, in order for a person to assert as a standard of value man's life *qua* man, he must know what man *is*. But, as we have seen, Rand was unable to distinguish man from lower life forms on the basis of volitional consciousness. Now she seems to think that her definition of man as a rational being is sufficient to define conduct appropriate to man. Unfortunately, it isn't. As Gordon Clark says: "If anyone should try to preserve the unity of morality by subsuming all moral actions under a general principle of rationality, the reply is that an atheist, a Roman Catholic, and a Buddhist each has his own conception of what it means to act rationally."[41] As we noted earlier, *reason* has a variety of meanings. And even those who subscribe to the Objectivist definition of reason—sensation plus abstraction—often reach different conclusions about ethical questions. This discrepancy merely serves to confirm that *rationality* is often used as a weasel word to legitimize whatever one wishes to advance as the correct morality.

Of course, Rand's aim all along was to legitimize some *quality* of life as a standard of value in morality. She was not interested in

---

[40] "The Objectivist Ethics," *The Virtue of Selfishness*, p. 23.
[41] *An Introduction to Christian Philosophy*, p. 47.

defending life at any price—few people are. The question is *not* whether she advocated a particular morality, but whether she was able to demonstrate that the kind of life man *qua* man that she advocated logically followed from her premises. Robbins makes this observation on the previously quoted passage:

> In making such a statement Rand begged all ethical questions. By what steps did the argument move from physical survival as the ethical standard to "man *qua* man," that is, to a standard already bristling with value judgments? Rand provided no steps. It was one small step for Rand, but one giant leap for logic. Making this substitution permitted Rand to attack as "evil" an action that leads to physical survival, because it does not lead to the quality of life she implicitly and without argument selected as proper for man. Rand smuggled ethics into her system by the backdoor: She switched the fundamental ethical standard from survival to the highest quality of life.[42]

Just as Rand had earlier made a decision "to live," which she could not substantiate, so now she asserts a quality of life man *qua* man without any effort to prove that such a life is indeed proper for man. Thus, Rand's vision of what a life man *qua* man ought to be, however appealing and heroic it may appear, remains simply *her* vision. She failed to justify it from first principles; and on her empirical and observational premises, her definition of man *qua* man has no more validity than any other definition.

The Predator and the Prey

Rand's concept of a life proper to a rational being bears further analysis. According to her, "[T]he two essentials of the method of survival proper to a rational being are: thinking and productive work."[43] Rand defined the good man as one who chooses to think, because the choice to think is the choice to live. If a man thinks and pursues the cardinal values of reason,

---

[42] *Without a Prayer*, pp. 172–173.
[43] "The Objectivist Ethics," *The Virtue of Selfishness*, p. 23.

purpose, and self-esteem, the cardinal virtues of rationality, productivity, and pride automatically follow.[44] By contrast, an evil man does not think.[45] He may imitate and repeat what the productive man has shown him, but he neither initiates nor creates anything of value. Such is the life of a parasite. For Rand, looters represented another class of evil men. They create no wealth but survive by stealing from the productive. Neither the looters nor the parasites could survive if they were on their own. They exist only by destroying the productive. Thus, evil men act like predators, and the productive serve as their prey.

If Rand hoped that the analogy to predator and prey would help us accept the Objectivist distinction between the two types of men, she was mistaken. Earlier, in our evaluation of the Objectivist concept of volitional consciousness, we concluded that volitional consciousness is a myth and man is merely an advanced animal who possessed an automatic code of survival. However, if men are only advanced animals, then no moral distinctions can be made between men as predators (looters and parasites) and men as prey (producers). The predator-prey analogy destroys the Objectivist system of morality. Here is why.

Consider the predator-prey paradigm. Each species of animal acts according to its automatic code of survival with its own biological life serving as its standard of value. Take, for example, the simplified model of the rabbit and the wolf. The rabbit acts for its own good, by consuming foliage and producing offspring, but it faces the possible evil of being eaten by a wolf. (Remember, the good is that which furthers the life of an organism, and evil is that which threatens it.) The wolf also acts for its own good and survives by preying on rabbits, thus avoiding the evil of starvation. However, strictly speaking, it would be incorrect to accuse the wolf of acting immorally when it hunts rabbits. After all, it is acting according to its nature wolf *qua* wolf. Nor can we consider the rabbit evil when it feeds excessively on foliage and neglects

---

[44] "The Objectivist Ethics," *The Virtue of Selfishness*, p. 25.
[45] "The Objectivist Ethics," *The Virtue of Selfishness*, pp. 23–24.

ecological principles. After all, the rabbit is acting according to its nature rabbit *qua* rabbit. Nevertheless, some people are fond of rabbits and consider the wolves evil for preying upon them. However, others admire the wolves for their cunning and strength. Strictly speaking, we cannot assign good or evil to either animal's behavior. The science of observation merely tells us that the predator-prey cycle occurs. It does not tell us what value judgment to make regarding the participants. In fact, the cycle is seen by environmental scientists as a self-regulatory phenomenon of nature. Now, if men are indeed advanced animals, and by Rand's own admission they are predator and prey, then the predator-prey paradigm demonstrates that there can be no moral distinctions between men as predators and men as prey.

But suppose this objection is raised: Wolves and rabbits are different species, whereas man is one species. And since man is one species, the predator-prey analogy using rabbits and wolves does not apply. After all, wolves do not prey upon other wolves, and rabbits do each other no harm. First, we should note that it was Rand who chose to use this analogy. We have merely followed where she has led us. Second, the observation that wolves and rabbits do not harm members of their own species may be correct, but other examples of intraspecies conflict and predator-prey practices within species cannot be ignored. Ants wage war against each other and even make slaves of other ants.[46] Male lions on occasion will eat the young cubs of their pride.[47] Chickens will peck a sick and weak chicken to death. Alligators cannibalize other alligators until they reach a certain size. "Bachelor" crows in Scotland kill the innocent and defenseless chicks of their "married" neighbors in order to drive them from their scarce and coveted treetop nests. Are men exceptions? Hardly. Julian Huxley observed that ants and man are the only species that habitually wage war.[48] Leakey and

---

[46] Julian S. Huxley, *On Living in a Revolution* (New York: Harper and Brothers Publishers, 1942), pp. 76–77.
[47] Leakey and Lewin, *Origins*, p. 220.
[48] *On Living in a Revolution*, p. 76.

Lewin explained that lions and man are the only mammals that practice cannibalism.[49] There seems to be abundant evidence for what Tennyson observed: Nature is red in tooth and claw. And man appears to be a full participant in that nature.

Moreover, the objector cannot even assume the unity of the human species. The evolutionary hypothesis implies that men may have evolved from different ancestors. Perhaps looters are men who have evolved from more aggressive and predatory ancestors. Perhaps productive men evolved from more industrious and constructive ancestors. Looters and producers may look like they belong to one species, but they really are not. Both types of men act to further their biological lives. And it remains to be seen whether one group will ultimately triumph in the struggle to survive, or if the two groups will simply coexist in a predator-prey cycle relationship. Perhaps a new breed of men, productive yet with the capacity on occasion for acting in an aggressive and predatory manner, will surpass them all. The predator-prey paradigm merely corroborates what Robbins has concluded:

> Perhaps it is best to emphasize here that the *physical* survival of man is in fact the survival of man *qua* man. After all, man does not become a plant or an animal simply because he wants to survive at any price. Rand, however, denied that physical survival and the survival of man *qua* man are equivalent. Therefore, what Rand meant by the phrase "man *qua* man" is already ethically loaded.[50]

Eric Mack concurs in *The Philosophic Thought of Ayn Rand*:

> [I]f there really are different types of survival, the basis for one's preference for one type over another cannot be in terms of survival. If there is human survival and subhuman survival, one's preference for the former must be in terms of the greater value of humanness over subhumanness. There is need to appeal to a

---

[49] Leakey and Lewin, *Origins*, p. 220.
[50] *Without a Prayer*, p. 173.

principle—humanness is better than subhumanness—which is quite independent of the endorsement of survival.[51]

Indeed, this distinction between humanness and subhumanness has important implications for Rand's theory of rights, and we will revisit it later in this chapter.

Another issue that needs to be addressed is Rand's statement that productive men think whereas parasites and looters don't. On the contrary, evil men do think. They just use their reason to devise a scheme for survival that differs from the scheme that the productive members of society have adopted. Criminals can be extremely intelligent. In fact, they may be quite innovative. They merely use their creative abilities for death and destruction. Surely, Hitler was innovative in his conduct of mass genocide during the Second World War. Few have surpassed his efficiency. Furthermore, it is false to say that parasites and looters cannot survive on their own. Even though they may *now* survive at the expense of the productive, they are not prevented from *switching* to an alternative mode of survival under different circumstances.

Rand also says, "Such looters may achieve their goals for the range of a moment, at the price of destruction: the destruction of their victims and their own. As evidence, I offer you any criminal or any dictatorship."[52] But this charge is simply not true. Did Rand think that Hitler planned his conquest for the range of a moment? No indeed. Hitler plotted his rise to power over several years and intended the Third Reich to last a millennium. Hitler had a glorious decade as the terror of Europe, and his death at the end of the war is no argument against predatory activities. For example, Stalin used his abilities so well—compromising when he had to—that he lived to a ripe old age. Stalin merely acted according to his nature better than Hitler acted according to his.

---

[51] Eric Mack, "The Fundamental Moral Elements of Rand's Theory of Rights," *The Philosophic Thought of Ayn Rand*, p. 138.
[52] "The Objectivist Ethics," *The Virtue of Selfishness*, p. 24.

Our discussion takes us back to an important question in Objectivist ethics. Is physical survival related to the quality of life
that Rand assumed is proper for a rational human being? Ronald
Merrill suggests that it is.[53] In *The Ideas of Ayn Rand*, he argues that
for every Stalin and Mao who lives to old age, there are dozens of
Trotskys whose lives are cut short by their own immoral behavior.
Therefore, in the long run, those who lead productive and rational
lives will increase the probability of their own longevity.[54] A person like Bertrand Russell, whom many Objectivists consider evil
and who happened to live to old age, "was lucky, that's all."[55]

But how could Merrill know that Russell was lucky unless he
had already decided which morality was correct? And on what
basis could he assert that Objectivist morality was the correct
one? As we have seen, it certainly is not because of logical argu-
mentation. Perhaps Merrill would argue that the virtues advocated by Rand have been scientifically demonstrated to increase
the length of peoples' lives. But where are the data? Where is the
controlled experiment that verifies this claim?

For one thing, Objectivism does not have exclusive claim to
the virtues of productivity and rationality. Christian morality also
upholds these virtues, among others. Moreover, Objectivism advocates behavior other than productivity and rationality as morally good. Can it be demonstrated that these additional behaviors
do not detract from longevity? In addition, Merrill would have to
demonstrate that productivity and rationality led to increased
survival in the pre-Objectivist era despite the mixed premises
that men may have held in the past. Moreover, that longevity of
life would have to be substantiated not only for the free societies
of the West, but also for the repressive societies of the East.

I wonder how many millions of rational, productive citizens
have died at the hands of dictators in the Soviet Union, Nazi Ger-

---

[53] When Ronald Merrill suggests a reformulation of Rand's argument by saying
that "morality consists not just of preserving life (MQM), but of maximizing
life (MQM)," he simply continues to beg the question as to what *is* or is *not* life
man *qua* man (MQM) [*The Ideas of Ayn Rand*, p. 112].
[54] *The Ideas of Ayn Rand*, pp. 114–116.
[55] *The Ideas of Ayn Rand*, p. 114.

many, and China? Didn't Ayn Rand herself say that she could never have survived in Soviet Russia?[56] Presumably she would have attempted to practice rationality and productivity even there. But how many have succumbed to the temptation to behave in a parasitic and criminal manner? Such activities may indeed be more advantageous under Communist rule. Perhaps rational men would have tried to escape Communism. But how many would have died in the attempt like Kira Argounova in *We the Living*?[57]

The questions seem endless. Does the fact that average life spans in the West exceed those of the East lend credence to the connection between longevity and rationality? Even Rand would admit that most people in the West hold mixed philosophical premises. Which of these premises are responsible for longevity? The calculations are as impossible as those of utilitarianism. Moreover, such calculations, even if they were possible, would make ethics a matter of probability. What may be true of most people may not be true of an individual. How does Merrill know that an individual will not have the ruthlessness and resourcefulness to succeed as Stalin did? Therefore, we must conclude that the connection between longevity and the quality of life that Rand envisioned remains unsubstantiated.

Planning for a Lifetime

Furthermore, not only are the rational and the productive men not guaranteed longevity of life, they are not promised even a tomorrow. Men are subject to disease, natural disasters, and indiscriminate violence. In the light of such uncertainties, how can Objectivism recommend planning for a lifetime instead of living for the range of a moment?[58] Even if it were true that criminals live moment by moment, who could fault them for it? Hitler did not have to worry about the human cost of his actions. Once he was dead, others could pick up the pieces. Obviously, Stalin's policies worked well enough to sustain him for a lifetime. He did not

---

[56] Barbara Branden, *The Passion of Ayn Rand*, p. 72.
[57] *We the Living*, pp. 442–446.
[58] "The Objectivist Ethics," *The Virtue of Selfishness*, p. 24.

have to worry about the eventual collapse of the Soviet Empire after his death. So why should we choose to live the life of an Objectivist, planning "in the context and terms of a lifetime"?[59] Even if productivity, honesty, and integrity contributed to lifelong success, we may not find lifelong success a compelling reason for practicing these virtues if we cannot guarantee long life. In the short run, we may suffer for practicing such virtues. The following attitude may be more appropriate: "Let us eat and drink, for tomorrow we die."[60]

Perhaps a compromise is in order. As Mack suggests:

> Given that rationality and productiveness are the characteristic survival traits for human beings, if survival is the goal, then each person should *as a matter of general strategy* foster rationality and productiveness in himself. But this in no way excludes the value of animalistic and parasitic courses of action when they are demanded by the longevity criterion.[61]

Again, the difficulty with prescribing rationality and productivity as virtues resurfaces as a result of confusion over the meaning of *virtue*. Are rationality and productivity to be regarded as virtues because they constitute a quality of life that is to be pursued regardless of the implications for survival? (Here life man *qua* man is the standard.) Or are they virtues because they are likely means for perpetuating length of life? (Here biological life and longevity is the standard.) On the first interpretation, one should never abandon virtuous living even if biological survival is threatened. However, then the virtues become evil by the Objectivist criterion, since they threaten the biological survival of the person who practices them. On the second interpretation, the virtues are not absolutely necessary to the perpetuation of biological life. They may as a general rule enhance the likelihood of biological survival. But, as Mack writes, "If on occasion the prospects for biological

---

[59] "The Objectivist Ethics," *The Virtue of Selfishness*, p. 24.
[60] 1 Corinthians 15:32.
[61] Eric Mack, "The Fundamental Moral Elements of Rand's Theory of Rights," *The Philosophic Thought of Ayn Rand*, p. 140.

survival would be enhanced by abandoning reason and productivity, then on those occasions these traits should be abandoned."[62] It is up to the individual to decide when and where such ethical principles should be suspended. But such relativism provides no basis for a morality of absolutes. In fact, it provides no morality at all.

Sensations and Emotions: Pleasure and Happiness

Perhaps the most controversial aspect of Objectivist ethics concerns its advocacy of rational selfishness. Rand holds that "the achievement of his own happiness is man's highest moral purpose."[63] When a morality aims at an individual's own good or self-interest, it is called *egoism*. However, Rand is not the only thinker ever to have advocated egoism. Self-interest, or egoism, by itself is a very generic term, and different philosophers have offered as many definitions of what constitutes an individual's good. Where did Rand stand on this issue? What did Rand define as an individual's good?

We have seen how Rand began with an amoral choice "to live" and then stressed physical survival of the individual as the standard of value. Subsequently, she inserted, without warrant, a quality of life man *qua* man as the standard of good. While this quality of life includes such admirable virtues as honesty, integrity, and productivity, how these virtues logically follow from holding physical survival of the individual as the standard of value has not been demonstrated. Consequently, the quality of life that Rand advocates as an individual's good remains an unsubstantiated one, and our analysis along these lines must end. But perhaps we can better understand Rand's version of egoism, not by looking at the virtues of honesty, rationality, and productivity that she advocates, but by examining how an individual guided by Objectivist morality is supposed to make his basic choices.

The reader will recall what Rand said. "An organism's life is its *standard of value*: that which furthers its life is the *good*, that which

---

[62] Eric Mack, "The Fundamental Moral Elements of Rand's Theory of Rights," *The Philosophic Thought of Ayn Rand*, p. 137.
[63] "The Objectivist Ethics," *The Virtue of Selfishness*, p. 27.

threatens it is the *evil*."[64] But how does an organism determine
what furthers or threatens its life?

> The physical sensation of pleasure is a signal indicating that the
> organism is pursuing the *right* course of action. The physical
> sensation of pain is a warning signal of danger, indicating that
> the organism is pursuing the *wrong* course of action. . . .[65]

Apparently, the same mechanism occurs in man.

> Now in what manner does a human being discover the concept
> of "*value*"? By what means does he first become aware of the
> issue of "*good or evil*" in its simplest form? By means of the physi-
> cal sensations of *pleasure* or *pain*. Just as sensations are the first
> step of the development of a human consciousness in the realm
> of *cognition*, so they are its first step in the realm of *evaluation*.[66]

However, as Robbins points out, if sensation is the sole pathway to knowledge, and if physical sensations of pleasure and pain
are trustworthy guides to morality, then what we have in Rand's
morality is a formulation of ethical hedonism.[67] To be sure, ethical
hedonism is a version of egoism, but it is hedonism nonetheless.
Yet Rand denied that she advocated ethical hedonism.[68] However,
if pleasure and pain are the means by which human beings become aware of good and evil, it is difficult to comprehend how
Rand's morality can avoid ethical hedonism. Perhaps the confusion centers on Rand's use of the phrase *first step*. What Rand seems
to be saying is that sensations of pleasure and pain do not by themselves help us decide what is good or evil. Such evaluations of
good and evil are made at a later stage of consciousness, of which
sensations are only a first step. Perhaps by making moral evaluation the province of a level of consciousness beyond the sensory
stage, Rand thought she had avoided hedonism.

---

[64] "The Objectivist Ethics," *The Virtue of Selfishness*, p. 17.
[65] "The Objectivist Ethics," *The Virtue of Selfishness*, pp. 17–18.
[66] "The Objectivist Ethics," *The Virtue of Selfishness*, p. 17.
[67] *Without a Prayer*, pp. 156–159.
[68] "The Objectivist Ethics," *The Virtue of Selfishness*, pp. 29–30.

But let us consider her argument closely. The pleasure-pain mechanism, according to Rand, is hardwired into man's body.[69] This mechanism lets him know whether things are for him or against him. Man has no ability to alter the pleasure-pain mechanism of his body. However, those mechanisms are only the first steps in the development of his evaluative capabilities. There is another set of evaluative tools: emotions. According to Rand, emotions are the end products of man's conscious and subconscious thought processes. Here is support for its conscious nature:

> Man's emotional mechanism is like an electronic computer, which his mind has to program—and the programming consists of the values his mind chooses. . . . [M]an chooses his values by a conscious process of thought—or accepts them by default, by subconscious associations, . . .[70]

And here is support for its subconscious nature:

> Emotions are the automatic results of man's value judgments integrated by his subconscious; emotions are estimates of that which furthers man's values or threatens them, that which is *for* him or *against* him—lightning calculators giving him the sum of his profit or loss.[71]

Notice, however, this last definition of emotional states is not altogether different from Rand's earlier definition of the pleasure-pain mechanism as a reliable guide to good and evil. And it seems to suggest that emotions are the higher level evaluative tools that allow an individual to determine what is good or evil. The distinction between emotions and sensations appears to be that emotions *follow* from value judgments whereas sensations *precede* them. Presumably, value judgments begin with information provided by the senses. Man contributes to this information through either the conscious or subconscious programming of values. The results are

---

[69] "The Objectivist Ethics," *The Virtue of Selfishness*, pp. 27–28.
[70] "The Objectivist Ethics," *The Virtue of Selfishness*, p. 28.
[71] "The Objectivist Ethics," *The Virtue of Selfishness*, p. 27.

subsequently integrated in the subconscious mind, and emotions are produced. The sequence appears as follows:

> Automatic sensation : volitional (conscious) programming and subconscious (automatic) integration : automatic emotional response.

However, this argument depends on the validity of volitional consciousness. To emphasize the point made earlier, volitional consciousness is a myth if one accepts the primacy of matter. Since Rand was unable to extricate consciousness as epiphenomenon from the deterministic mechanism of unconscious matter, she could not justify free will. Therefore, we cannot accept the distinction she tried to draw between sensations and emotions based on the volitional nature of emotions. Sensations are hardwired, but emotions are supposed to result from volitional programming. However, on Rand's view of consciousness as an epiphenomenon of matter, the programming that man does is itself predetermined by the way his brain is structured. That structure was inherent in his genes (nature) and modified by the environment (nurture). Therefore, the programming of value judgments that result in emotions is not volitional but involuntary. Thus the schema for the relationship between sensation and emotion may be more accurately represented by the following:

> Automatic sensation : automatic response programming and integration : automatic emotions.

On this view, emotions are merely advanced forms of sensation. The two occur in a repetitive cycle of cognition and evaluation.

> Automatic sensations/emotions : automatic response programming and integration : automatic sensations/emotions.

Therefore, sensations and emotions represent a continuum of the pleasure-pain mechanism. However, if sensations cannot be distinguished from emotions, then the two forms of pleasure (sensational and emotional) cannot be distinguished either. Consequently, Rand's emotional states of *for* or *against* are really just advanced forms of sensory pleasure and pain. Therefore, Rand's formulation of morality depends, from the first steps of sensation to the last stages of emotion, on pleasure and pain, and her morality cannot fail to degenerate into ethical hedonism.

Even if we did not concern ourselves with the difficulties just mentioned and looked exclusively at Rand's theory of emotions, we would still find numerous disconcerting problems. First of all, Rand herself never seemed completely sure what purpose emotions were supposed to serve in ethics. She had said that emotions represented estimates of good or evil for a human being. However, *estimates* appears to be a weasel word. Are emotions "estimates" in the sense that they are accurate and therefore serve as infallible guides to good and evil? Or, are emotions "estimates" in the sense that they are inaccurate approximations of which one can never be certain? Rand takes this latter view when she says, rather vehemently:

> Emotions are not tools of cognition; to be guided by whims—by desires whose source, nature and meaning one does not know— is to turn oneself into a blind robot, operated by unknowable demons (by one's stale evasions), a robot knocking its stagnant brains out against the walls of reality which it refuses to see.[72]

But Rand cannot have it both ways. Either emotions are accurate estimates and hence tools of cognition, or they are untrustworthy whims and therefore not tools of cognition.

Rand attempted a solution. The difference may be one of programming. According to Rand, man cannot avoid feeling some emotions. What he can control is the programming of the internal standards that give rise to emotions. If we program the correct thoughts and standards into our minds, we will automatically experience the correct emotions.[73] (But as we have already seen, the

---

[72] "The Objectivist Ethics," *The Virtue of Selfishness*, p. 29.
[73] "The Objectivist Ethics," *The Virtue of Selfishness*, p. 28.

idea of volitional consciousness and programming is a contradiction in Objectivist epistemology.) These "correct" emotions can
then be trusted. Indeed, that is what the virtue of rationality should
produce for us in the realm of values. However, Rand also writes:

> [The virtue of rationality] means a commitment to the principle
> that all of one's convictions, values, goals, desires and actions
> must be based on, derived from, chosen and validated by a pro-
> cess of thought. . . .[74]

Naturally, this means that emotions (desires) must also be derived from and validated by a process of thought. Mack describes
this theory of emotions as *promulgative*.[75] On this view, emotions
are not to be trusted unless the antecedent processes of thought
that led to such emotions can be validated. Two things may be said
against this theory. First, from a practical point of view, no one can
perform the kind of self-psychologizing this theory requires and
still function. For example, if a person experiences the emotion of
elation or triumph, he could not allow himself to feel a sense of
"that which is for him" until he has had a chance to analyze and
justify those emotions rationally. His emotional apparatus would
be paralyzed by the validation process. Second, such a theory means
that emotions can never serve as an estimate of good or evil, since
a person can never be 100 percent certain that his emotions are the
end result of a proper sequence of thought. Even if a person's past
conduct and volitional programming had been consistent with the
life of a rational being, it is possible that some irrational impulse
has worked its way into his subconscious on this particular day.
Remember, "emotions are the automatic results of man's value judgments integrated by his *subconscious*" (emphasis added). The subconscious, by definition, is that which cannot be accessed
immediately and requires psychological methods of inquiry and
analysis for extraction. Even if a person were proficient at self-

---

[74] "The Objectivist Ethics," *The Virtue of Selfishness*, p. 26.
[75] Eric Mack, "The Fundamental Moral Elements of Rand's Theory of Rights,"
The Philosophic Thought of Ayn Rand, p. 146.

analysis, he would still be uncertain as to whether all of the value judgments integrated by his subconscious had been uncovered and validated. Consequently, Rand's promulgative theory of emotions undercuts her attempt to provide a rational man with a measure of confidence in the emotions he experiences.

But perhaps it was never Rand's intention to show us how we can have confidence in our emotions. It seems that Rand wanted to become the ultimate arbitrator of emotional responses. *She* would decide whether a person's emotional response was validated by a rational sequence of thoughts. Consider Barbara Branden's description of how Rand performed this analysis on others:

> [Rand] had said, . . . that the validity of one's musical tastes could not be philosophically demonstrated: not enough was understood about the mechanism by which music was interpreted by the brain and translated into emotional responses. Yet if one of her young friends responded as she did to Rachmaninoff, . . . she attached deep significance to their affinity. On the other hand, if a friend did not respond as she did, she left no doubt that she considered that person morally and psychologically reprehensible.[76]

This tendency to psychologize and arbitrate emotions continued in later years.

> Ayn had returned to her former "psychologizing"—the translation of ideas and attitudes she thought irrational into psychological and psycho-epistemological terms—and her friends had to endure constant discussions of their "failings" and "betrayals." . . . "Her discussions of our [Allan and Joan Blumenthal's] artistic and musical choices grew very difficult," Allan was to say, "and often heated and condemning. She was relentless in her pursuit of so-called psychological errors."[77]

Obviously, Rand felt that her analysis of the Blumenthals' artistic emotional response was accurate. However, the Blumenthals—note

---

[76] *The Passion of Ayn Rand*, p. 268.
[77] *The Passion of Ayn Rand*, pp. 386–387.

that Allan Blumenthal is a psychiatrist—considered Rand's judgment too simplistic. Each person believed his own artistic attitudes and emotional responses to be rational. This disagreement merely demonstrates the inability of *reason* to validate emotions and the insanity of allowing emotions to become a cognitive tool in the realm of ethical evaluation. Rand would no doubt have agreed with the latter half of my statement. In order to discredit the whim-worshipers, she disparaged their dependence on emotions as cognitive tools. However, in doing so she cut the ground from under her own belief that happiness signaled an individual's attainment of abundant life.

Consider this passage from *The Virtue of Selfishness:*

Happiness is that state of consciousness which proceeds from the achievement of one's values. If a man values productive work, his happiness is the measure of his success in the service of his life. But if a man values destruction, like a sadist—or self-torture, like a masochist—or life beyond the grave, like a mystic—or mindless "kicks," like the driver of a hotrod car—*his* alleged happiness is the measure of his success in the service of his own destruction. . . . Neither life nor happiness can be achieved by the pursuit of irrational whims. . . . "Happiness is a state of non-contradictory joy. . . . Happiness is possible only to a rational man, . . ." The maintenance of life and the pursuit of happiness are not two separate issues. . . . Existentially, the activity of pursuing rational goals is the activity of maintaining one's life; psychologically, its result, reward and concomitant is an emotional state of happiness. It is by experiencing happiness that one lives one's life, in any hour, year or the whole of it.[78]

In making such a statement Rand begged all questions about emotions. How did the argument move from happiness as a positive or pleasurable emotion that arises when anyone achieves his values, to happiness as an emotion possible only to a rational man who achieves rational values? Just as Rand had earlier substituted the quality of life of man *qua* man in place of physical survival as

---

[78] "The Objectivist Ethics," *The Virtue of Selfishness*, pp. 28–29.

the standard of ethical conduct, she now makes a similar substitution in her theory of emotions. This substitution allowed Rand to label as "alleged happiness" and "contradictory joy," or to attack as "whim," any positive emotions a person may experience if they result from thoughts or actions that she disagreed with. In other words, happiness is not genuine unless it is the emotion one experiences as a result of pursuing the life of a rational being as defined by Objectivism. Noncontradictory joy is possible only for the likes of John Galt and Howard Roark. Thus, what non-Objectivists experience as happiness is merely a delusion. What Rand has done is to switch the fundamental emotional gauge of successful living from generic happiness to the quality of happiness experienced by man *qua* man.

Purpose and Standards

In conclusion, Rand asserts: "'Happiness' can properly be the *purpose* of ethics, but *not* the *standard*. The task of ethics is to define man's proper code of values and thus to give him the means of achieving happiness."[79] Now this statement is problematic for a number of reasons. First, why is the emotion of happiness made the *purpose* of Objectivist ethics? There are many rational emotions possible to a rational man besides happiness. Surely, fear is an appropriate response to that which threatens one's life. Surely, there is a state of noncontradictory lament just as there is a state of noncontradictory joy. Yet we do not say that fear or lament is the purpose of one's life. Why is it necessary to posit happiness as life's purpose? Moreover, instead of the extremes of happiness and suffering, why should one not strive for peace and tranquillity?

Furthermore, Rand seems to suggest that successful living is not to be measured by the occasional or even the frequent occurrence of happiness. Instead, the continuous experience of happiness appears to be the goal. "It is by experiencing happiness that one lives one's life, in any hour, year or the whole of it."[80] How-

---

[79] "The Objectivist Ethics," *The Virtue of Selfishness*, pp. 29–30.
[80] "The Objectivist Ethics," *The Virtue of Selfishness*, p. 29.

ever, does Rand really want us to believe that a man is not living a successful life if he does not experience happiness during any hour, year, or the whole of his life? This statement could not possibly be true, even by her own standards. Was Dagny happy late one night in the office of the John Galt Line when she experienced loneliness?[81] When Francisco cried out at the thought of losing Dagny because of the strike, was he experiencing joy?[82] Even though they each acted rationally under the circumstances, neither Francisco nor Dagny experienced happiness with any immediacy. What happened to the joy that they were supposed to feel in the act of living? More than most people, the two of them had correctly programmed their emotional apparatus with the appropriate value judgments. Why could they not trust their negative emotions to tell them that they were pursuing the wrong course of action? If happiness really is a measure of successful living in any hour of one's life, happiness should be sought diligently *every* hour of one's life. But that makes happiness the goal and standard of one's activities in every hour of one's life. What is a person to do if he is unhappy? If a person is not happy, he cannot argue that his actions are rational and that he will experience happiness *someday*. By definition, the absence of happiness means that he is not living fully. He needs to do something to make happiness happen *now*.

This discussion points to a further difficulty in Rand's distinction between happiness as the *purpose* of one's life, and life man *qua* man as the *standard* of ethics. Just what does it mean to say that happiness is the purpose instead of the standard of ethics? Let us be reminded of Rand's definition of ethics. "[Ethics] is a code of values to guide man's choices and actions—the choices and actions that determine the purpose and the course of his life."[83] On this scheme, the initial selection of a code of values (based on some *standard*) determines choices and actions : choices and actions determine *purpose* and course of life. An Objectivist will of course select a code of values based on the standard of life man *qua* man.

---

[81] *Atlas Shrugged*, p. 209.
[82] *Atlas Shrugged*, p. 113.
[83] "The Objectivist Ethics," *The Virtue of Selfishness*, p. 13.

The choices and actions that result from adopting this code of values will determine the purpose and course of his life. And Rand says that the purpose of the Objectivist's life will consist of his own happiness. However, if one has previously decided to make happiness the purpose of one's life, then the decision to follow a particular code of ethics must be pursuant to that goal of happiness. It is useless to advocate a morality based on the standard of life man *qua* man if such a standard does not achieve the purpose of happiness. Moreover, unless one knows ahead of time that one's choice of morality will achieve happiness, one cannot proceed to advocate that particular morality.

But how can a person know that a morality based on the standard of life man *qua* man will accomplish the goal of happiness? One cannot know except for the fact that Rand had already appropriated the term *happiness* and defined it in such a way as to make it possible only for a person who practices her philosophy. Consequently, she could indeed argue that her morality based on the standard of life man *qua* man would achieve the purpose of happiness. In fact, hers is the *only* code of values that will achieve happiness.

Moreover, Rand could also argue for happiness as the purpose of ethics. After all, happiness is possible only if one selects the Objectivist standard of life man *qua* man as the standard for ethics. So if one's purpose in life is happiness, that purpose will imply adopting the Objectivist standard of morality. Once Rand's circular definition of happiness is recognized, it is easy to see that the distinction between purpose and standard disappears. And if we reject Rand's assertion that only her standard of morality leads to happiness, the choice of happiness as purpose implies that happiness also has to be the standard. The following scheme more accurately describes the situation:

Choice of *purpose* is the *standard* that determines code of values : code of values determines choices and actions that accomplish *purpose*.

Now, when happiness—and here we are speaking of generic happiness, not the Objectivist version—is made the purpose of ethics, only happiness as an immediate goal makes any sense. Indeed, Rand herself requires the immediate experience of happiness in any hour of one's life to verify successful living. Also, no one can know with certainty that a particular course of action will result in a future state of happiness that justifies passing up the experience of short-term happiness. One final point. Since our earlier analysis exposed Objectivism's artificial distinction between sensations and emotions, we must conclude that the emotion of happiness is just another form of sensory pleasure. And that makes pleasure the purpose of Objectivist ethics. Now, unless one is prepared to maintain Rand's unsubstantiated and narrow definition of happiness, upholding happiness and pleasure as the purpose of morality necessarily leads to ethical hedonism and subjectivism.

Summary

Ayn Rand began with an attempt to provide a rational, scientifically demonstrable ethics. She ended with an untenable morality of rational self-interest that leads logically to ethical hedonism. Her failure could have been predicted from her choice of an empirical epistemology, for observation and induction never provide absolutes. Michael Shermer, a skeptic writing from the same empirical premises as Rand, had this to say about her in *Why People Believe Weird Things:*

> The great flaw in her philosophy is the belief that morals can be held to some absolute standard or criteria. This is not scientifically tenable. Morals do not exist in nature and thus cannot be discovered. . . . Its absolutism was the biggest flaw in Ayn Rand's Objectivism, the unlikeliest cult in history. The historical development and ultimate destruction of her group and philosophy is the empirical evidence that documents this assessment. . . . What separates science from all other human activities (and morality has never been successfully placed on

a scientific basis) is its commitment to the tentative nature of all its conclusions. There are no final answers in science, only varying degrees of probability.[84]

Shermer thus confesses to the skeptical nature of any moral assertions *including* his own. Rand had once said, "If man is 'gray' by nature, no moral concepts are applicable to him, including 'grayness,' and no such thing as morality is possible."[85] What Rand failed to understand was that *her epistemology* arrived at no truth and therefore yielded a "gray" world where no morality was possible.

Aside from this initial, devastating, epistemological flaw in Rand's choice of methods, we also discovered other difficulties with her ethical theory. Rand's materialist first principles undercut her theory of free will. And according to her, there is no possibility of morality without free will. In addition, our analysis demonstrated that Rand's morality is not deduced from her axioms, but rests on a metaethical, amoral choice "to live." If Rand had been consistent, she would not have condemned altruism as a morality of death, for the choice of life or death as the standard of value is by her own admission an amoral choice. And even if physical survival does serve as a legitimate standard of value in ethics, it does not imply the quality of life man *qua* man that Rand endorsed. Clearly, Rand also failed in her attempt to surmount the *is-ought* gap. Moreover, the question "What is man?" was never satisfactorily answered by her. Our consideration of the predator-prey paradigm and the evolutionary hypothesis reduced man to an advanced animal, and animals do not possess a code of morality. Consequently, Rand's moral distinction between looters as predators and producers as prey cannot be maintained. Finally, it was shown how the Objectivist morality of rational self-interest leads to ethical hedonism, not the list of virtues Rand advocated. Hence, we must conclude that Rand was unsuccessful in her attempt to formulate an ethical theory just as she was unsuccessful at formulating a theory of knowledge.

---

[84] *Why People Believe Weird Things*, pp. 123–124.
[85] "The Cult of Moral Grayness," *The Virtue of Selfishness*, p. 76.

The implications of the Objectivist ethics for its political theory should be quite obvious. If Rand could not define good and evil for individuals, how could she construct a theory of government that defines interpersonal relationships and reciprocal obligations among men? If we went no further, this criticism alone would cripple Rand's political theory. Nevertheless, because part of Rand's fame is derived from her commitment to *laissez-faire* capitalism, we will do well to examine the political theory that undergirds it.

Politics

Rand's ethical theory has profound implications for the political system she advocated. As she says, "Every political system is based on some code of ethics."[86] In morality, Rand was persuaded that she had established the life of man *qua* man as the standard of ethics and successfully argued for an individual's happiness as the moral purpose of his life. Therefore, in politics she argues, "There is only *one* fundamental right (all the others are its consequences or corollaries): a man's right to his own life."[87] And because life, in her view, is a process of self-sustaining and self-generated action, a man's right to his life means that he has "the freedom to take all the actions required by the nature of a rational being for the support, the furtherance, the fulfillment and the enjoyment of his own life."[88] In addition, Rand asserted that each man is an end in himself, and no one has the right to violate the rights of another person while pursuing his own goals. Consequently, Rand advocated *laissez-faire* capitalism as the political system that logically follows from her ethics of rational self-interest. The political principle that originated with Rand was later adopted by the Libertarians and designated as the *nonaggression axiom*: "[N]o man may *initiate* the use of physical force against others."[89]

---

[86] "Man's Rights," *Capitalism: The Unknown Ideal*, p. 320.
[87] "Man's Rights," *Capitalism: The Unknown Ideal*, p. 321.
[88] "Man's Rights," *Capitalism: The Unknown Ideal*, p. 322.
[89] "The Objectivist Ethics," *The Virtue of Selfishness*, p. 32; Murray Rothbard, *For a New Liberty*, p. 23.

However, in order for Rand's argument for *laissez-faire* capitalism to go through, she had to demonstrate the validity of the transition she made from assertions about an individual's right to the pursuit of his own life and happiness, to the necessity of respecting other individuals as ends in themselves. Indeed, Rand argues, "'Rights' are a moral concept—the concept that provides a logical transition from the principles guiding an individual's actions to the principles guiding his relationship with others. . . ."[90] However, as we demonstrated in the section on ethics, Rand never succeeded in validating her version of life man *qua* man as the standard of value in ethics. At most, she was able to demonstrate that physical survival is of value to the individual. Even then, physical survival is of value only to those who wish to live.

We also saw how the pursuit of physical survival, self-fulfillment, and happiness as the purpose of an individual's life degenerated quickly into ethical hedonism. And that seems incompatible with an obligation to respect the rights of others. For if the standard of value for an individual is his own physical survival and happiness, why should that individual regard another person as an end in himself? Why should he take another person's physical survival into consideration when contemplating a course of action? For example, we might agree that three hypothetical persons—Brown, Colton, and Davis—each are right to pursue their own lives. However, it does not follow from this premise that Colton or Davis should respect Brown's pursuit of his own life and refrain from interfering in it or obstructing it.[91] If the situation warrants it, why should Colton not use Brown as a means of achieving some goal that would be advantageous to Colton's survival? The idea of "the end justifying the means" may be distasteful to some, but distaste is no argument against the logical implications of Rand's theory. If the choice is between Brown's life and Colton's, why should Colton not interfere with Brown's life in order to preserve

---

[90] "Man's Rights," *Capitalism: The Unknown Ideal*, p. 320.
[91] Eric Mack, "The Fundamental Moral Elements of Rand's Theory of Rights," *The Philosophic Thought of Ayn Rand*, p. 152.

and further his own? Other philosophers have also found Rand's argument unconvincing.[92]

What has happened is this: Rand has introduced into her concept of life man *qua* man a respect for other peoples' lives that cannot be justified by viewing an individual's physical survival as the standard of value. To be sure, many people feel a healthy respect toward their fellow man. The question is not whether an underlying ethos in our culture sustains that respect. No doubt that ethos exists—though it appears to be disappearing rapidly. The question is where such a climate of respect came from and whether the Objectivist theory of ethics can justify the warm and kindly disposition toward others that Rand wanted her readers to feel. To answer such questions, we need to better understand Objectivism's theory of rights and its view of reciprocal obligations among men.

Individual Rights: Source and Definition

Where do rights come from? Man's nature, according to Rand, is the source of individual rights.[93] Rights are neither the gift of society, nor of the Congress, nor of God. They are inherent in man's nature by virtue of the law of identity. However, Rand's reference to man's nature and the law of identity assumes that she had a correct understanding of man's nature and identity. As we saw earlier, Rand's conception of the nature of man is fraught with contradiction. We need not revisit that failure now; however, we do need to examine her definition of rights.

One of the statements crucial to Rand's formulation of rights is found in *Atlas Shrugged* and quoted in her essay "Man's Rights":

> If a man is to live on earth, it is *right* for him to use his mind, it is *right* to act on his own free judgment, it is *right* to work for his values and to keep the product of his work. If life on earth is his purpose, he has a *right* to live as a rational being: nature forbids him the irrational.[94]

---

[92] J. Charles King, "Life and the Theory of Value: The Randian Argument Reconsidered," *The Philosophic Thought of Ayn Rand*, pp. 119–120.

[93] "Man's Rights," *Capitalism: The Unknown Ideal*, pp. 322–323.

[94] "Man's Rights," *Capitalism: The Unknown Ideal*, p. 323; *Atlas Shrugged*, p. 986.

As John Robbins points out, Rand's theory of rights depends on an equivocation of the word *right*.[95] *Right* in the first three propositions in the above paragraph is used as an adjective describing the correctness of certain actions. In the final instance, *right* is used as a noun describing the freedom and liberty that ought to be available to a man living in society. There is a difference in the two meanings of *right*. Eric Mack concurs: "[T]o establish that a person is right to do *x* is neither to establish that he has a right to do *x* nor to establish that others have a right that he do *x*."[96]

Furthermore, Robbins and Mack have each explained the difficulties associated with Rand characterizing political rights as being justified by the performance of "right" actions. ("Right" actions, of course, are those that meet Rand's standard of rationality and productivity.) For if freedom and rights are intimately tied to the concept of rationality and productivity, then, in some sense, individuals "only have the right to do what they should. . . ."[97] If that were truly the case, then an individual who performed "wrong" actions could be regarded as the violator of his own rights. (Recall the case of our hypothetical golfer in chapter 4.) Given this understanding, an agency that forces an individual to perform right actions would not necessarily be evil. If it seems equitable, as Rand had said, for nature to forbid man the irrational, why should other men (also part of nature) not forbid an individual from acting irrationally? As Robbins observes: "Let us assume, *arguendo,* that Rand had demonstrated that it is right for a person to use his mind. How does it follow that it is wrong for another person to force him to use it in a specified way?"[98] If it is right for a person to use his mind, to earn his own living, etc., why is it not then a political right for others to force him to use his mind, to earn his own living, etc.? Why should not the Objectivist government, whose purpose is allegedly to secure the rights

---

[95] *Without a Prayer*, pp. 183–184.
[96] Eric Mack, "The Fundamental Moral Elements of Rand's Theory of Rights," *The Philosophic Thought of Ayn Rand*, p. 151.
[97] Eric Mack, "The Fundamental Moral Elements of Rand's Theory of Rights," *The Philosophic Thought of Ayn Rand*, p. 155.
[98] *Without a Prayer*, p. 184.

of the individual, not force each person to accomplish all those things that Objectivism deems right?[99]

Rights: Inalienable or Conditioned?

Let us set aside for the moment this preliminary confusion over "right" action and political rights, and turn to Rand's theory of inalienable rights. Rights, Rand believed, have their source in the nature and identity of man. They are also inalienable. What does inalienability mean? She writes: "Since Man has inalienable individual rights, this means that the same rights are held, individually, by every man, by all men, at all times. Therefore, the rights of one man cannot and must not violate the rights of another."[100] Already, this passage suggests a contradiction. The last sentence appears to conditionalize rights while the first sentence asserts the inalienability of individual rights. Elsewhere, Rand shows no tolerance for such a conditioning of rights:

> Inalienable means that which we may not take away, suspend, infringe, restrict or violate—not ever, not at any time, not for any purpose whatsoever.[101]

> You cannot say a thing such as "semi-inalienable" and consider yourself either honest or sane.[102]

> Either man's rights are inalienable, or they are not. . . . When you begin making conditions, reservations and exceptions, you admit that there is something or someone above man's rights, who may violate them at his discretion.[103]

---

[99] *Without a Prayer*, p. 185.

[100] "Textbook of Americanism," pamphlet, p. 6 as quoted in *The Ayn Rand Lexicon*, edited by Harry Binswanger, p. 215.

[101] "Textbook of Americanism," pamphlet, p. 12 as quoted in *Without a Prayer*, p. 189.

[102] "Textbook of Americanism," pamphlet, p. 12 as quoted in William O'Neill, *With Charity toward None*, p. 207.

[103] "Textbook of Americanism," pamphlet, p. 12 as quoted in *With Charity toward None*, p. 204.

Of course, Rand is correct in one respect: If rights are inalienable, then they can never be violated or set aside.[104] If rights are not inalienable, then they are subject to the rules and regulations imposed by other individuals, society, or God. Unfortunately, Rand contradicts herself. "The Right to the Pursuit of Happiness means man's right to live for himself, to choose what constitutes his own private, personal, individual happiness and to work for its achievement, *so long as he respects the same right in others*" (emphasis added).[105] But to say that the rights of an individual are inalienable *except* when they violate the rights of others is to have already made those supposedly inalienable rights conditioned upon a predetermined notion of respect for others. As William O'Neill demonstrates, Rand repeatedly asserts the inalienability of individual rights and then proceeds to conditionalize those rights as if she had already solved the problem of what constitutes reciprocal obligations between men.[106]

Where do such obligations come from? Rand gives a pat answer: "The only 'obligation' involved in individual rights is an obligation imposed, not by the state, but by the nature of reality. . . ."[107] Again, Rand seemed to think that by attributing obligations to the nature of reality, she had legitimized her contradictory concept of inalienable yet conditionalized rights. But it is precisely the deduction of rights and obligations from the nature of reality that Rand never performed. Moreover, such an argument presupposes agreement on the nature of reality and the nature of man. If anyone thinks that such an agreement can be reached from the observation of reality, a reconsideration of the earlier section on morality, especially the predator-prey paradigm, ought to dissuade him.

---

[104] *Without a Prayer*, p. 189.

[105] "Textbook of Americanism," pamphlet, p. 5 as quoted in *The Ayn Rand Lexicon*, pp. 214–215.

[106] *With Charity toward None*, pp. 204–211.

[107] "The Wreckage of the Consensus," *Capitalism: The Unknown Ideal*, p. 227.

Inalienable Rights: Implications

What implications does the concept of inalienable rights have in practice? Rand writes: "Man's rights can be violated only by the use of physical force."[108] Using the crime of murder as an example, Robbins shows clearly what this principle would entail.[109] First, Robbins points out that a man does not lose his inalienable rights simply by committing murder. If words have any meaning, inalienable rights must mean just that; they cannot be alienated at any time, for any reason. The murderer was using his free judgment and pursuing his own life when he found it necessary to extinguish the life of another. The victim was also pursuing his own life and values when his path crossed with the murderer. Obviously, the victim failed to evade the murderer or defend himself successfully against attack. (Like the rabbit that failed to outrun the wolf, the victim was unsuccessful in his bid to survive.) However, the murderer does not thereby lose his inalienable rights just because he has violated the rights of another. Inalienable rights mean just that. They cannot be violated regardless of one's actions.

Moreover, if the police or family were to retaliate against the murderer, they would be violating the murderer's inalienable rights. Consequently, the idea of inalienable rights destroys the distinction between the initiation of physical force and the retaliatory use of physical force. It abolishes the difference between crime and punishment. In some respects, both the murderer and the police violate inalienable rights—the rights of another to live and pursue his life. Thus their actions are both unjustified and reprehensible. However, both uses of force are also justifiable because they occur in the context of each person—whether it is the murderer or the policeman—acting on his own judgment in the pursuit of his own values. Such is the confusion that results from the concept of inalienable rights. Yet this confusion foreshadows Rand's attempt at a solution to the problem. Since it is the murderer's *nature,* as man, that validates his claim to inalienable rights, the murderer's in-

---

[108] "The Nature of Government," *Capitalism: The Unknown Ideal*, p. 330.
[109] *Without a Prayer*, pp. 186–190.

alienable rights could be revoked if he somehow lost his identity as man. If the murderer were no longer human, the police would violate no rights in apprehending him. We will return to this topic in detail later.

Inalienable Rights: The Derivation of Government

Rand also believed that government derives its just powers from the consent of the governed.[110] In this, she thought that she shared the view of the Founding Fathers. They regarded government not as the ruler, but as the servant of the people.[111] As such, the government's functions are limited to those duties assigned to it by the citizens. Government was instituted to secure the rights of individuals. It provides protection against foreign aggressors and internal criminals and operates a court system to settle disputes.

However, this view of a limited government does not appear to be consistent with Rand's view of inalienable rights. For why should sovereign individuals ever give up their inalienable rights to the government? If individuals are prior to the state, why should they ever submit themselves to the state? If the government is derived from the consent of the governed, then what happens when the consent is withdrawn? If, for some reason, individuals did delegate those rights to government, would they not be justified in taking those rights back whenever they pleased? Do they even need to take back those rights, since inalienable rights reside within the individual and cannot be revoked at any time? For example, can an individual refuse to observe traffic laws whenever he pleases? Can individuals or a number of individuals secede from the Union simply because they feel the government no longer serves their interest? These are important questions that must be asked concerning the Objectivist view of government, given Rand's stance on inalienable rights.

Let us consider Rand's attempt to justify government. It takes the following form. In any society, there exist evil men, and there-

---

[110] "The Nature of Government," *Capitalism: The Unknown Ideal*, p. 332.
[111] "Man's Rights," *Capitalism: The Unknown Ideal*, p. 323.

fore conflicts among men must exist. Evil men have to be re-strained. However, the retaliatory use of force is too great and dangerous a power to be left in the hands of any individual; there-fore, it has to be entrusted to government.[112] However, placing that power in the hands of a group of individuals does not seem to remedy the difficulty either, for the government's monopoly over the use of force poses an even greater danger than an individual's use of force. Indeed, governments have historically shown a tendency toward corruption. Consequently, Rand argues that the government's use of force has to be very carefully con-trolled and subordinated to law.

However, this line of reasoning still fails to answer the funda-mental question. Why should sovereign individuals ever give up their rights or delegate it to so dangerous an entity as the state? Why is anarchy not the political ideal for Objectivism? These dif-ficulties with Rand's theory of inalienable rights have led a num-ber of Libertarian thinkers to advocate stateless societies that are supposed to fall short of anarchy. One example of such a stateless society is the concept of multiple, competing governments. Now, Rand rejected such proposals even as she had repudiated the Lib-ertarian movement. She illustrates the problem with such scenarios by posing an example of two individuals named Smith and Jones subscribing to different Governments A and B:

> [S]uppose Mr. Smith, a customer of Government A, suspects that his next-door neighbor, Mr. Jones, a customer of Govern-ment B, has robbed him; a squad of Police A proceeds to Mr. Jones's house and is met at the door by a squad of Police B, who declare that they do not accept the validity of Mr. Smith's com-plaint and do not recognize the authority of Government A. What happens then? You take it from there.[113]

The situation would lead to anarchy and erupt in violence.

It is interesting to consider how the Libertarians have attempted to defend a stateless society in spite of Rand's criticism. In *For a*

---

[112] "The Nature of Government," *Capitalism: The Unknown Ideal*, p. 331.
[113] "The Nature of Government," *Capitalism: The Unknown Ideal*, p. 335.

New Liberty, the Libertarian Murray Rothbard attempts to demonstrate the viability of the competing government theory in the context of natural rights. The model he chooses in support of his thesis is the ancient Celtic system of *tuaths*. In this system, individuals belong to clans, or *tuaths*; each tuath is headed by a king whose powers are delegated to him and limited by the tuath. Individuals may freely move from one tuath to another. Well-reputed and independent judges known as *brehons* roam the country and settle disputes according to a body of natural and common law. Individuals belong to insurance companies called *sureties*, which guarantee that the brehons' decisions are enforced.

However, this system of voluntary government is susceptible to a number of criticisms. First, it is not at all clear that all brehons, even if they were otherwise flawless in their logic and free from prejudice, will agree to begin their deliberations from the same body of natural law. Second, why should a defendant even agree to appear before a brehon and submit to judgment? If person A murdered person B's father, person A has nothing to gain from appearing before a brehon who considered murder evil. Surely person B will not appear before a brehon who condoned murder. The problem with selecting brehons who judge rightly is not solved by the suggestion that brehons known for their integrity will survive better on the free market. Only if both parties feel they have something to gain from appearing before a just brehon will they voluntarily submit to his judgment. Person A is under no obligation to appear before a brehon at all. In the absence of agreement over the choice of a brehon, does person B have the right to appear before a brehon with person A *in absentia*? Or, does person B have the right to force person A's appearance before some particular brehon?

This last question points out some other difficulties with Rothbard's theory. Even on the view that retaliatory use of force is appropriate, apprehension of a person for the purpose of trial is not thereby sanctioned. Apprehension is itself the initiation of the use of physical force and a violation of rights, for the defendant has yet to be convicted of murder. On the basis of natural rights and the nonaggression axiom, person B has no right to apprehend person A and bring him to trial. Nevertheless, Rothbard writes: "The victim [person B] would gather his sureties around him and proceed to apprehend the criminal [person A] or to proclaim his suit publicly and demand that the defendant submit to adjudication of their dispute with the brehons."[114]

But if rights are inalienable, how can person B have the right to apprehend the defendant, person A? Person A and his clan simply may not recognize the authority of the brehons or the sureties to judge him. Only if person B and his surety had the right to either apprehend or threaten apprehension would person A be required to attend court and submit to the decision of the brehons. However, this represents the use of force by person B; and as we showed before, no distinction can be made between the initiatory and retaliatory use of force once natural, inalienable rights are accepted.

Nevertheless, Rothbard continues: "If [the defendant] did not [submit to judgment], he was considered an 'outlaw' by the entire community; he could no longer enforce any claim of his own in the courts, and he was treated to the opprobrium of the entire community." Again, why should person A, the defendant, care what the entire community thinks? Person A may have sufficient resources and power to obviate the need for dealing with the rest of the community. He may have a sizable army with which to accomplish his goals and enforce his claims without resorting to the courts.

Rothbard's scenario appears plausible only because it rests upon a number of assumptions present in his Celtic society that do not necessarily inhere in the state of affairs today. The Celtic society appears to be a manifestation of what Alasdair MacIntyre called a "heroic society" in his book *After Virtue*.[115] (It may even have been influenced by biblical law.) Individuals in these societies accepted as norms the moral precepts given to them by their community. There was general agreement on morality. Each man knew his obligations toward other men and submitted to tribal or intertribal

---

[114] *For a New Liberty*, p. 233.
[115] *After Virtue*, pp. 121–130.

regulations and judgments. Indeed, a man who failed to abide by those commonly held regulations and judgments would be ostracized by the community and regarded as an outsider. For that man, such opprobrium would constitute a profound loss of identity, from which he could not easily recover psychologically.

However, this argument based on guilt and conscience would not go very far in contemporary political debate. Our earlier discussion on ethics and the theory of rights showed that no agreement on morality could be reached from the observation of nature. And the idea of natural rights imposes no obligations on the individual to submit to the judgment of others. Today there may be no body of shared beliefs pervading society as it once did in the Celtic heroic society. (If there is a body of shared beliefs, it is a faint memory of America's Christian heritage.) By itself, the concept of natural rights leads to anarchy. As Thomas Hobbes points out in *Leviathan*, in the natural state of affairs, the individual's pursuit of his own life and happiness leads to a war of every man against every other man.[116]

But let us return to the main point. Rand opposed the institution of multiple, competing governments, and she eschewed the chaos and anarchy that would follow. However, she advanced a peculiar view of government financing that made anarchy all but certain. Rand made the purpose of government one of enforcing contractual agreements between citizens.[117] Such a government would provide its services for a voluntary fee; taxes (a form of initiation of force) would eventually be abolished under the Objectivist system. However, this notion of a government that provided its services on a voluntary basis contradicts Rand's opposition to multiple, competing governments. A government that provided voluntary services would not be able to keep other governments out of its territory and maintain its monopoly on the use of force. A government has to initiate or threaten force in order to keep competing governments out and ensure compliance with its own

[116] *Leviathan*, pp. 101–106.
[117] "Government Financing in a Free Society," *The Virtue of Selfishness*, pp. 116–120.

laws. As Robbins points out, taxation, apprehension of suspects, and the issuance of subpoenas are all examples of the initiation of physical force. If a government has no right to initiate physical force, it would not be much of a government.[118] Hence, Rand's support for inalienable rights and voluntary taxation leads logically to anarchy, not limited government.

Moreover, whether she realized it or not, Rand also depicted the ideal of anarchy, not limited government, in her fiction. Indeed, Rand says, "Art is the indispensable medium for the communication of a moral ideal."[119] Perhaps there is no better example of this literary principle than Rand's depiction of the ideal society, Atlantis, in *Atlas Shrugged*. As both Robbins and Merrill have demonstrated, there are no rules in Atlantis, and its inhabitants voluntarily submit to Judge Narragansett as the arbitrator of disputes.[120] This can be regarded as a description of nothing other than anarchy. Consequently, we must conclude that the political ideal of Objectivism is anarchy.

Inalienable Rights: How They Are Lost

Earlier, we saw how the concept of inalienable rights made it impossible to distinguish morally and politically between the initiation of force and the retaliatory use of force. Rand attempted to circumvent that difficulty in two ways. First, she merely conditionalizes her inalienable rights to exclude actions that she deems reprehensible from legal protection—that is, she assumes reciprocal obligations that she could not logically justify on the basis of inalienable rights. Second, since inalienable rights are derived from the nature and identity of man, it stands to reason that such rights can only be taken away if a man stops being man. Can man become *non*man? This possibility is inherent in Rand's concept of volitional consciousness. Remember, during every moment of his life, a man has to make the primary choice to think or not to think.

---

[118] *Without a Prayer*, pp. 198–203.

[119] *The Romantic Manifesto*, p. 21.

[120] *Without a Prayer*, pp. 199–200; *The Ideas of Ayn Rand*, p. 146.

This choice determines whether he lives as a man or as a subhuman creature, an entity or a zero. Thus, criminal action or nonrational thought strips a man of his nature and identity as man. Since a subhuman entity has no rights at all, there is no problem with punishing him. Using physical force against such an entity would violate no rights.

However, there are several difficulties with such a view. We have already shown that criminals do indeed think; they merely think differently from the standard that Rand has set for man *qua* man. However, as we also saw, Rand was unable to justify her notion of man *qua* man, and no agreement on what constitutes the nature and identity of man could be found on an empirical basis. Without such agreement, we could not decide whether a man had indeed become subhuman.

However, if we assumed that Rand and the Objectivists were able to distinguish between man and nonman, where would that lead us? As Robbins shows, this doctrine on the forfeiture of rights has far-reaching consequences. If a man can lose his rights by behaving in nonhuman fashion, by choosing not to think or by acting in a way that Rand deemed criminal, then those rights may not have been his to begin with. He may have acquired those rights at a time when he first chose to think and act rationally. If man can *unmake* himself, he may have had to *make* himself. But when does a man become man and acquire rights? The reader will have to indulge an excursion into the subject of abortion, for in this discussion much can be learned about Rand's theory of rights.

According to Rand, man does not acquire rights by merely being conceived. Rand apparently believed that a fetus was "not-yet-living" and therefore "cannot acquire any rights until it is born."[121] Rand did not consider a fetus an *actual* human being, but only a *potential* human being; consequently, she did not regard abortion as murder. But if the fetus is not an actual human being, what is it?

Obviously, it is a living tissue of some kind. Physicians, whether they support abortion or not, would hardly debate whether the fetus was a living thing. The question is, What kind of living thing is it?

---

[121] "Of Living Death (II)," *The Objectivist*, October 1968, p. 534.

Is the fetus merely a part of the mother's body that can be mutilated or destroyed? (As Robbins points out, one would be hard pressed to regard the fetus, an entity that has all the features of a human being, a brain, eyes, heart, etc., as merely part of the mother's body.[122])

Is it some indistinct organism that is making a transition from a single cell to some subhuman species that has no rights? (Rand contradicted herself on occasion by implying that the fetus was a distinct human entity with rights. She comments: "Observe that Mr. Cohen's (and the egalitarians') view of man is literally the view of a children's fairy tale—the notion that man, before birth, is some sort of indeterminate thing, an entity without identity, something like a shapeless chunk of human clay, and that fairy godmothers proceed to grant or deny him various attributes. . . ."[123] Might such attributes include *inalienable rights?*)

Or is the fetus human thereby making abortion murder? Since Rand did not regard the fetus, the child, as having any rights until it is born, she must have believed that the fetus was subhuman.

But let us look at the development of a fetus. Its heart develops into the typical four-chambered structure by the seventh week of gestation. A heartbeat is discernible on examination at six weeks. The basic structure of the brain is developed by six to ten weeks, although continued development obviously takes place throughout the rest of gestation. Pregnant women recognize their baby as already possessing a personality, even while in the womb. When it is delivered, even prematurely, it looks and acts like a human baby. How then can we conclude that the fetus is not human?

A change in the location of the fetus is apparently the primary reason for Rand's position on abortion. The decision to abort or not was to be left solely to the mother because the fetus is *in* the mother.[124] However, that consideration is irrelevant. As we noted before, it is the humanity of the fetus that is the relevant question here. And why should a change in the baby's location alter its hu-

---

[122] *Without a Prayer*, p. 207.
[123] "An Untitled Letter (II)," *The Ayn Rand Letter*, February 12, 1973, p. 169.
[124] "Of Living Death (II)," *The Objectivist*, October 1968, p. 534.

manity? The change is primarily one of physiology. After the baby exits the mother's womb, it is able to breathe independently and its circulatory system no longer draws upon that of the mother. These are the primary physiological differences. But they do not have a bearing on whether the fetus is human.

If the success of these physiological changes were the criterion for the assessment of humanness in the fetus, then we could make the argument that anyone wishing to have an abortion ought to at least submit themselves to an induced delivery so that the child might be given an opportunity to breathe on its own and demonstrate its humanity. If it is successful in the bid, it is human. If not, it is subhuman. (Of note, some premature infants are sustained in hospital intensive care units and given respiratory support because they cannot breathe independently; yet we consider these infants human.)

Of course, we could deny the fetus the opportunity to breathe on its own and thereby eliminate the test of his humanity altogether. However, that would be akin to defining man as a rational creature and then denying him the opportunity to prove his rationality through communication by plugging his ears, shading his eyes, gagging his mouth, and cutting off his fingers. Since he has not demonstrated his rationality, obviously he is not human. But notice: This is precisely what is currently done in the case of late-term, partial-birth abortions. The baby's head is partially delivered from the womb. Since it is technically still in the womb and has not yet undergone the postpartum physiological changes, the dissection and destruction of its brain is not seen as infanticide and murder.

With regard to Rand's repeated characterization of the fetus as a *potential* being, we also need to realize that a child does not complete its biological and mental development merely by exiting the birth canal. Many aspects of development, for example in the eyes and the brain, hidden from view, are not completed until weeks after birth. And quite obviously, a child continues to grow over time and develop characteristics that are an outworking of the potential already present within it. In this regard, it should be noted that genetic diseases and birth defects may kill a child within a few years of life, but they also may not become manifest until decades later. Also, devastating learning disabilities may not be identified for years. Where then does one draw the line in distinguishing the *actual* from the *potential*? And is an *actual* human being a person devoid of genetic and intellectual flaws? Who will set the minimum standards? And at what stage of life will these standards be applied and enforced? Thus we see that Rand's definition of humanness based on the concept of potentiality is not very helpful. In the final analysis, the decision to categorize a fetus as human or otherwise depends solely on the mother. One pregnant woman regards the baby as human while another considers it subhuman, depending on her view of abortion. Each person becomes the arbiter of human nature and of morality and of political rights. Is this not a most absurd example of subjectivism?

But the absurdity does not end there. The categorization of individuals as human or subhuman can logically be extended to infants and children as well, as the preceding discussion on potentiality and actuality has suggested. Indeed, since man is only man if he subscribes to the life of man *qua* rational being, one wonders why Rand regards infants and children as human. After all, how can we tell if infants and young children are applying Aristotelian logic? If they do think in terms of logic, they do not seem to apply it as frequently or as consistently as adults. Some suggest that infants exhibit nonrational, emotive modes of behavior.[125] By Objectivist criterion, this lack of consistent rationality makes infants and toddlers subhuman. And that makes them as vulnerable to killing as the subhuman fetus.

Moreover, even if an infant were somehow accorded the status of humanity, that status would not offer him much protection. Biologically, infants cannot sustain an independent existence. An infant who is not nourished or given covering will soon perish; it cannot find its own food or grow it. It can express its need only by crying. But remember, Objectivism teaches that a need does not justify a claim on anyone's life. Consequently, just because an in-

---

[125] *With Charity toward None*, p. 121.

fant is considered human, his humanity would not obligate an Objectivist to care for him. One wonders where Leonard Peikoff got his idea that a mother who gives birth to a child is morally obligated to take care of the child for the next twenty-one years?[126]

But let us return to the main point. If the preceding discussion is correct concerning the acquisition and loss of man's nature, and therefore the acquisition and loss of inalienable rights, then other conclusions follow. As Robbins points out, Objectivism must logically approve of certain types of murder:

> Because men make themselves, some men are better made than others, who are rather shoddy merchandise. Some are not men at all. Logically then, Objectivists must approve the liquidation of imbeciles, morons, idiots, the retarded, the mediocre who don't think, . . . [127]

This conclusion may seem shocking, but it is the logical consequence of Rand's ethical and political theory. If some men fail to think in the manner prescribed by Objectivism, they lose their identity as man and, consequently, their inalienable rights. As non-humans, they are vulnerable to treatment normally reserved for animals. Whether such a distinction, between the killing of a sub-human man as opposed to the murder of a man *qua* man, is maintained by a government will depend ultimately on whether the Objectivist view of man and inalienable rights prevails.

Recapitulation

Rand had hoped to ground her political theory of limited government and *laissez-faire* capitalism on an ethics of rational self-interest. Unfortunately, she could not justify her moral ideal of life man *qua* man as the standard for man's life. Consequently, her ethical theory is based on the physical survival of the individual and his attainment of happiness. However, if physical sur-

---

[126] Leonard Peikoff, in the debate "Capitalism or Socialism? Which is the Moral System?" 1984; tape on file with author.
[127] *Without a Prayer*, p. 209.

vival is the goal of each individual, there can be no such thing as reciprocal obligations between men to respect each other as ends in themselves. Rand could not and did not show that individuals in the pursuit of their lives must respect the lives of others. She was unable to demonstrate why one person, as a sovereign individual, must give up anything with regard to the pursuit of his own life. Moreover, we have seen how Rand's concept of inalienable rights obliterates the distinction between the initiatory and retaliatory use of physical force. It renders crime and punishment indistinguishable, and it makes government impossible. Logically, the theory of inalienable rights leads to anarchy and sanctions a tyrannical destruction of lives that do not live up to the Objectivist standard of man *qua* man. Consequently, the political theory of Objectivism cannot produce the republican form of government that the Founding Fathers envisioned and which Rand applauded.

A Christian Construction

The failure of Objectivism in ethics and politics began with its choice of method. For the reasons we previously discussed, empiricism must fail in its bid to provide universal ethical principles. In contrast, Christian theism offers hope where Objectivism and empiricism fail.

First, with respect to systematization, the axiom of revelation positing the Bible as the revealed word of God provides a starting place from which universal ethical principles may be deduced. There is no problem with induction and observation. Moreover, one does not have to bridge the gap between the *is* and the *ought*. The Scriptures reveal both what man *is* and what he *ought* to do. The Ten Commandments, for example, are a logical consequence of accepting the axiom of revelation.[128] They inform us as to our rights *and* obligations as creatures made in the image of God.

Second, as Gordon Clark shows in *A Christian View of Men and Things*, the Scriptures provide numerous case examples and considerable detail for the application of moral principles. The difficulties of applying the utilitarian calculation of Jeremy Bentham

---

[128] Exodus 20:1–17.

and of universalizing the categorical imperative of Immanuel Kant are thereby avoided.[129] Thus morality becomes possible for the common man as well as the elite. Christian ethics succeeds both theoretically and practically.

It should be noted, however, that Christianity advocates an ethical system quite different from what most people might imagine from having read Rand. After reading *Atlas Shrugged* and Rand's nonfiction essays, I was under the impression that Christianity necessarily advocates a morality that gives rise to socialism. However, as I discovered later, this could not be further from the truth.[130] The Scriptures abound with examples to the contrary. The commandments "You shall not steal" and "You shall not covet . . . anything that belongs to your neighbor" not only forbid thievery but establish private property. Working and prospering from one's work (the Protestant work ethic) were principles well established in the Book of Genesis. Man was given dominion over all of creation and commanded to bring it to maximum fruitfulness. Moreover, Christ clearly advocated investment, risktaking, and the rewards of enterprise in the Parable of the Talents.[131] "For to everyone who has shall *more* be given, and he shall have an abundance." This saying cannot possibly imply economic egalitarianism. In addition, laziness is not condoned. As Paul says, "If anyone will not work, neither let him eat."[132] Whatever a man finds to do, he is commanded to do with all of his might as unto God and not unto men.[133] Thus, Christianity does not advocate socialism.

Moreover, it may be seen that the Scriptures neither argue against self-interest nor disparage prosperity. Christianity advocates a form of egoism, which as we saw earlier merely means the pursuit of an individual's "good" leaving open the question: What

---

[129] *A Christian View of Men and Things*, pp. 110–116, 119–124.

[130] A number of scholars have argued convincingly that the Protestant Reformation contributed significantly to the development of capitalism. Compare Max Weber, *The Protestant Ethic and the Spirit of Capitalism*, and Gottfried Dietze, *In Defense of Property*, pp. 17–19, 36.

[131] Matthew 25:14–30.

[132] 2 Thessalonians 3:10.

[133] Colossians 3:17, 23.

is good? However, Christianity does not appeal to a self-interest based on hedonism. Instead, Christianity appeals to genuine self-interest limited by God's law. First, in contrast to Objectivism, the Scriptures clearly define an individual's reciprocal obligations ("You shall not murder," "You shall not steal," "You shall not covet," etc.) toward other men even as the individual pursues his own life, liberty, and happiness. This kind of ethics gives ample room for self-interest in the context of clearly defined reciprocal obligations toward others. (However, these reciprocal obligations are derived from God's moral commandments, not from natural, inalienable rights.)

Furthermore, the appeal to genuine self-interest is based on a system of rewards and punishments that will not only be revealed in eternity, but is partially manifested even in this world. For example, the command "Honor your father and mother" carries with it a promise: "that your days may be prolonged in the land which the Lord your God gives you."[134] Deuteronomy chapter 28 laid before the nation of Israel the alternative of obedience attendant with rewards, or disobedience resulting in curses. Psalm 1 describes a man who adheres to the law of the Lord and thereby prospers in all that he does. Proverbs 31 describes a diligent woman who brings blessing and abundance to her family and community. Christ himself said: "Seek first His kingdom and His righteousness; and all these [temporal, material] things shall be added to you."[135] Thus it may be seen that the self-interest to which Christianity appeals is not merely pie-in-the-sky, but real, tangible, and down-to-earth.

Moreover, sacrifices, as we saw in chapter 3, are not encouraged for the sake of attaining lesser values. They are the means by which greater values, either spiritual or material, may be realized. And even if temporal and material desires are not ultimately satisfied in this life, God's justice will ultimately be revealed in eternity. As Clark points out, "The Gospel of Christ demands sacrifices of men, but it demands no ultimate sacrifice."[136]

---

[134] Exodus 20:12.

[135] Matthew 6:33.

[136] *A Christian View of Men and Things*, p. 124.

The question of sacrifice requires that we take a slight detour into the question of charity, for which Objectivism has often been criticized. Rand's ethics of rational selfishness does not seem to allow for the practice of charity. However, Rand claimed that freedom and the attitude of rational selfishness present in her ideal society would create the necessary conditions for generosity and benevolence between rational men. Consequently, she believed that her morality does make room for charity. Besides, Rand regarded charity as essentially a marginal issue: If the majority of mankind needed charity, we simply would not survive as a species. Therefore, an Objectivist government presumably would dismantle the welfare state and depend on private charities to solve the problem of the poor.

However, Rand's definition of the conditions under which charity can be practiced makes it all but impossible to practice charity:

> There is nothing wrong in helping other people, if and when they are worthy of the help and you can afford to help them.[137]

> It is morally proper to accept help, when it is offered, not as a moral duty, but as an act of good will and generosity, when the giver can afford it (i.e., when it does not involve self-sacrifice on his part), and when it is offered in response to the receiver's virtues, *not* in response to his flaws, weaknesses or moral failures, and *not* on the ground of his need as such.[138]

Unfortunately, the people who usually need help are precisely those who fall short of Objectivist standards and exhibit "flaws, weaknesses or moral failures." Therefore, they would not be worthy of help. We should also remember, "A trader is a man who earns what he gets and does not give or take the undeserved."[139] Would not the practice of charity then merely serve to sustain the kind of subhuman life and behavior that Objectivism detests? And if a candidate for charity were merely a rational man caught in

---

[137] "*Playboy's* Interview with Ayn Rand," pamphlet, p. 10 as quoted in *The Ayn Rand Lexicon*, p. 69.
[138] "The Question of Scholarships," *The Objectivist*, June 1966, p. 92.
[139] *Atlas Shrugged*, p. 948.

unforeseen, unfavorable circumstances, would not his ability to surmount those difficulties on his own be a good test of his rationality and resolve? Moreover, when is it ever not a sacrifice to help someone? Every dollar that I give away represents a dollar that I could have used to further *my* life or save up for an uncertain future. To merely give money away is a sacrifice. Perhaps a loan is in order. But is the person a good risk? The interest will have to be calculated accordingly. . . . Ah, but that is no longer charity.

In contrast to the Objectivist view, the Scriptures command individuals to be charitable and generous. (Again, the commandments generally do so with a view to the blessings that would attend such behavior. For example, Jesus said, "Give, and it will be given to you."[140]) As a practical example, the ancient Israelites were commanded as individuals to leave certain portions of their fields unharvested so that the needy may gather their sustenance from them.[141] Helping to feed and clothe the poor is legitimized, even commanded, as one of man's responsibilities before God.[142] However, note that such charity is to be performed by the individual and the religious institutions; it is not an activity to be coerced by the state. We are all familiar with the fraud and waste of the welfare state. Part of the requirements of good stewardship recommends that even charity be performed with financial responsibility and accountability.[143] Resources are not to be squandered.

The foregoing discussion has established morality on the basis of the objective revelation found in the Scriptures. But how is this

---

[140] Luke 6:38. In the lecture "The Philosophical Base of Capitalism," Leonard Peikoff comments during the question and answer period: "If farmers had a fire in the nineteenth century, it became a legend that they were richer after the fire than before because their neighbors from all over inundated them with help in that kind of disaster. There was a great deal of benevolent good will among people because they were free. . . ." Even though Peikoff's comments about the effect of freedom on charity may be partially true, freedom does not by itself engender benevolence or charity. It is much more likely that the pervasive sense of generosity engendered by Christianity in that era spurred men on to love their neighbors as themselves. See also chapter 3.

[141] Leviticus 19:9–10; Ruth 2.

[142] Matthew 25:35–46.

[143] Luke 12:42.

related to a theory of government? The solution comes from the recognition that the laws and commandments are applicable not only to individuals, but also to leaders. Kings, priests, and prophets, including Moses himself, were subject to the laws revealed by God. "It is an abomination for kings to commit wickedness, for a throne is established on righteousness."[144] If an individual was not allowed to steal, neither was the government. Coercive taxation may be a legitimate source of revenue for sustaining the government's legitimate functions. (And these functions are clearly spelled out in the Scriptures. It consists primarily of punishing evildoers and providing security from external enemies.[145]) However, a government's theft of its citizens' moneys through inflationary tactics and the deficit spending of Keynesian economics is contrary to the eighth commandment as surely as embezzlement or larceny. Christianity, which posits God alone as sovereign, subjects both individuals and governments to his laws. Therefore, it lays the only legitimate foundation for a limited government. As Clark explains, all secular attempts at political philosophy fail in this regard. They tend either toward anarchy or totalitarianism depending on whether the individual or the state is considered sovereign.[146]

Rand did not appear to understand this fundamental problem in political philosophy. She says, "The most profoundly revolutionary achievement of the United States of America was *the subordination of society to moral law.*"[147] But where does this moral law come from? As we have demonstrated in this chapter, absolute, objective moral law cannot be had on the basis of Objectivist epistemology, ethics, and politics; it can only be had on the basis of scriptural revelation. It is ironic that Rand, who praised the United States as the first moral society in history, failed to appreciate the Christian philosophy on which it is founded.[148]

Some historical details may be helpful. Of the fifty-five men who gathered to write the Constitution of the United States, over

---

[144] Proverbs 16:12.
[145] Romans 13.
[146] *A Christian View of Men and Things,* pp. 61–95.
[147] "Man's Rights," *Capitalism: The Unknown Ideal,* p. 321.
[148] "Man's Rights," *Capitalism: The Unknown Ideal,* p. 321.

90 percent were devout Christians.[149] And their Christian background cannot be dismissed as hypocritical formality. In the political writings and speeches of the Founding Fathers, the Bible
was the most frequently cited resource; it represented 34 percent
of the references.[150] Paying lip service to religion does not necessitate such extensive documentation. Thus it is more than a plausible hypothesis that the limited government devised by American
statesmen had its origins in the Scriptures.

Indeed, the American system was heavily influenced by the
Judeo-Christian worldview. As Francis Schaeffer points out, Henry
de Bracton's *De Legibus et Consuetudinibus* (c. A.D. 1250) documents
the biblical influence that gave rise to the English Common Law
and the Magna Carta. Bracton's work reflects a nearly universal
view of law and government that was present in England at that
time. Schaeffer summarizes this view:

> ... God in His sheer power could have crushed Satan in his revolt
> by the use of that sufficient power. But because of God's charac-
> ter, justice came before the use of power alone. Therefore Christ
> died that justice, rooted in what God is, would be the solution. ...
> Therefore, power is not first, but justice is first in society and law.
> The prince may have the power to control and to rule, but he
> does not have the right to do so without justice.[151]

Thus God's law and justice is considered sovereign over all
men—both rulers and subjects. Four hundred years later, Samuel

[149] M.E. Bradford, *A Worthy Company* (NH: Plymouth Rock Foundation, 1982),
pp. viii–ix as quoted in David Barton, *The Myth of Separation*, pp. 24–25.
[150] John Eidsmoe, *Christianity and the Constitution: The Faith of Our Founding
Fathers* (Grand Rapids, MI: Baker Book House, 1987), pp. 51–52, 54–62 as
quoted in D. James Kennedy and Jerry Newcombe, *What If Jesus Had Never
Been Born?* pp. 70–71. Of note, the two academicians, Charles S. Hyneman and
Donald S. Lutz, who analyzed the references also edited the two volume anthology: *American Political Writing during the Founding Era, 1760–1805*. A quick
glance at its contents will show the pervasive influence of the Scriptures on the
cultural climate of that era as evidenced in the writings and speeches of that
time. Compare Ellis Sandoz, *Political Sermons of the American Founding Era,
1730–1805*.
[151] *A Christian Manifesto*, pp. 27–28.

Rutherford, a Scotsman, wrote *Lex Rex*. Up to that time, it had been supposed that the king was law, or *rex lex*. In *Lex Rex*, Rutherford asserts that law, Divine law, is king. Subsequently, John Locke and Thomas Jefferson drew heavily upon the Christian principles found in the works of Rutherford and other Scottish Covenanters and incorporated them into their secularized theories of government.[152] This is how government and society were subordinated to moral law. Contrary to Rand's belief, "The Divine Right of Kings," if it refers to absolute monarchy, is nowhere to be found in the Scriptures.[153] One merely has to consider the reigns of Saul and David, the kings of Israel, to substantiate this.[154] God alone is the source of rights, and he is the legislator of rights to both men and governments.

Rand's appreciation for the Constitution extended to its view of government as servant. In the United States, for the first time in history, "the government's function was changed from the role of ruler to the role of servant."[155] However, Rand and her followers seem to think that this view of the government's role as servant came about as a resurgence of Aristotelian reason.[156] However, Aristotle advocated totalitarianism; and the ancient civilizations, with the exception of the Hebrews, held no such enlightened view of government as the servant of the people.[157] With this background in mind, what Jesus said stands out as truly remarkable and revolutionary:

> You know that the rulers of the Gentiles lord it over them, and *their* great men exercise authority over them. It is not so among you, but whoever wishes to become great among you shall be

---

[152] *A Christian Manifesto*, p. 32; Gordon Clark, *Essays on Ethics and Politics*, pp. 127–128.

[153] "Man's Rights," *Capitalism: The Unknown Ideal*, p. 321.

[154] 1 Samuel chapters 12 to 24; 2 Samuel chapters 11 and 12; Isaiah 40:15–17, 23; Daniel chapters 4 and 5.

[155] "Man's Rights," *Capitalism: The Unknown Ideal*, p. 323.

[156] "Man's Rights," *Capitalism: The Unknown Ideal*, p. 322; Leonard Peikoff, *The Ominous Parallels*, pp. 328–338. Rand also wrote, "An 'Aristotelian statist' is a contradiction in terms. . . ." (*The Objectivist Newsletter*, May 1963, p. 19).

[157] *Politics*, 1337, a28–30.

your servant, and whoever wishes to be first among you shall be your slave; just as the Son of Man did not come to be served, but to serve, and to give His life a ransom for many.[158]

It is this biblical concept of the servant-leader that influenced the Founding Fathers of the United States.

In the fictional world of *Atlas Shrugged*, John Galt, Ragnar Danneskjöld, and Francisco d'Anconia attend the most distinguished institution of higher learning in the United States, the Patrick Henry University. Rand named the university after the famous Revolutionary War patriot and statesman. Perhaps she did not realize that Patrick Henry was also a Christian. However, Patrick Henry's faith was not mere formality. It embodied his values, political and otherwise. He says:

It cannot be emphasized too strongly or too often that this great nation was founded, not by religionists [pluralism], but by Christians; not on religions, but on the gospel of Jesus Christ! For this very reason peoples of other faiths have been afforded asylum, prosperity, and freedom of worship here.[159]

With reference to the Scriptures, he remarks, "Here is a book worth more than all the other books that were ever printed."[160] But Henry was not the only American statesman whose Christianity influenced his politics. The majority of the Founding Fathers were educated at three American universities: Princeton, Yale, and Harvard. It is interesting to note what such universities considered important. Princeton University's motto was emphatic. "Cursed be all learning that is contrary to the cross of Christ!" Princeton's president John Witherspoon, also a Presbyterian minister, not only signed the Declaration of Independence, but worked on key committees that laid the foundations for the fledgling nation. He applied Christian principles derived from his understand-

---

[158] Matthew 20:25–28; *Without a Prayer*, pp. 324–331.

[159] Steve C. Dawson, *God's Providence in America's History* (Rancho Cordova, CA: Steve C. Dawson, 1988), p. I:5 as quoted in *The Myth of Separation*, p. 118.

[160] William Wirt, *The Life and Character of Patrick Henry* (Philadelphia, PA: James Webster, 1818), p. 402 as quoted in *The Myth of Separation*, p. 119.

ing of Rutherford's *Lex Rex* to his political assignments and responsibilities, as did the many statesmen whom he trained.[161] At Yale University, the reading of the Scriptures and attendance at public prayer meetings was required of its students. Harvard University's College Laws of 1642 contain the following admonition:

> Let every student . . . consider well the main end of his life and studies is to know God and Jesus Christ which is eternal life, John 17:3, and therefore to lay Christ in the bottom, as the only foundation of all sound knowledge and learning. Seeing the Lord giveth wisdom, everyone shall seriously by prayer, in secret, seek wisdom of Him.[162]

Thus the influence of Christianity on the Founding Fathers was profound. But if that influence did not extend to the populace, it would be of no avail. John Adams, the second President of the United States, expressed his concern:

> We have no government armed with power capable of contending with human passions unbridled by morality and religion. Avarice, ambition, revenge, or gallantry, would break the strongest cords of our Constitution as a whale goes through a net. Our Constitution was made only for a moral and religious people. It is wholly inadequate to the government of any other.[163]

Adams's analysis was corroborated by the French historian Alexis de Tocqueville, who visited America in the early 1800s. He recorded his observations in his book *Democracy in America*:

> In the United States the sovereign authority is religious, and consequently hypocrisy must be common; but there is no country in the whole world, in which the Christian religion retains a greater influence over the souls of men than in America; and there can be no greater proof of its utility, and of its conformity

---

[161] *A Christian Manifesto*, pp. 31–34; *The Myth of Separation*, pp. 92–93.

[162] Harvard College Laws, 1642, as quoted in Kelly Monroe (editor), *Finding God at Harvard*, p. 14.

[163] John Adams, *The Works of John Adams, Second President of the United States*, edited by Charles Francis Adams (Boston, MA: Little Brown, 1854), Volume IX, p. 229, October 11, 1798, as quoted in *The Myth of Separation*, p. 123.

to human nature, than that its influence is most powerfully felt over the most enlightened and free nation of the earth.[164]

He adds:

> Thus whilst the law permits the Americans to do what they please, religion prevents them from conceiving, and forbids them to commit what is rash or unjust.[165]

De Tocqueville knew that truth very well. The bloody confusion and the murderous chaos of the French Revolution illustrated what happens when freedom is not sustained and restrained by the laws of God.[166]

Thus, contrary to what some have supposed, the testimony of history shows that Christianity was not about to be laughed out of existence at the time of the American Revolution.[167] Instead, it exerted a profound influence on the American people, its political system, and ultimately the rest of the world. The reader should be wary of Rand's argument that the elements of "reason" led to the creation of the greatest country on earth while the presence of a mixed premise, namely "faith," is the cause of its current demise. As our earlier discussion showed, a limited, republican form of government could never have arisen from the kind of political theory that Objectivism advocates. Implicitly and explicitly, it was an ethical and political philosophy based on biblical revelation that led to the development of America's republican form of government. It was biblical revelation that the Founding Fathers, America's first intellectuals, chose as their starting point for morality and government. Will the New Intellectuals now choose to continue their political line?

---

[164] *Democracy in America*, Volume I, p. 294.

[165] *Democracy in America*, Volume I, p. 296.

[166] See also *A Christian Manifesto*, pp. 44–45; Francis Schaeffer, *How Should We Then Live?* pp. 121–125.

[167] Leonard Peikoff, "The Philosophical Base of Capitalism;" tape on file with author. Compare *Political Sermons of the American Founding Era, 1730–1805*. For example, John Wingate Thornton writes, "To the Pulpit, the *Puritan Pulpit*, we owe the moral force which won our independence."

10
SCIENCE AND CHRISTIANITY

[O]ur attempts to see and to find the truth are not final, but open to improvement; that our knowledge, our doctrine, is conjectural; that it consists of guesses, of hypotheses, rather than of final and certain truths; and that criticism and critical discussion are our only means of getting nearer to the truth.

Karl Popper, *Conjectures and Refutations*

Any physical theory is always provisional, in the sense that it is only a hypothesis: you can never prove it. No matter how many times the results of experiments agree with some theory, you can never be sure that the next time the result will not contradict the theory. On the other hand, you can disprove a theory by finding even a single observation that disagrees with the predictions of the theory.

Stephen Hawking, *A Brief History of Time*

For the scientist who has lived by his faith in the power of reason, the story ends like a bad dream. He has scaled the mountains of ignorance; he is about to conquer the highest peak; as he pulls himself over the final rock, he is greeted by a band of theologians who have been sitting there for centuries.

Robert Jastrow, *God and the Astronomers*

I have spent most of my life dealing with science and medicine. Through a process of diligent study and participation in research, I believed I was contributing to the wider body of scientific knowledge and truth. Ayn Rand's fiction had instilled in me a certainty in science that I had not questioned. Galt's motor and Rearden Metal were the products of men in possession of the truth, and it never occurred to me that what science produced is not truth. Truth is fixed and immutable. That which is true is so for all times and all places. Is that not what science produces?

Before we address that question, I need to explain a preconceived bias that had prevented me from seriously considering Christianity. Almost everyone has heard of Galileo's treatment at the hand of the Inquisitors at the beginning of the seventeenth century. Galileo believed that the sun, not the earth, was the center of the universe. However, his heliocentrism brought him into conflict with the official position of the Roman Catholic Church-State. The Roman Catholic Church believed that the earth was the center of the universe and the stars revolved around it. Eventually, as a result of this conflict, Galileo was forced to retract his statements; and he even suffered house arrest for holding these scientific views. For me, Galileo's dilemma seemed to epitomize the conflict between science and Christianity, and his treatment at the hands of the religious authorities lent credence to Rand's claims that faith and force were corollaries.[1] Even before I came to understand the nature of science, I could see that the exclusive claims of science to the province of truth were at stake. Those were high stakes indeed.

Preliminary Problems

For me, the most obvious example of the conflict between science and Christianity had to do with the question of origins, *not* whether we could utilize science to master nature. Was the uni-

---

[1] "Faith and Force," *Philosophy: Who Needs It*, p. 80.

verse billions of years old? How long ago did the first human being appear? Was evolution a theory or a fact? Did any of the evidence conflict with the biblical account? In high school, I had learned about the primitive age of the universe. From my study of Objectivism, I had come to believe in the eternity of the physical universe.[2] The evolutionary account of the development of life and the primitive ancestry for man seemed beyond question. Various techniques for dating the universe appeared to confirm its primitive age. All of this, it seemed to me, sorely conflicted with Bishop Ussher's estimation of the biblical creation date at 4004 B.C. (The accuracy of Ussher's date is a question we will address later.)

Nevertheless, in reviewing these difficulties when I first reconsidered the claims of Christianity, I was struck by one of the problems with the methods for determining the age of specimens: its initial assumptions. Take, as an example, carbon-14 radiometric dating. The rationale for this technique is as follows.[3] Atmospheric nitrogen, under constant bombardment by cosmic neutrons, is converted into carbon-14. A percentage of atmospheric carbon dioxide contains this radioactive isotope of carbon. Carbon dioxide is consumed by plants, which in turn are consumed by animals. This is how carbon-14 is incorporated into living organisms. Now carbon-14 decays with a half-life of 5730 years; therefore, the level of carbon-14 radioactivity in a living organism eventually reaches steady-state as a result of continuous carbon-14 intake and spontaneous radioactive decay. When the organism dies, carbon-14 is no longer actively incorporated into the organism; however, the radioactive decay process continues at a uniform rate. Consequently, by measuring the amount of carbon-14 in a sample and extrapolating from the results in comparison with the level of carbon-14 in the atmosphere and the known rate of radioactive decay, scientists can determine a specimen's age.

However, the scientist makes a number of assumptions in the dating procedure. First, he assumes that the rate of conversion of

---

[2] Nathaniel Branden, "Intellectual Ammunition Department," *The Objectivist Newsletter*, May 1962, p. 19.
[3] Bruce Mahan, *University Chemistry*, pp. 854–857.

nitrogen to carbon-14 has remained relatively constant through-out the period of history in question. Second, he assumes that the rate of radioactive decay for carbon-14 is also a constant. Sampling error aside, it seemed to me that neither of these assumptions could be substantiated. How do we know that the conversion of nitrogen to carbon-14 and the rate of carbon-14 decay has been constant for thousands of years? After all, scientists have only been able to measure the atmospheric conversion process and the decay rate of carbon-14 for at most two hundred years. Now perhaps they have been able to corroborate the accuracy of the radiometric technique by applying it to objects, like wooden furniture and mummies, that have been reliably preserved and dated through alternative historical techniques. But this corroboration can only be valid for at most a few thousand years' worth of history. (Other radiometric techniques that allegedly allow us to see further back in time have no such corroboration from written human records.) Yet the scientist is asking us to believe that this technique for dating samples is accurate for tens of thousands of years. Can he prove his initial assumptions on the basis of his limited empirical observations? Where was he thousands of years ago when the measurements on carbon-14 conversion and decay should have been made? What we cannot ignore is that the scientist has introduced nonempirical and nonverifiable factors into his theory of radiometric dating.

As a result of these considerations, it occurred to me that science and Christianity may not actually conflict. Of note, one of my mentors in science suggested that the question of God's existence is perhaps beyond science. After all, you cannot perform a controlled experiment of the universe *with* and *without* God.[4] That satisfied me for the moment. However, several years later, I was reintroduced to the question of scientific truth through Gordon Clark's book *The Philosophy of Science and Belief in God*. This astonishing statement appears on its cover: "[S]cience can never discover truth. It is ever learning but never able to come to the knowledge of truth."[5] How can that be?

[4] See Charles Thaxton, Walter Bradley, and Roger Olsen, *The Mystery of Life's Origins*, pp. 202–206 for a discussion of the difference between origin science and operation science.
[5] *The Philosophy of Science and Belief in God*, cover.

One of the main points of the book is that the scientific method rests on a logical fallacy: the fallacy of asserting the consequent. What is the fallacy of asserting the consequent? In formal language, the fallacy takes the following form. If *A* is true, then *B* is true. Since *B* is true, then *A* is true. Perhaps an example would help. If there is poison in this apple, I will become ill after eating it. Since I became ill after eating this apple, there was poison in it. Obviously, this is fallacious, since I may have become ill for any number of reasons. My illness does not verify that there was poison in the apple. Even though the example just given is a simple one, it is not altogether different from the way in which all scientific laws are verified. Applying this example to the scientific situation, *A* represents the hypothesis and *B* represents the experimental observations. A scientist says, in effect, "I have a hypothesis. If that hypothesis is true, I would observe certain experimental results. In my observations, I do indeed see the expected experimental results. Therefore, my hypothesis is true." If *A* is true, then *B* is true. Since *B* is true, then *A* is true. This is the same fallacy. The scientist can only escape the charge of committing a logical fallacy by offering alternative explanations for his experimental results and by saying, "My limited observations suggest that the hypothesis may be true." However, this a tentative statement which does not purport to be the truth, immutable and absolute.

Science also commits the fallacy of induction—*i.e.*, the fallacy of arguing from the particular observations to a universal statement. For example, in a scientist's *particular* observations, he has observed only white swans. It may be a thousand observations; it may be a million. But if he were to conclude "All swans are white," he would be wrong. There is no guarantee that he may not see a black swan on the very next observation. In fact, neither he nor his colleagues have seen all swans, past, present, and future. Therefore, he cannot assert the *universal* statement "All swans are white." Thus we see the fallacy of scientific induction.

Somehow, as I pondered these statements on induction in Clark's book, the memory of my physical science class in high school returned. I recalled the introduction we had to the scientific method. (It is a peculiarity of scientific education that once you reach college, everyone assumes you understand the method. Very few basic science courses reconsider the scientific method, and few science students that I knew bothered to take a course on the philosophy of science.) The instructor described the basic steps of the process.

1. Formulate a hypothesis.
2. Plan an experiment to test the hypothesis.
3. Perform the experiment, and collect the data.
4. Interpret and discuss the results as they bear on the hypothesis.

If the results contradict the hypothesis, then the hypothesis is false. Now here is the *key*: If the results support the hypothesis, the hypothesis is not necessarily true. The experiment has to be repeated many times, and the results have to be verified by other scientists. If the hypothesis survives this verification process, it may eventually reach the status of a theory or law. However, it is not *law* in the sense that it is the truth. It is only law in the provisional sense that it has been verified repeatedly. The problems associated with induction and the logical fallacy of asserting the consequent prevent us from asserting the truth of the law. The laws of science are tentative, and the instructor was cognizant of the limits of science.

Yet, for some reason, the tentative nature of scientific investigation never occurred to me as I progressed toward my career in medicine. Suddenly, it became clear to me why papers in the experimental sciences, especially the biological sciences, were filled with phrases like "These results suggest . . ." However, biological systems are quite complicated and difficult to control for, and perhaps that explains the tentative nature of the experimental conclusions expressed in biology. But surely, physics, with its ability to measure minute phenomena precisely, has demonstrated its ability to attain to the truth, has it not? Yet even the brilliant physicist Stephen Hawking concedes that physics does not provide us with the truth. In *A Brief History of Time*, he writes:

Any physical theory is always provisional, in the sense that it is only a hypothesis: you can never prove it. No matter how many times the results of experiments agree with some theory, you can never be sure that the next time the result will not contradict the theory. On the other hand, you can disprove a theory by finding even a single observation that disagrees with the predictions of the theory.[6]

Hawking is merely pointing out the logical fallacy of induction. No one ever has enough experience of the past, present, and future to ensure that a scientific theory will always be true. Hawking then appeals to conclusions that had been formulated by Karl Popper, a prominent British philosopher of science:

Each time new experiments are observed to agree with the predictions the theory survives, and our confidence in it is increased; but if ever a new observation is found to disagree, we have to abandon or modify the theory. At least that is what is supposed to happen, but you can always question the competence of the person who carried out the observation.[7]

While Hawking's presentation of the way in which science abandons or modifies theories is a little simplistic (as we shall soon see), he is generally correct with regard to the difficulty of establishing scientific truth. Yet the layman and the expert scientist often gloss over statements such as his without giving them much thought. Enamored by the success of science, they remain unaware of the underlying problems of scientific epistemology. Indeed, science has helped us send probes to Mars and beyond, and here on earth its application has brought numerous technological conveniences. But science does not supply the truth. Physics, the most exacting of scientific disciplines, remains vulnerable to all of the fundamental criticisms of the scientific method, for induction and asserting the consequent are always logical fallacies. If Objectivists esteem logic, then they must recognize and acknowledge the dependence of science upon an illogical procedure for arriving at truth.

[6] *A Brief History of Time*, p. 10.
[7] *A Brief History of Time*, p. 10.

The Problem of Measurement and the Philosophy of Science

But other problems besides logic plague science. How many people have expressed a naive confidence in scientific observation by claiming the objectivity of the empirical approach? In fact, very few people understand that science is not a purely empirical endeavor. They are unaware of the many nonempirical factors that scientists themselves introduce into science. Moreover, these nonempirical factors do not occur merely at the interpretive and discussion phase of scientific inquiry. They are present at the very beginning, at the observational phase. As Brand Blanshard points out in *The Nature of Thought*, "That observation is thus selective, and that selection must be guided by theory is now recognized by science."[8] Observations are never purely empirical. Instead, we approach nature with hypotheses and probe her for answers. As Karl Popper explains in his book *Conjectures and Refutations*, "[L]acking such hypotheses, we can only make haphazard observations which follow no plan and which can therefore never lead us to a natural law."[9] Thus we see that observation in science begins in a nonempirical manner, with a theory in mind.

Moreover, the collection and organization of experimental data also occurs with the assistance of nonempirical factors. Let us begin with some elementary considerations. As Clark explains, all scientific measurements are in the final analysis the measurement of a line.[10] Whether it is the height of a mercury column in a thermometer, the deflection of a needle in response to current passing through an instrument, or the intensity of a particular band on an electrophoretic gel column, all significant scientific measurements are reduced to a number, the measurement of a line. However, no two measurements are ever the same, and the physical quantity to be measured is itself constantly changing. Moreover, no immutable and absolute standard exists in nature with which one might compare the physical quantity to be measured. Therefore, no mat-

---

[8] *The Nature of Thought*, Volume II, p. 84.

[9] *Conjectures and Refutations*, p. 189.

[10] *The Philosophy of Science and Belief in God*, pp. 58–60.

ter how carefully a scientist constructs an experiment, no matter how much he increases the power and precision of his apparatus for gathering the data, he will always obtain inexact measurements. That is why he repeats them. The only reason that some measurements have the same value is either because the numbers are rounded off or because the instrument is limited in its precision. Nevertheless, at the conclusion of an experiment, the scientist has generated a list of numbers, the data.

Because the scientist's measurements are inexact and many, he next attempts to determine a *central location* for the data generated in his experiment. He assumes that somewhere within the range of the numbers that he has collected lies the true answer. The scientist usually calculates a *mean*, which is simply the arithmetic average. However, the *mode* and the *median* are other determinants of central location available to him. (The *mode* is the most frequently occurring value in the data. When the numbers in the data are arranged according to magnitude, the *median* is the value such that half of the data are larger than it and half are smaller.) In fact, the mean, because it is an arithmetic average, may not even be one of the numbers that was generated in the experiment, whereas the mode actually occurred many times. Nevertheless, in most situations, the scientist chooses the mean because it is more amenable to mathematical manipulation. However, in doing so, he may have chosen to exclude some of his actual, empirical measurements in favor of a theoretical, nonempirical central location. As the reader can see, the scientist has already begun to impose nonempirical information on the data.

Next, in order to compare two sets of data so that meaningful statements about their relationship can be derived, the scientist calculates a *variable error*, which is a measure of the spread of the numbers in each data set. He begins by calculating the difference between each individual measurement and the mean; this he calls the *deviation*. However, because the sum of all the deviations from the mean in any given data set is zero, the deviation would be of no help in determining the spread of numbers in each set of data or in comparing two different sets of data.[11] Therefore, the scientist squares all of the deviations (why not use the cube or the fourth power of the deviations?) and adds them up. This sum is *not* zero; therefore, comparison between two data sets is possible. After dividing this sum by the total number of measurements minus one, the scientist now has the *sample variance*, which he then transforms into the *sample standard deviation* by taking the square root of the sample variance. The sample standard deviation allows the scientist to determine the relationship between two data sets according to statistical theories. However, these statistical theories are derived strictly from mathematical considerations. Once again, a nonempirical grid is being imposed on the data.

Let us review what the scientist has done.

1. He has performed measurements that are inexact.
2. He imposed a nonempirical concept of central location.
3. He chose a method for calculating a standard deviation that is convenient for mathematical manipulation.
4. He later imposed a theory of statistics derived from nonempirical mathematical considerations.
5. And finally, he inferred properties of the underlying distribution of his data set by way of inductive reasoning; that is, he tried to determine which probability model best fits the data. [12]

Thus, from the beginning, science has shown itself not to be a purely empirical enterprise.

Now, let us suppose the scientist is interested in deriving a mathematical formula or law that will describe his entire collection of data. Once again, Clark offers a detailed analysis of this process.[13] Consider figure 10.1. At a single position along the x axis, the scientist makes several measurements along the y axis. From these results, he determines a mean and a standard devia-

[11] Bernard Rosner, *Fundamentals of Biostatistics*, pp. 8–19.

[12] *Fundamentals of Biostatistics*, p. 137.

[13] *The Philosophy of Science and Belief in God*, p. 60; *A Christian View of Men and Things*, pp. 137–139.

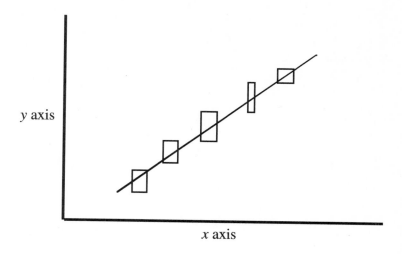

y axis

x axis

Figure 10.1. The scientist makes a series of measurements that are represented by rectangular areas. Then he attempts to calculate or plot a best-fit line through the data.

tion. This would ordinarily be represented by a single point with vertical error bars. However, since the value measured along the x axis is likewise not exact and subject to error, a mean and standard deviation is also generated in the horizontal direction. The combination of a horizontal and a vertical mean and standard deviation is best represented by a rectangular area. The scientist then repeats this process at different positions along the x axis thereby generating an entire series of areas. Finally, he derives a mathematical formula from the data by plotting a best-fit line through the series of areas. The mathematical formula that represents this line he calls a scientific law.

However, an infinite number of lines can actually be drawn through the data,[14] even though an infinite number of other lines can also be excluded from consideration (see figure 10.2 on the next page).

Clark observes: "Even through a series of points apparently on a straight line it is equally easy to pass a straight line or a sine

---

[14] *A Christian View of Men and Things*, pp. 138–139.

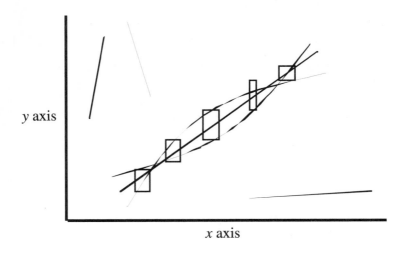

Figure 10.2. An infinite number of lines can be passed through the data. Therefore, an infinite number of mathematical formulas or laws can describe the data, even though an infinite number of other formulas can also be rejected.

curve. In fact, it is to be particularly noted that through a series of areas [a series of means and standard deviations] an infinite number of different curves may be passed. The empirical data do not necessitate any given curve."[15] Yet, out of the infinite number of lines that can be drawn through the data set, the scientist picks one formula. The formula may indeed be a statistical best fit, but again statistical considerations are nonempirical. Moreover, simplicity and elegance (which is what a statistical best fit often implies), as Clark shows, are important factors in the final selection of a scientific law. But whoever said nature was simple or elegant?

The way in which scientific laws are chosen raises further difficulties for the concept of scientific truth. As Popper explains, scientific laws are not only false, they cannot even be said to have a high degree of probability:

> We may also compare, say, two theories in order to see which of them has stood up better to our severest tests—or in other words,

---

[15] *The Philosophy of Science and Belief in God*, p. 60.

which of them is *better corroborated* by the results of our tests. But it can be shown by purely mathematical means that *degree of corroboration can never be equated with mathematical probability*. It can even be shown that all theories, including the best, have the same probability, namely zero.[16]

Why is the probability zero? As Clark shows, the probability of any scientific law is zero because an infinite number of lines, each representing a law or theory, can be drawn through the graphical representation of any data set. Hence, the probability of any given mathematical law being true is one divided by infinity, that is, zero.[17]

Now some may object to the notion of science as an empirical attempt at fitting lines to the data. For example, while it is true that Boyle's inverse law for the ideal gas was initially obtained by fitting lines to the empirical data, it is also true that the law can be derived mathematically by making some fundamental assumptions about the behavior of a single gas molecule. Then the overall behavior of the gas can be calculated by summing up the effect of all of the gas molecules in a given volume.[18] In this case, the scientific law is apparently not obtained simply by fitting lines to the data.

However, this objection can be met by two considerations. First, the assumption that individual molecules behave in a certain way is itself a theoretical construction. Hence, nonempirical information has been introduced once again. Second, the logical fallacy of asserting the consequent is still being committed. Look at the format of the argument: The simplified model of the behavior of gas particles is put forth as a hypothesis. If the model is true, a law that is mathematically derived from that model should correlate with the empirical formula obtained from the observational data (the best-fit line drawn through the data). Since the mathematical law derived from the model and the empirical formula do indeed correlate, the model is true. If A is true, then B is true. Since B is true, then A is true. Quite obviously, the fallacy is still being committed. Moreover, there are other difficulties. We have to recognize that

---

[16] *Conjectures and Refutations*, p. 192.
[17] *The Philosophy of Science and Belief in God*, p. 60.
[18] *University Chemistry*, pp. 48–54.

the model of the behavior of gas molecules is a construction in the mind of the scientist that does not exist in reality. Furthermore, the assumptions of the model, even if they are true, can be true only under very special circumstances. How then can the model and the law be extended to cover all gases under all situations?

Indeed, Clark offers a similar criticism of classical mechanics. The physical law governing the relationship between the period of the pendulum and its length has to be false. Why? The law assumes a tensionless string and a pendulum bob whose mass is evenly distributed about its center. No such pendulum exists, even in the best of laboratories. It follows that the law of the pendulum, created in the imaginary and mathematical world of the scientist, does not apply to pendulums in the real world.[19]

Similarly, Popper offers several criticisms of Isaac Newton's theory of mechanics. One point he emphasizes, in opposition to Francis Bacon's view of science, is the impossibility of deriving a theory from observations. Let us suppose that Newton did in fact derive his theory from observations. However, observations are always inexact. How was it possible for Newton to come up with a theory from *inexact* observations that then made *exact* predictions? Moreover, it is incredible that a theory supposedly derived from inexact observations should later be verified by even more accurate observations. (Indeed, some historians claim that Newton fudged his data to make his theory look more impressive than it actually was.[20]) In addition, the theory claims to be applicable in all circumstances, even though only specific instances are ever measured. As Popper points out, "[A]n observation is always made under very special conditions, and that each observed situation is always a highly specific situation. . . . Moreover, observations are always *concrete*, while theory is *abstract*. For example we never observe mass points but rather extended planets."[21] Thus, the Baconian myth that induction can arrive at theory from observations is demolished by Popper's analysis.

---

[19] *The Philosophy of Science and Belief in God*, pp. 57–58.
[20] William Broad and Nicholas Wade, *Betrayers of the Truth*, pp. 27–28.
[21] *Conjectures and Refutations*, p. 186.

Popper, like the philosopher Immanuel Kant, recognizes that scientific laws are not derived from nature, but instead are invented by the human mind. Unlike Kant, who believed that such laws are invariably successful, Popper understands that such laws are mere conjectures.[22] Scientific laws cannot be proven true. But perhaps they can be proven false. Popper writes:

> We have seen that theories cannot be logically derived from observations. They can, however, clash with observations: they can contradict observations. This fact makes it possible to infer from observations that a theory is *false*. The possibility of refuting theories by observations is the basis of all empirical tests. . . . From a logical point of view, all empirical tests are therefore *attempted refutations*.[23]

On the surface, Popper appears to be right. Consider the scientific argument: A hypothesis implies certain experimental results. But the experiment does not yield those results; therefore, the hypothesis is false. If *A* is true, then *B* is true. Since *B* is false, then *A* is false. Notice, this argument does not commit the fallacy of asserting the consequent. It is, in fact, a valid argument termed *denying the consequent*.[24] However, the situation is not as simple as one might suppose. As Imre Lakatos and Alan Musgrave show in *Criticism and the Growth of Knowledge*, the process by which a scientific theory is rejected is much more complicated than that.[25] Scientists often do not permit a theory to be refuted by a single experiment or even a group of experiments that yield a negative result. A negative result *could* be an experimental error. If a negative result obtained in the first series of experiments conducted to test an idea was always permitted to refute a theory, many scientific theories would never have become mainstream. Without a certain tenacity on the part of some scientists regarding their theories, a useful

---

[22] *Conjectures and Refutations*, pp. 191–192.
[23] *Conjectures and Refutations*, p. 192.
[24] *The Philosophy of Science and Belief in God*, p. 71.
[25] Imre Lakatos, "Methodology of Scientific Research Programmes," *Criticism and the Growth of Knowledge*, pp. 91–132.

idea would never get off the ground. Moreover, even if the negative result were trustworthy, scientists often create secondary, auxiliary hypotheses to explain away the inconsistency. As Thomas Kuhn explains in his book *The Structure of Scientific Revolutions*, scientists many times cling tenaciously to their adopted theoretical paradigms until enough evidence accumulating from multiple sources discredits the currently held theory and makes room for a new theory that then violently overthrows the old.

Furthermore, as Lakatos shows, experiments are necessarily complex.[26] An experiment that is designed to test a given scientific hypothesis simultaneously tests other scientific theories, which the experimental scientist often treats as background "factual" knowledge. Thus, when an experiment yields a negative result, it may not be the hypothesis in question that is false. Instead, it may well be that the scientific theories that had been accepted as background factual knowledge are false, and this explains the inconsistency in the experimental data.

Clark gives the following example. Scientists in the nineteenth century assumed that Newtonian mechanics was true. This assumption represented background factual knowledge for them. Now, Newton also advanced the corpuscular theory of light—*i.e.*, light behaves as a particle. When Leon Foucault in 1850 tested the corpuscular theory of light by comparing the speed of light in air and in water, the experimental results contradicted the theory. The experiment appeared to refute the corpuscular theory of light and, instead, establish the wave theory of light. However, in 1902, a crucial experiment on the photoelectric effect was performed by Philipp Lenard. His findings gave renewed support to the corpuscular theory of light. How do we explain this inconsistency? Is the corpuscular theory of light valid or not?

As Clark explains, "The strict argument in 1850 should have been: The corpuscular theory of light plus all Newtonian mechanics implies what the experiment denied; therefore, either the corpuscular theory is false or something is wrong with Newtonian

---

[26] Imre Lakatos, "Methodology of Scientific Research Programmes," *Criticism and the Growth of Knowledge*, pp. 116–118.

mechanics, or both."[27] The reader will recall that the Newtonian theory of mechanics was erroneously assumed to be background factual knowledge. So entrenched was Newton's theory in the minds of scientists that they assumed the crucial experiment of 1850 proved the corpuscular theory of light false when in fact the problem may have been with Newtonian mechanics. It remained for Einstein to show in 1905 that the corpuscular theory is a viable theory if Newtonian mechanics were discarded. Today, Newton's theory has indeed been overthrown. As Paul Feyerabend observes, new theories are often "out of phase" with the rest of scientific knowledge.[28] Therefore, a new theory may not be invalid, but simply inconsistent with what is currently accepted in science; and it may have to wait for the rest of science to catch up before it gains acceptance. Thus we see the process by which scientific knowledge advances is much more complicated than the idea of simple conjecture and refutation put forth by Popper. Nevertheless, Popper writes:

> [O]ur attempts to see and to find the truth are not final, but open to improvement; that our knowledge, our doctrine, is conjectural; that it consists of guesses, of hypotheses, rather than of final and certain truths; and that criticism and critical discussion are our only means of getting nearer to the truth.[29]

But even that seems too optimistic. How does Popper know that he is getting closer to the truth? After all, a person can only know that he is getting nearer the truth if he is in possession of the truth to begin with. Moreover, we have seen that Popper's idea of falsification and simple refutation is untenable. Perhaps we may conclude with Lakatos that *"scientific theories are not only equally unprovable, and equally improbable, but they are also equally undisprovable."*[30]

---

[27] *The Philosophy of Science and Belief in God*, p. 71.

[28] Paul Feyerabend, "Consolations for the Specialist," *Criticism and the Growth of Knowledge*, p. 205.

[29] *Conjectures and Refutations*, p. 151.

[30] Imre Lakatos, "Methodology of Scientific Research Programmes," *Criticism and the Growth of Knowledge*, p. 103.

Therefore, science can only reach tentative conclusions. And by its very nature, science utilizes nonempirical factors from start to finish. Yet many scientific leaders remain blinded by the myth that science is objective and true, and they confidently assert its freedom from nonobservational authority. For example, A. J. Carlson, former president of the American Association for the Advancement of Science, writes:

> What is the method of science? In essence it is this—the rejection *in toto* of all non-observational and non-experimental authority in the field of experience. . . . When no evidence is produced other than personal dicta, past or present, "revelations" in dreams, or the "voice of God," the scientist can pay no attention whatsoever, except to ask: How do they get that way? . . . The scientist tries to rid himself of all faiths and beliefs. He either knows or he does not know. If he knows there is no room for faith or belief. If he does not know he has no right to faith or belief.[31]

But clearly, the reader must conclude from our discussion up to this point that Carlson is sadly mistaken with regard to scientific methodology. If science is the rejection of all nonempirical authority, it would have to reject itself. The method of science requires the use of nonobservational factors. The scientist cannot rid himself of all faith and belief. In fact, such faith and belief is necessary to the advancement of science. However, sometimes such preconceptions do more to earn our distrust than our confidence in science. Paul Davies and John Gribbin point out in *The Matter Myth:*

> The philosopher Thomas Kuhn believes that scientists adopt certain distinct paradigms that are tenaciously retained and are abandoned only in the face of glaring absurdities. These paradigms help to shape scientific theories, and exercise a powerful influence over the methodology of science and the conclusions drawn from experiments. Experimental scientists pride themselves on their objectivity, yet time and again they unwittingly massage their data to fit in with preconceived ideas. Sometimes,

---

[31] A. J. Carlson, "Science and the Supernatural," *Science* 73: 217–225, 1931.

several different independent experimenters will carefully measure the same quantity and consistently get the same *wrong* answer, because it is the answer they have come to expect.[32]

Anyone who denies the power of presuppositions needs only to examine *Betrayers of the Truth* by William Broad and Nicholas Wade in order to see how such biases have influenced even the best of scientists to deceive both themselves and others.

The Success of Science versus the Truth of Science

The purpose of the discussion up to now has been to point out the limitations of science. Science is logically invalid. However, the falsity of scientific laws does not prevent them from being useful. Popper writes:

> [F]alse theories often serve well enough: most formulae used in engineering or navigation are known to be false, although they may be excellent approximations and easy to handle; and they are used with confidence by people who know them to be false.[33]

Scientific theories enable man to operate in the environment and to dominate nature on the basis of tentative, inexact rules. However, the success of scientific theories does not prove the truth of science. Hawking explains:

> Einstein's general theory of relativity predicted a slightly different motion [of the planet Mercury] from Newton's theory. The fact that Einstein's predictions matched what was seen, while Newton's did not, was one of the crucial confirmations of the new theory. However, we still use Newton's theory for all practical purposes because the difference between its predictions and those of general relativity is very small in the situations that we normally deal with. (Newton's theory also has the great advantage that it is much simpler to work with than Einstein's!)[34]

[32] *The Matter Myth*, p. 23.
[33] *Conjectures and Refutations*, p. 56.
[34] *A Brief History of Time*, p. 10.

Einstein's theory of relativity is considered to be closer to the truth than Newtonian mechanics; however, Newton's theory is used because the difference between the two theories is insignificant in this particular instance and because Newton's theory is easier to use. So perhaps we may conclude that we have succeeded in landing a man on the moon on the basis of a false theory. Perhaps John Galt's motor in *Atlas Shrugged* converts atmospheric static electricity into useful energy on the basis of an inexact law. Perhaps Rearden Metal possesses its unusual strength because of tentative metallurgical principles. Utility and success, as we can see, are not dependent upon truth. Of interest, Newton's theory of mechanics was known in his lifetime to contain illogical and incompatible presuppositions.[35] However, his theory's incredible predictive power overshadowed its logical inconsistencies; consequently, those inconsistencies generally went unnoticed until the early part of the twentieth century. Yet many scientists operate on the assumption that such inconsistencies no longer exist in science. But, in fact, they do exist. Regarding the two currently held fundamental theories of physics, the general theory of relativity and the theory of quantum mechanics, Hawking says:

> The general theory of relativity describes the force of gravity and the large-scale structure of the universe, ... Quantum mechanics, on the other hand, deals with phenomena on extremely small scales, such as a millionth of a millionth of an inch. Unfortunately, however, these two theories are known to be inconsistent with each other—they cannot both be correct.[36]

Our previous discussion about the nature of science should lead us to the conclusion that both theories are false, even though they are both extremely useful in their respective areas of application. But even if a particular scientific theory could be true, the incompatibility of general relativity and quantum mechanics implies that they cannot both be true. Either one or the other must

---

[35] *The Philosophy of Science and Belief in God*, p. 68.
[36] *A Brief History of Time*, pp. 11–12.

be false. Hawking hopes someday to find a grand unified theory that will reconcile those two partial theories. However, his own statements about the provisional nature of all physical laws and the fundamental criticisms of scientific epistemology offered by Clark, Popper, and Lakatos will prevent any new theory from being assured of the final status of truth.

Christianity and the Rise of Modern Science

Popper suggested that conjectures and refutations could get us closer to the truth. It is this belief, that there is a truth that could be approximated, if not reached, and that the universe is ultimately rational, that urges us onward in the field of science. But isn't that belief a kind of faith, a presupposition that is not empirically verifiable? How does one derive a belief in the rationality and uniformity of nature from empirical observation? Indeed, how can an Objectivist, who trusts in the senses and insists upon a blank mind, believe in uniformity without resorting to *a priori* information? Certainly, these are not beliefs that men have always held. Perhaps we can examine history to find out where these beliefs came from and what preconditions were necessary for the development of modern science.

In *Science and Creation*, Stanley Jaki asks just that question: What were the preconditions that helped science become a self-sustaining and dynamic force? He observes:

> In a world history that had witnessed at least half a dozen great cultures, science had as many stillbirths. Only once, in the period of 1250–1650, did man's scientific quest muster enough zest to grow into an enterprise with built-in vitality.[37]

After a masterful study of the great ancient cultures, including the Chinese, Indian, Babylonian, and Greek civilizations, Jaki comes to this astounding conclusion: The precondition for the emergence of science was that for the first time in history the belief in a personal, rational, and transcendent Creator permeated an entire cul-

---

[37] *Science and Creation*, p. viii.

ture, the European culture. The modern mind must greet this conclusion with incredible skepticism; however, this conclusion was not reached by Jaki alone but has been noted by several other historians. It was the Judeo-Christian worldview that provided the necessary stimulus for the development of science.

What are some of the ingredients in this worldview? First in this list is the Hebrew concept of *ex nihilo* creation (creation out of nothing). As Jaki points out, this idea may seem simple, but it had no precedent in human history. Yet we see this concept clearly explained in the first two chapters of Genesis, where the Hebrew God is revealed as the "sole and supreme Lord of all."[38] No force or principle complements his power. He had a singular destiny for the universe and for mankind. In contrast to the prevailing belief systems found in other cultures, Jaki writes, "[N]othing could be more alien to the biblical outlook than the prospect of an endless tug of war between opposite cosmic and moral forces."[39] The pantheistic and animistic view of nature held by other cultures resulted in a cosmology that taught a "treadmill of perennial, inexorable returns."[40] Such a cosmology could not foster the presuppositions necessary for the development of science. In contrast, the concept of an omnipotent, transcendent, rational Creator, as the eminent physicist Carl-Friedrich von Weizsäcker points out in his book *The Relevance of Science*, completely divested nature of its divinity and destroyed the concept of nature as a "house of gods."[41] It paved the way for nature to be seen as the orderly creation of a rational, transcendent God. Consequently, even the non-Christian philosopher Alfred North Whitehead was compelled to concede that "faith in the possibil-

---

[38] *Science and Creation*, p. 140. The reader may also wish to contrast the lucid description of creation found in Genesis 1 with the capricious and gory account given in the Babylonian cosmogonical poem of *Enuma Elish* in *The Babylonian Genesis: The Story of Creation,* translated by Alexander Heidel (Chicago, IL: University of Chicago Press, 1942).

[39] *Science and Creation*, p. 140.

[40] *Science and Creation*, p. viii.

[41] *The Relevance of Science*, pp. 93, 121.

ity of science, generated antecedently to the development of modern scientific theory, is an unconscious derivative from medieval theology."[42] In *Foolishness to the Greeks*, Lesslie Newbigin expands on this view:

> [I]f the world is not rational, science is not possible; if the world is not contingent, science is not necessary. . . . [A] scientist faced with an apparent irrationality does not accept it as final, nor does he take refuge in the idea of arbitrary divine intervention. He goes on struggling to find some rational way in which the facts can be related to each other, some formula or mathematical equation that will tie them logically together. This struggle is a deeply passionate one, sustained by the faith that there must be a solution even though no one can yet say what it is. Without that passionate faith in the ultimate rationality of the world, science would falter, stagnate, and die—as has happened before. Thus science is sustained in its search for an understanding of what it sees by faith in what is unseen. The formula *credo ut intelligam* is fundamental to science.[43]

Credo ut intelligam, "I believe in order to understand," was the formulation of the eminent theologian Aurelius Augustine (A.D. 354–430). It was, however, not that of the Aristotelians. In the midst of refuting the skepticism of his day, Augustine, like others, searched for a source of absolute truth. He found that truth in the revelation of the Scriptures.[44] Not only does belief in the Scriptures reveal truth whereas science fails to furnish it, but belief in the rationality of the God who created nature also provides one of the preconditions necessary for the pursuit of science. Augustine saw every event as a work of God, but he also saw in God a source of stability and regularity in the midst of apparent irregularity in nature. Whatever may have been Augustine's shortcomings with regard to either his interest in or his pursuit of science, modern

---

[42] "Science and the Modern World," in *Alfred North Whitehead: An Anthology*, p. 374.
[43] *Foolishness to the Greeks*, pp. 70–71.
[44] See chapter 8 on reason and reality with regard to the axiom of revelation.

science owes him a debt of gratitude.[45] As W. T. Jones observes in *A History of Western Philosophy*:

> The perpetuation through the Middle Ages of this Augustinian belief in the regularity of nature made possible, when men's minds finally turned away from the other world towards this one, the scientific achievement that followed. Without this fixed belief— this faith that all oddities are only apparent—modern science could never have taken even its first steps.[46]

But Jones's comments raise an interesting question. If Augustine's *credo ut intelligam* was such an important condition for the development of modern science, why did science not emerge during the Middle Ages, after Augustine's death? Since science only began to gain vitality around the time of the Renaissance and the Reformation, it behooves us to examine this period of history carefully and contrast it with that of the Middle Ages, which preceded it.

Augustine lived in the fourth and fifth centuries. After suffering intense persecution for nearly three centuries after the time of Jesus, Christianity was finally gaining some acceptance and influence during Augustine's lifetime. Augustine's belief in the rationality of God and of the world that he created would later be essential to the development of modern science. Unfortunately, Augustine left behind him no one of substantial intellectual ability who could carry on his work and sustain this Christian belief. With his death, the West entered a period known as the Dark Ages. By the late sixth century, the foundational teachings of the Scriptures—especially the belief in a transcendent, rational Creator—were being distorted. While Christianity continued to spread to the West and began to transform Europe, its doctrines were not always transmitted in purity. They had become tainted with an admixture of paganism and the occult.[47]

---

[45] *A History of Western Philosophy*, Volume II, pp. 128–133.

[46] *A History of Western Philosophy*, Volume II, p. 133. As I pointed out in chapter 4, a concern with the other world need not have conflicted with a concern for this world. This false dichotomy does not exist in Christianity.

[47] Francis Schaeffer, *How Should We Then Live?* pp. 30–35.

As Carlos Eire points out in his book *War against the Idols*, by the late Middle Ages the medieval theology of the Roman Catholic Church had degenerated to such an extent that immanence rather than transcendence was the prevailing view.[48] Under the influence of such teachings, the masses as well as the clergy once again saw divinity as being invested in objects of nature. Relics and graven images were thought to possess magical powers. They could work miracles and accumulate indulgences for their owners. There was a patron saint for everything: as a cure for particular diseases as well as favor for success in certain types of animal husbandry. The cult of the saints, as Jacques Toussaert says, had become a form of "parapolytheism."[49] Once again, nature had become a house of gods. Keith Thomas also observes that religion in the late medieval period was consumed with the magical. Ultimately, the difference between the priests and the magicians had less to do with what they alleged they could do than what they claimed as the source of their authority and power.[50] This was the pathetic state to which medieval theology had fallen.

What happened in the Renaissance? And why did the scientific revolution first begin to assert itself at that time? Perhaps it was the rediscovery of the Greek heritage and classical learning— what Jones called a turning of men's minds away "from the other world towards this one"—that ushered in the era of modern science. While this may seem plausible initially, several historians of science have shown that the Greek heritage contributed little to the emergence of modern science during the Renaissance. As von Weizsäcker observes, the atomism of Democritus taught that only atoms are real, whereas mathematics is imaginary; therefore, the atomist school could not see the relevance of mathematics to the

---

[48] *War against the Idols*, pp. 8–27. Biblical Christianity teaches an immanent-transcendent God in contrast to the nonimmanent, transcendent god of deism and the nontranscendent, immanent god, or gods, of medieval Roman Catholicism, pantheism, and polytheism.

[49] Jacques Toussaert, *Le Sentiment Religieux en Flandre à la Fin du Moyen Age* (Paris, 1963), p. 586 as cited in *War against the Idols*, p. 12.

[50] Keith Thomas, *Religion and the Decline of Magic* (New York, 1971), p. 49 as cited in *War against the Idols*, p. 11.

physical world.[51] Aristotle's preconceived ideas of celestial spheres and of motion as a constantly applied force could not provide the paradigm necessary for the development of modern scientific thinking.[52] Moreover, Aristotle was in many ways too empirical. He relied too much on common-sense experience and hence was unable to conceive of a world based on mathematical laws, which lay beneath the world as revealed by our common-sense perceptions.[53] Thus von Weizsäcker concludes, "[T]he concept of exact mathematical laws of nature which was only dimly present in Greek thought gained far greater convincing power by means of the Christian concept of creation. Thus I think it is a gift of Christianity to the modern mind."[54] Indeed, "To Christians God has made everything. Hence man, made in his image, can understand all created things, that is, certainly the whole material world."[55]

Jaki concurs with this analysis and interpretation. The classical, pagan Greek heritage conveyed to Europe a message about reality that was distinctly different from that of the Christian faith.[56] The former reintroduced the idea of cycles of recurrences and fostered an enthusiasm for numerology and astrology, whereas the latter emphasized the creative and redemptive work of an omnipotent and rational God. The "interlude" of the Renaissance, to borrow Jaki's terminology, was therefore one of uneasy tension between the revival of Greek learning and the resurgence of biblical Christianity over medieval Roman Catholic theology.

But gradually, biblical Christianity gained the ascendancy. Once again, Augustine's transcendent Creator was being proclaimed and affirmed. And the Reformation, as Eire shows, finally succeeded in abolishing the superstitious and the magical. Relics lost their power. The cult of the saints was vanquished. Divinity resided in God

---

[51] *The Relevance of Science*, pp. 69–70.
[52] Charles Thaxton, "Christianity and the Scientific Enterprise," in *Finding God at Harvard*, edited by Kelly Monroe, p. 264; *Science and Creation*, pp. 110–112.
[53] *The Relevance of Science*, p. 104.
[54] *The Relevance of Science*, pp. 120–121.
[55] *The Relevance of Science*, p. 107.
[56] *Science and Creation*, pp. 248–257.

alone, not in his creation. This cessation of the superstitious made way for the concept of a rational universe made by a rational God. And this idea, which was necessary for science to progress, gradually spread across Europe.

Other ideas, however, were necessary for the development of science. The Greeks did have a semblance of science, but several factors hindered its growth. Chief among them was the Greek view of the purpose of science. Here is how Jaki describes the Greek attitude:

> One could speculate about nature in order to understand it, but one was not supposed to supplement his speculations about nature by submitting them to tests consisting in changes imposed systematically on nature. . . . While nature was thought to be repetitive, that is cyclic, artificially produced recurrences of events (or systematic experimentation) were considered contrary to nature and the dictates of reason.[57]

Thus science was seen as an academic, speculative enterprise to be pursued for the sake of satisfying the rational, contemplative nature of man, but not to be applied to the domination of nature.

This view was prevalent in ancient Greece. The great engineer Archimedes, for example, refused to write a manual on engineering because he deemed as vulgar any profession that dealt with the crude necessities of life. Aristotle seemed to accord special status to the "superior" sciences, those which did not aim at invention and practical use but instead speculated about ultimate principles and causes. And, according to him, these superior sciences developed during the times of leisure that men had *after* they had attained to the basic needs of life.[58] This two-fold tendency of the Greeks—first, to avoid submitting nature to systematic tests and, second, to view practical utility and invention as somehow a less worthy pursuit—stunted the growth of science.

---

[57] *Science and Creation*, p. 130.
[58] *Metaphysics*, 981, b13–35.

However, these two concepts—science as a tool of dominion over nature and the nobility of the scientific profession—in addition to the rationality of the Creator and his creation, were necessary for the development of modern science. And they were uniquely brought to bear on the European mind by the initial stirrings of the Christian Reformation during the Renaissance. First, the concept of the Judeo-Christian God not only divested nature of its divinity, but it also invested man with a God-given authority over nature.[59] Whatever scientific progress was made during the Renaissance, it was due to an implicit faith in the intelligibility of the world *as well as* a dualistic view of nature and man, of faith in human volition, and man's ability to utilize his God-given creative and imaginative powers to dominate nature. The great scientists of that era, including Copernicus, Galileo, da Vinci, Kepler, Bacon, and Newton all shared this view.[60] Jaki writes: "Therein lay the factor that made a world of difference and ultimately a different world. In that world, science became the implementation of the age-old drive sparked by the hallowed injunction: 'Fill the earth and conquer it.'"[61]

However, the Reformation contributed further to this mandate to transform nature by teaching the priesthood of all believers and hence the sanctity of all vocations, not merely the "religious" vocations as taught by the medieval church.[62] John Calvin wrote that one did not have to be a monk or a nun and live in isolation and idleness in order to please God.[63] Thus the people of that era came to believe that learning and science, when joined to the moral principle of loving one's neighbor as oneself, could potentially bring prosperity and progress to all. The Reformation systematized these truths and disseminated them across Europe, thus solidifying the foundations of modern science.

---

[59] *The Relevance of Science*, pp. 50–51.
[60] *Science and Creation*, pp. 259–269.
[61] *Science and Creation*, p. 269.
[62] 1 Peter 2:9.
[63] *Institutes of Christian Religion*, Book IV, chapter 12, Sections 23–28, pp. 468–471; Book IV, chapter 13, Sections 10–21, pp. 480–490.

Yet, as von Weizsäcker observes, there is a tendency for men to forget the heritage of rationality and dominion that they inherited from the Christian worldview:

> Now we see how this inherited gift is used against the religion whence it came. And this killing of one's own parent by the weapon inherited from him becomes more and more naive. . . . Modern scientists in general find it very difficult to think of a religious interpretation of natural law as anything but an additional tenet, probably mythical and certainly not logically connected with the concept of laws of nature. . . . Science does not prove the existence of God. . . . [But] it was a sort of Christian radicalism which transformed nature from the house of gods into the realm of law.[64]

Thus the development of science, noted initially by Whitehead to be an unconscious derivative of medieval theology, was, as Jaki points out, in fact "*a most conscious derivative* from the tenets of medieval theology on the 'Maker of Heaven and Earth.'"[65] Modern science was then given its final shape and impetus by the Christian Reformation.

With the benefit of hindsight and a greater appreciation for the logic and process of scientific discovery, we might even reprove some Christians from the period of the Renaissance and the Reformation for being too naive and optimistic about the ability of science to discover truth. Science does not discover truth. However, nothing in what we discussed previously concerning the limitations and utility of science disposes of the debt owed to Christianity for making modern science possible. Modern science, as von Weizsäcker concludes, is a "legacy, I might even have said a child, of Christianity."[66]

Galileo versus Aristotle

But what about Galileo? Was his treatment at the hand of the Inquisitors not an example of the conflict that inevitably arises

---

[64] *The Relevance of Science*, p. 121.
[65] *Science and Creation*, p. 231.
[66] *The Relevance of Science*, p. 163; Charles Thaxton, "Christianity and the Scientific Enterprise," *Finding God at Harvard*, p. 266.

between science and Christianity? Not necessarily. Christianity does indeed maintain that the Scriptures represent the revelation of God and the touchstone of truth, but it also leaves men free to develop scientific theories that allow them to dominate and subdue the earth. As Jaki explains, even while Augustine maintained the supremacy and truth of the Scriptures, he did not use it as a bludgeon against scientists. "When some statements of the Bible collided with the latter [scientific observations and hypotheses about nature], Augustine urged caution."[67] For example, if the Scriptures' description of God stretching forth the heavens as a tent seems to contradict the sphericity of the earth, we should not jump to hasty conclusions. As Augustine points out, even if it could be demonstrated that the heavens were spherical, "it remains to be shown that what is spoken of as a tent, does not contradict those true demonstrations [of science]."[68] (One might add that some portions of the Scriptures clearly imply the sphericity of the earth.[69]) Ironically, Galileo referred to these statements of the great Christian theologian in his own defense when faced with the Inquisition of the Roman Catholic Church-State.[70]

Moreover, it should be noted that Thomas Aquinas, whom Ayn Rand admired, was the person who made Aristotelianism the official philosophy of the Roman Catholic Church. Yet few people who cite Galileo as the classic example of the conflict between science and religion understand that the Roman Catholic Church attacked the heliocentric position of Galileo and Copernicus not because their description of nature contradicted the Scriptures, but because it contradicted the Aristotelian dogma.[71] It was the speculative reasoning of the Aristotelian tradition that had come to dominate the Roman Catholic Church, not the original Augustin-

---

[67] *Science and Creation*, p. 182.

[68] *Sancti Aureli Augustini De Genesi ad litteram libri duodecim*, edited by J. Zycha, in *Corpus Scriptorum Ecclesiasticorum Latinorum*, Vol. XXVIII, Sec. III, Pars. 1 (Vienna: F. Tempsky, 1894) p. 46 (Book II, chapter 9) as quoted in *Science and Creation*, p. 183.

[69] Isaiah 40:22.

[70] *Science and Creation*, pp. 182–183.

[71] *How Should We Then Live?* p. 131; see also Charles Thaxton, "Christianity and the Scientific Enterprise," *Finding God at Harvard*, pp. 261–266. Indeed, it

ian position of scriptural truth, that led to the conflict. Atheists who attack biblical Christianity on this account should review the details of history.[72] But alas, as Charles Thaxton describes, "In 1572, a new star appeared in the skies over Europe. The star remained visible for a year and a half, even in the daytime. The star hovered clearly above the moon. Yet, according to established Aristotelian views, the heavens were supposed to be changeless. . . . [I]t was clear evidence that the Aristotelian system was in deep trouble."[73] Ironically, it was Aristotle's philosophy, the one that garners the most praise from Objectivism, and not biblical Christianity, which had stood in the way of science.

Resolution of Conflict

Much of this chapter has been devoted to demonstrating the limits of science. What science produces are useful theories that cannot claim to be truth. Furthermore, not only are scientific theories and laws tentative, but even if they corroborated current experimental results, they cannot logically be extended to all unobserved events of the past, present, or future. This understanding of the nature and limits of science will now be applied to several areas of alleged conflict between Christianity and science.

The Laws of Thermodynamics

The Genesis description of creation *ex nihilo* was unprecedented in human history. The first law of thermodynamics, it is

---

should be noted that even the heroic Galileo was not as objective as the textbooks portray him to be. Citing the historian I. Bernard Cohen, Broad and Wade point out in *Betrayers of the Truth* that Galileo probably never performed the experiments that he claimed supported some of his theories. Galileo liked to perform "thought" experiments, and the rough experimental conditions that were available to him could never have yielded many of the exact laws that he proposed (*Betrayers of the Truth*, pp. 26–27). Finally, it should be noted that modern astronomy now discounts both the geocentric and the heliocentric models of the universe. In fact, the center of the universe cannot be determined.

[72] George Smith, *Atheism: The Case against God*, pp. 113–114.

[73] Charles Thaxton, "Christianity and the Scientific Enterprise," *Finding God at Harvard*, pp. 265–266.

said, contradicts creation out of nothing. The first law states that the total amount of energy and matter in the universe is constant. Energy and matter may be converted from one form into another, but the total amount of energy and matter remains the same. (However, even now this law is being rendered suspect. As Davies and Gribbin point out, quantum mechanics allows energy and matter to appear spontaneously out of nothing as long they disappear again quickly.[74]) However, as we discussed previously, a scientific law is based on induction; therefore, it cannot be universally true. Even though numerous experiments have been performed that appear to verify the first law of thermodynamics, there are thousands of years' worth of unmeasured events that limit the universality of this law. Furthermore, unless a scientist is able to conduct a measurement at the time of an alleged violation, he cannot claim that the law continued to hold during the event in question. He can only conclude that *in his limited experience* no such violation has actually occurred. However, he could not assert on purely empirical grounds that creation *ex nihilo*, miracles, and the resurrection are impossible. Neither can he categorically deny the possibility of the soul surviving death or the future creation of a new heaven and a new earth as depicted in the Bible.[75]

Indeed, the nonbeliever's appeal to the universality of scientific laws appears to be a modern version of an old argument against miracles. In his day, the philosopher David Hume denied the possibility of miracles by an appeal to the uniformity of nature. According to Hume, a miracle always has a naturalistic explanation (although he seems to allow for the possibility of the miracles attested to by the Scriptures). However, the problem is that no amount of human experience can ever demonstrate what *is* or is *not* the uniformity of human experience. No one has ever experienced all time and all space to justify such a claim. On a purely empirical basis, such a claim is invalid. In order for a person to deny that miracles can happen, he would have to be omniscient and om-

---

[74] *The Matter Myth*, p. 142.
[75] Luke 16:22–31; Revelation 21:1; Isaiah 65:17, 66:22.

nipotent. In short, the skeptic would have to be God. Moreover, such a denial of the possibility of miracles contains nonempirical presuppositions. In *Miracles*, C. S. Lewis observes:

> Now of course we must agree with Hume that if there is absolutely "uniform experience" against miracles, if in other words they have never happened, why then they never have. Unfortunately we know the experience against them to be uniform only if we know that all the reports of them are false. And we can know all the reports to be false only if we know already that miracles have never occurred. In fact, we are arguing in a circle.[76]

The same criticism applies to anyone who claims that the physical universe is eternal. Such a claim is made not on the basis of empirical observation but on an *a priori* choice.

Now let us turn our attention to the second law of thermodynamics. The second law states that the *entropy*, or randomness, of the universe is increasing. This law, it is said, denies the possibility of a spontaneous increase in the *order* of the universe. For example, gases do not flow from cold to hot; houses fall apart but do not spontaneously build themselves. Hence, a miracle, the resurrection, and the future creation of a new heaven and a new earth are also specifically denied by the second law. However, the general comments regarding the first law of thermodynamics apply equally to the second law. The second law cannot be extended to all experience simply because no one has ever experienced all. Once again, the denial of miracles on the basis of the second law is a nonempirical choice.

Now with regard to the second law, some theists have asserted its truth in an effort to prove that the universe had a beginning. The argument goes like this: The second law says that the overall order of the universe must decrease with time. If the universe has been in existence for an eternity, then the order of the universe, and consequently its temperature, should have reached a minimum by now. If so, the universe should have suffered "heat death"

---

[76] *Miracles*, p. 102.

long ago, and we would not exist. However, George Smith claims in *Atheism: The Case against God* that the assertion of the truth of the second law would make it applicable even to God, and foil the case for Christianity. God would also have suffered "heat death" and hence could not have existed for an eternity.[77] But it is obvious that the second law applies only to our physical universe and not to an immaterial reality like God. Therefore, in making such an argument, Smith reveals his own materialistic presuppositions.

Moreover, the Christian need not claim the universal truth of the second law in order to prove that the universe had a beginning. Rather, he appeals to revelation for the truth of creation *ex nihilo*. In fact, Christianity specifically denies the truth of the second law because science does not produce truth. It is the skeptic who runs into danger if he wishes to claim the truth of the second law. For the reasons given above, he would then have to deny the eternal existence of the universe and accept its beginning in a finite past.

Smith attempts to circumvent this conclusion by arguing that the second law of thermodynamics does not apply to the universe as a whole.[78] The second law, he says, applies only to closed systems, and the universe is not a closed system. This argument is specious. If the universe contains everything that exists, as Smith claims it does, then how can it not be a closed system? Is it connected to something else? If so, then the universe cannot be everything that exists. Is that the conclusion Smith wants us to draw? However, if the skeptic now admits that the second law of thermodynamics is not universally true—and our analysis of the nature of the scientific method requires this conclusion—then he must concede that miracles, the resurrection, and the new creation are all possible.

Creation and Evolution

In chapter 8, we saw that Christianity does not require empirical verification in order to assert its veracity. Christianity and empiricism have no presuppositions in common. Christianity claims

---

[77] *Atheism: The Case against God*, pp. 252–255.
[78] *Atheism: The Case against God*, pp. 255–256.

that truth is a gift of God and that one arrives at truth by accepting the axiom of revelation and proceeding with the use of deductive logic. The epistemological problems associated with empiricism have been discussed in previous chapters, and the tentative nature of all scientific theories has been emphasized in the preceding section. Empiricism and scientism, both of which are incapable of providing the truth, are not the method of Christianity. Nevertheless, it is noteworthy that on the basis of the information and the methodology provided by scientists themselves some of the major points of contention between Christianity and science can be reconciled. In the remainder of this chapter we will address two major issues, creation and evolution, and see that opposition to Christianity cannot be maintained on the basis of the evidence.

The Creation Event

"In the beginning God created the heavens and the earth."[79] The Hebrew phrase for "the heavens and the earth," *shamayim erets,* means the entire physical universe.[80] The Bible declares that the universe had a beginning. Yet former Objectivists like Nathaniel Branden and Libertarians like George Smith claim that the universe had no beginning. They believe it is eternal.[81] Smith writes: "The universe, then, has always existed and always will exist."[82] But on what basis is such a statement made? Is it a nonempirical choice that seeks to avoid the creation event and hence the Creator, or is it an opinion borne out by the scientific evidence?

In *The Creator and the Cosmos*, Hugh Ross chronicles many of the scientific evidences that suggest the universe had a beginning. Only the most pertinent will be briefly discussed here. First, a problem known for the last two centuries as "Olber's paradox of the

---

[79] Genesis 1:1.

[80] Harris, R. Laird, Archer, Gleason L., and Bruce K. Waltke (editors), *Theological Wordbook of the Old Testament* (Chicago, IL: Moody Press, 1980), Volume II, p. 935.

[81] Nathaniel Branden, "Intellectual Ammunition Department," *The Objectivist Newsletter*, May 1962, p. 19; see a discussion of the first-cause argument in chapter 11 of this book.

[82] *Atheism: The Case against God*, p. 241.

dark night sky" should have alerted scientists and skeptics to the possibility that the universe had a beginning.[83] Paul Davies gives a detailed explanation of this paradox in *The Last Three Minutes*. In the sixteenth century, scientists thought the universe was static. The galaxies and stars remained in essentially fixed positions. However, if the universe were static, stars would tend to collapse toward the center of the universe. In response to this difficulty, Newton postulated a universe that was infinitely large and uniform in all directions. In that scenario, the gravitational effect of all the stars would presumably cancel out and prevent the universe from collapsing. However, this explanation created other difficulties. If the distribution of stars were indeed uniform in all directions in an infinitely large universe, the night sky would not be dark. It would be infinitely bright. Why is this so?

Imagine an infinite number of stars evenly distributed throughout space. Now imagine the earth, in the midst of all those stars. One can then visualize an infinite number of concentric, spherical shells surrounding the earth, and each one of those shells contains some number of stars. The number of stars in the shells increases according to the square of a particular shell's distance from the earth. At twice the distance, there are four times the number of stars; at three times the distance, there are nine times the number of stars, etc. However, the brightness of the stars as observed from earth decreases according to the inverse-square law—a star that is twice as far away from the earth is only one-fourth as bright, a star that is three times as far away is only one-ninth as bright, etc. But these two effects of distance—the number of stars increases with the square of the distance while the brightness of the stars decreases with the inverse square of the distance—cancel each other out. Consequently, the total amount of light reaching the earth from the stars within any particular concentric shell is the same as for any other shell, regardless of distance. And since the universe is infinitely large, the total amount of light coming from an infinite number of such shells would make the night sky infinitely bright.

---

[83] *The Creator and the Cosmos*, p. 50; *The Last Three Minutes*, pp. 14–18.

Even taking into account other minor adjustments in this model, the entire night sky ought to be at least as bright as the sun. Yet we experience the night sky as dark. How do we explain this paradox?

Olber's solution was to propose the existence of intergalactic dust clouds that absorbed the heat and the light emanating from the stars. However, thermodynamic principles require that the dust clouds eventually give off as much heat and light as they absorbed. The night sky should still be as bright as the sun, and the earth should be uncomfortably hot. As Davies points out, the flaw in the scientific thinking had more to do with a belief in infinite time than in infinite space. The scientists assumed that the universe had been in existence for an eternity. But it is obvious that the universe cannot be eternal. Stars cannot burn forever. If the universe had been in existence for infinite time, the stars would have run out of fuel by now. Therefore, the universe must have had a beginning. The solution to Olber's paradox lies in understanding that light from distant stars takes time to reach earth. If the universe were, say, 10 billion years old, the light from stars more than 10 billion light years away may not have reached the earth as yet. The same is true of heat. It takes time to heat up the universe. If the universe has not been in existence for an eternity, thermodynamic equilibrium may not have been reached. Therefore, Olber's paradox implies a finite age for the universe.

Olber's paradox should have alerted scientists to the possibility that the universe had a beginning, but it was Einstein's theory of relativity that forced this conclusion by predicting a universe that was simultaneously expanding and decelerating in its expansion.[84] Einstein's results implied that the universe began in an explosion: the big bang. However, Einstein was reluctant to accept his own theory because a beginning implied a Beginner who created the universe. Moreover, as Hawking explains, Einstein's preconceived notion of a static, eternal universe was so strong that he was willing to deny the implications of his own theory by introducing an antigravity force into his equations.[85] However, in 1929,

---

[84] *The Creator and the Cosmos*, p. 52.
[85] *A Brief History of Time*, p. 40.

Edwin Hubble discovered that the galaxies were moving away from each other; the universe was indeed expanding. This observation corroborated the predictions of Einstein's initial, unmodified theory. As a result, Einstein reluctantly acknowledged that the universe had a beginning; however, it is doubtful that he ultimately came to believe in God.[86]

Subsequently, the big bang theory has been confirmed by a number of other experiments. If the universe did in fact begin as an explosion, physicists reasoned that it should be cooling off. As Ross points out, this means that the universe resembled a hot kitchen oven whose door had been opened to permit the dissipation of heat. The universe should resemble what physicists call the perfect radiator.[87] In 1965, Arno Penzias and Robert Wilson, two physicists at Bell Laboratories succeeded in measuring the cosmic background radiation. Their measurements were consistent with the temperature of the universe as predicted by other physicists on the basis of the perfect radiator model and the relative abundance of various elements known to exist in the universe. In 1990, results from the Cosmic Background Explorer (COBE) confirmed the findings of Penzias and Wilson. Subsequently, in 1992, the COBE detected minor irregularities in the distribution of the background radiation that also seemed to explain the clustering of galaxies. The big bang theory was receiving striking experimental confirmation. However, the evidence for a beginning was not restricted to the physical dimensions of the universe. Three British physicists, Stephen Hawking, George Ellis, and Roger Penrose, had previously extended Einstein's theory of relativity to the analysis of time; and their work suggested that time also had a beginning.[88]

Now, of course, as we saw earlier, all of these scientific theories and experiments commit the fallacy of asserting the consequent. Therefore, they cannot purport to be truth. However, the point I

---

[86] *The Creator and the Cosmos*, pp. 52–54.
[87] *The Creator and the Cosmos*, pp. 19–29.
[88] *The Creator and the Cosmos*, p. 73.

wish to make is this: According to the best contemporary scientific theories, the entire space-time continuum appears to have begun in the explosion of the big bang.[89] Therefore, contrary to what Branden and Smith have said, the evidence suggests the temporal and contingent nature of the physical universe rather than its eternity. Could it be that science has now come full circle by corroborating what had been revealed in Genesis 1 all along? As Robert Jastrow writes in *God and the Astronomers:*

> For the scientist who has lived by his faith in the power of reason, the story ends like a bad dream. He has scaled the mountains of ignorance; he is about to conquer the highest peak; as he pulls himself over the final rock, he is greeted by a band of theologians who have been sitting there for centuries.[90]

The Six Days of Creation

Thus we see that the scientific evidence suggests there was indeed a beginning to the physical universe, and this description is consistent with the one found in the Bible. However, two questions inevitably arise with regard to the Genesis description: Does the description of creation in Genesis 2 contradict Genesis 1? And did creation occur in six literal, twenty-four-hour periods?

First, the description of creation in Genesis 2 does not contradict Genesis 1; Genesis 2 describes the spiritual order of creation, not the chronological order of creation. It describes how Adam was *introduced* to inanimate objects, plants, animals (sentient beings), and woman (spiritual being) in sequential order.

---

[89] Since his original work demonstrating that time had a beginning, Hawking has been trying to find a loophole in the theory that would free time and the physical universe from the necessity of creation. "Only if we could picture the universe in terms of imaginary time would there be no singularities" and no beginning and end to the universe. However, Hawking concedes that we do not live in imaginary time, but in real time. Using real time, there is no way of avoiding a beginning to the universe (*A Brief History of Time*, pp. 138–139).
[90] *God and the Astronomers*, p. 116.

Second, the Bible does describe creation in six literal, twenty-four-hour periods. Let me briefly outline the Genesis description.

1. First, Genesis 1:1 establishes the creation of the entire physical universe. "In the beginning God created the heavens and the earth." Next, Genesis 1:3 describes the creation of light on day 1. "Then God said, 'Let there be light'; and there was light."
2. On the second day, water is separated into subterranean and surface components (Gen. 1:6–8).
3. On the third day, dry land appears as the great ocean basins are formed and the surface waters gather to one place (Gen. 1:9); vegetation also appears on land (Gen. 1:10–13).
4. On the fourth day, the stars, the sun, and the moon are formed (Gen. 1:14–19).
5. Subsequently, on the fifth day, the birds and the sea creatures (Gen. 1:20–23), including lower vertebrates, reptiles, and amphibians, are formed.
6. The appearance of livestock and wild animals follows on the sixth day (Gen. 1:24). And finally, man and woman are created (Gen. 1:27).

Notice the straightforward chronological description in this account. Moreover, there is nothing inherently impossible in this sequence of events. One objection that is often raised against the biblical account is the fact that the sun and the moon (day 4) are said to be created after the plants (day 3). Isn't sunlight required for photosynthesis? Plants cannot survive in the dark, can they? However, notice that the plants would only have to survive for one day in darkness before sunlight becomes available, that is, if six literal days of creation is accepted. And that is certainly possible. Only if one hypothesizes that each day of creation represents an epoch lasting thousands, perhaps millions, of years, does the creation of the sun after the creation of plants become problematic. Moreover, Genesis 1:3 specifically states that light was created on day 1. But what could have caused light besides the luminous bodies formed on the fourth day? An explosion could have. An explosion in the initial moments of creation (the big bang) could easily explain the presence of light on day 1, and that light might still have been available on day 3 to sustain plant life until the luminous bodies were formed. Thus we see there is nothing inherently impossible in this sequence of events.

But isn't the universe billions of years old? Accepting six literal days of creation and the biblical genealogies would mean that the universe is at most tens of thousands of years old, would it not? How does one reconcile science and the Bible on this point? To begin with, since written human history only goes back at most to ten thousand years, no written confirmation of the earth's history prior to that time exists.[91] As we saw previously, scientific laws derived from the inductive method cannot be extended beyond actual experience, and all theories about the primitive earth and the origin of the universe depend on assumptions and experimental inferences that cannot be verified. Earlier, we saw the difficulties with the assumptions of the carbon-14 dating technique. Similarly, none of the assumptions made in any other radiometric dating technique can be validated for the time periods in question. Other methods of dating the earth also encounter such difficulties. For example, the believer in the uniformitarian theory of geology may claim that the rate at which the geologic strata currently forms implies a primitive earth. But let him explain how he knows the rate of strata formation has remained constant for millions of years. Did he make the measurements at the appropriate times in history? And how does he propose to explain away the evidences for a catastrophic flood?[92]

But surely, it is sometimes said: Since there are galaxies billions of light years away from us, and since we see their light that has

---

[91] It is interesting that works such as Bernard Grun's *The Timetables of History* (New York: Touchstone, Simon and Schuster, 1975) and Will Durant's *The Story of Civilization 1: Our Oriental Heritage* (New York: Simon and Schuster, 1954) begin their description of human history and civilization at about 4 to 5 thousand B.C.

[92] See, for example, Walt Brown, *In the Beginning: Compelling Evidence for Creation and the Flood* (Phoenix, AZ: Center for Scientific Creationism, 1995).

taken billions of years to reach us, the universe must be at least several billion years old. However, this conclusion assumes that the speed of light has always been the same. But there is no *a priori* reason for this belief. Who was around to make the measurements? In fact, there is some evidence to suggest that the speed of light has slowed down during the last three hundred years.[93] Moreover, even if these measurements on the speed of light were inaccurate and the speed of light has actually been a constant for the last three hundred years, there is no reason why the speed of light could not have been dramatically different during the six days of creation. (Even theoretical physicists believe that the laws of physics break down at 10^{-43} seconds after creation; they do not know what the laws and the physical constants of the universe were prior to this moment.) And if the speed of light has indeed slowed down, then galaxies that we have heretofore believed to be a certain distance from earth, based on calculations utilizing the current speed of light, may in fact be much further away. Thus it is possible that heaven and earth were created in six literal days and the experimental assumptions we use for dating the universe are simply incorrect.

Evolution

It is commonly supposed that evolution is true. It is not. Evolution is a hypothesis. As such, it is false, just as all scientific theories are false. If anyone remains unconvinced, he will have to

---

[93] M. E. J. Gheury de Bray, "The Velocity of Light," *Nature 133*: 464, 1934; M. E. J. Gheury de Bray, "The Velocity of Light," *Nature 127*: 522, 1931; "The Velocity of Light," *Science 66*: Supplement, x, 1927. Of note, there has been no appreciable decay in the velocity of light in measurements made since 1960; however, as Setterfield points out, the techniques used for measuring the speed of light since 1960 utilize the oscillating frequency of the cesium clock as the definition of a second (see also David Halliday and Robert Resnick, *Physics*, pp. 924–926). And if the speed of light is decreasing, then the atomic frequencies in these clocks may also be decreasing (velocity of light = wavelength x frequency). Since the quantity measured and the tool used to make the measurement are interdependent and changing at the same rate, no relative change would be detected in the speed of light (see *In the Beginning: Compelling Evidence for Creation and the Flood*, pp. 158–159.)

reconsider the detailed analysis of scientific epistemology given earlier in this chapter. As we also pointed out before, scientists cling tenaciously to their adopted paradigms; and the passionate adherence to the evolutionary model by some antitheistic paleontologists is a measure of their prior commitment to naturalism, *not* to some objective standard of truth. In fact, their prior commitment to naturalism distorts their understanding of the nature of science and their view of evidence. It seems to me, nowhere is this misunderstanding more apparent than in the conflict that arose between scientists over an exhibit called "Man's Place in Evolution" presented by the British Museum of Natural History in the early 1980s.

As Berkeley law professor Philip Johnson describes in his book *Darwin on Trial*, the exhibit at the British Museum displayed a sign that asked:

> Have you ever wondered why there are so many different kinds of living things?
>
> One idea is that all the living things we see today have EVOLVED from a distant ancestor by a process of gradual change.
>
> How could evolution have occurred? How could one species change into another?
>
> The exhibition in this hall looks at one possible explanation—the explanation of Charles Darwin.[94]

An adjacent poster suggested as an alternative hypothesis that God may have created everything. According to Johnson, "The general tenor of the exhibit was that Darwinism is an important theory but not something which it is unreasonable to doubt."[95] However, in a letter to *Nature*, the preeminent British scientific journal, paleontologist L. B. Halstead responded passionately and critically to the exhibit's tentative statements.[96] The exhibit also used a classification scheme known as *cladism*. This scheme iden-

---

[94] *Darwin on Trial*, p. 135.
[95] *Darwin on Trial*, p. 136.
[96] L. B. Halstead, "Museum of Errors," *Nature* 288: 208, 1980.

tifies resemblance between species but never ventures to hypoth-
esize an imaginary common ancestor. Advocates of Darwinism,
of gradual change from one species to another, objected to the
cladist implication that no species can be identified as the ancestor of any other species. Halstead, for one, felt this was tantamount to an abdication of Darwinism and capitulation to the
creationists.

The dialogue between the two sides, as it appeared in the pages
of *Nature,* is instructive. The comments made in one of the
Museum's films regarding the status of evolution was reported by
Barry Cox:[97]

> The Survival of the Fittest is an empty phrase; it is a play on
> words. For this reason, many critics feel that not only is the idea
> of evolution unscientific, but the idea of natural selection also.
> There's no point in asking whether or not we should believe in
> the idea of natural selection, because it is the inevitable logical
> consequence of a set of premises. . . .

> The idea of evolution by natural selection is a matter of logic,
> not science, and it follows that the concept of evolution by natural
> selection is not, strictly speaking, scientific. . . .

> If we accept that evolution *has* taken place, though obviously
> we must keep an open mind on it. . . .

> We can't prove that the idea is true, only that it has not yet been
> proved false. . . .

> It may one day be replaced by a better theory, but until then. . . .

The exhibit also displayed the following passage:

> Biologists try to reconstruct the course of evolution from the
> characteristics of living animals and plants and from fossils,

[97] Barry Cox, "Premises, Premises," *Nature 291:* 373, 1981.

which give a time scale to the story. If the theory of evolution is true . . .[98]

Now the tentative tone of these statements is quite proper if one recalls the nature of scientific inquiry as discussed in the first part of this chapter. However, the author of an editorial in *Nature*, "Darwin's Death in South Kensington," seemed quite oblivious to the limits of science. He wrote:

Nobody disputes that, in the public presentation of science, it is proper whenever appropriate to say that disputed matters are in doubt. But is the theory of evolution still an open question among serious biologists? And, if not, what purpose except general confusion can be served by these weasel words?[99]

But numerous scientists wrote in defense of the Museum's exhibit. A French paleontologist said, "Halstead presents gradualism [Darwinism] as evidence, and cladism as a crime against evidence. But where is the evidence of gradualism? There is almost none, or rather it is everywhere one wants to see it."[100] An American scientist also lent his support. "The British Museum (Natural History) is to be congratulated for bringing epistemology into its exhibits and teaching visitors that science is a method, not a body of revealed knowledge."[101] Another American scientist had this to say regarding Halstead's belief in evolution as truth:

This is certainly the news Biology has waited for, the moment when the Truth can at last be known so that all this difficult and extremely tiresome theory can be dispensed with. Until now my colleagues and I had always imagined that to doubt something was "to be uncertain as to a truth or fact" and the notion that distinguishes science from, say, politics is that in science uncertainty about the truth must remain or progress ends.[102]

---

[98] As quoted in "Darwin's Death in South Kensington," *Nature* 289: 735, 1981.
[99] "Darwin's Death in South Kensington," *Nature* 289: 735, 1981.
[100] Philippe Janvier, "French Museums," *Nature* 289: 626, 1981.
[101] Malcom C. McKenna, "More Museums," *Nature* 289: 626–627, 1981.
[102] Donn E. Rosen, "Museum Policy," *Nature* 289: 8, 1981.

Furthermore, the distinguished scientists responsible for the exhibit at the Museum responded to the *Nature* editorial by saying:

> You suggest that most of us would rather lose our right hands than begin a sentence with the phrase "If the theory of evolution is true . . ." Are we to take it that evolution is a fact, proven to the limits of scientific rigour? If that is the inference then we must disagree most strongly. We have no absolute proof of the theory of evolution. What we do have is overwhelming circumstantial evidence in favour of it and as yet no better alternative. But the theory of evolution would be abandoned tomorrow if a better theory appeared.[103]

Argument and counter argument illustrate what we have been discussing in this chapter all along. The scientific method never arrives at the truth. All theories are provisional. No amount of observation can ever prove a hypothesis true. Furthermore, even if a scientific law described current phenomena accurately, it would be illogical to claim that this law is universally true and applicable to past events of which we have no direct evidence. Those events include the alleged transformation of one species into another by naturalistic mechanism. Who has ever seen such a transformation? Moreover, if physicists who work in the most exacting of experimental conditions acknowledge the limitations of science in their field of study, why should paleontologists claim more certainty for their relatively inexact area of study? Are we to suppose that a paleontologist reconstructing the past on the basis of geological assumptions and incomplete fossils is on a par with a physicist testing out his theories in supercolliders? Are we to suppose that Einstein's *theory* of relativity has less experimental support than the "fact" of evolution? I'm afraid not. Evolution remains a theory. And as the museum scientists rightly point out in their film, evolution is not even strictly a science. It is an *a priori* commitment to the principle and tautology of naturalism: Man evolved

---

[103] Ball H. W., Gray A., Mound L. A. *et al*, "Darwin's Survival," *Nature 290*: 82, 1981.

from lower animals, which in turn evolved from inorganic molecules in the prebiotic soup by natural mechanisms.

A scientist operating under such a premise will be biased to interpret all experimental data as verifying the evolutionary theory, because it is the only alternative to theistic creation. For example, Darwin's theory of evolution implies gradual change from one species to another.[104] Historically, when transitional forms between species were not found in the fossil record, evolutionists did not at first abandon their theory; instead, they proposed that further excavation would eventually produce the intermediate forms. When an insufficient number of intermediate forms turned up after more extensive excavation, many scientists still adhered firmly to their belief in Darwinian evolution. Instead of looking for evidence that could falsify the theory, they merely looked for evidence that supported it. Darwinism had indeed become a tautology. To repeat what the French paleontologist said: "But where is the evidence of gradualism? There is almost none, or rather it is everywhere one wants to see it."[105] However, some scientists have since modified Darwinism to allow for *saltations* (sudden, large-scale modifications from one species to another) and *punctuated equilibrium* (the stability of new species after they have been formed by saltations). The reader will notice the continual development of auxiliary hypotheses in an attempt to patch up Darwinism. However, such modifications of the original theory may in fact be problematic for the advocates of naturalism. As Johnson explains: "[A] saltation is equivalent to a miracle. At the extreme, saltationism is virtually indistinguishable from special creation. If a snake's egg were to hatch and a mouse emerge, we could with equal justice classify the event as an instance of evolution or creation."[106]

Natural Selection

A second major area of confusion with regard to evolution has to do with a misapplication of the principles of natural selection to

[104] *Darwin on Trial*, pp. 45–62.
[105] Philippe Janvier, "French Museums," *Nature 289*: 626, 1981.
[106] *Darwin on Trial*, pp. 32–33.

the origin of species. Natural selection, the process whereby organisms with advantageous traits are preserved while those with disadvantaged traits are reduced or removed, should not be misunderstood as a confirmation of evolution. Kettlewell's famous observations of the peppered moth serve as a classic example of natural selection.[107] Kettlewell found that the survival of dark-colored moths were favored when air pollution from industrial smoke darkened the trees to which such moths attached. The moths' natural predators had difficulty seeing the dark-colored moths against a dark background. At the same time, light-colored moths were at a disadvantage because they were visible to the predators. When the trees became lighter in color because of an improvement in air quality, the light-colored moths were favored instead. Thus the prevalence of light- or dark-colored moths varied depending on the level of air pollution and the color of trees. However, throughout the experiment, both light- and dark-colored moths were present. The advantageous traits may indeed have been favored by the environmental conditions; however, these traits were already present in the population. The confirmation of natural selection in this and many other examples, as Johnson observes, does not provide "any persuasive reason for believing that natural selection can produce new species, new organs, or other major changes, or even minor changes that are permanent."[108]

Let me emphasize this point: The advantageous traits were *already* present at the outset of the experiment and *remained* present so long as the conditions that favored them persisted. No new traits were produced. While scientists may have succeeded in genetically engineering new traits in the laboratory, the development of new traits or new species has never been documented in nature. Only extinctions have taken place. Johnson asks: "Why do other people . . . think that evidence of local population fluctuations confirms the hypothesis that natural selection has the capacity to work engineering marvels, to construct wonders like the eye and the wing?"[109]

---

[107] H. B. D. Kettlewell, "Selection Experiments on Industrial Melanism in the *Lepidoptera*," *Heredity 9:* 323–342, 1955.
[108] *Darwin on Trial*, p. 27.
[109] *Darwin on Trial*, p. 27.

The answer, as before, has to do with an *a priori* commitment made by some scientists to the principle of naturalistic evolution.

Prebiotic Soup and Probabilities

The theory of naturalistic evolution has also gained support from the common misperception that scientists have demonstrated the spontaneous appearance of life from nonliving molecules. This myth has been perpetuated by the limited findings of the famous Miller-Urey experiment. In the 1950s, Stanley Miller and Harold Urey simulated what they thought was the atmosphere of primitive earth by mixing hydrogen, methane, and ammonia with water in a closed chamber.[110] (How do they know this was the case?) Lightning, also presumed to be present in the early atmosphere, was simulated by discharging electricity through the vapor phase of the mixture. When Miller and Urey subsequently examined the composition of the prebiotic soup, they found that a small amount of five amino acids were produced along with other compounds that could potentially be used in forming amino acids and nucleic acids. However, the experiment provides no convincing evidence for the theory that life spontaneously evolved from prebiotic soups.

First, even if a few peptides (a short sequence of amino acids) could be formed from the amino acids generated in the experiment, difficult questions remain. In their textbook *Molecular Cell Biology*, Darnel, Lodish, and Baltimore acknowledge some of the difficulties: "Among the many unsolved problems pertaining to how random peptide assembly could have developed into ordered synthesis is the evolutionary choice of L[left-handed]- compared to D[right-handed]-amino acids. Random polymers would have contained either, of course, but only L-amino acids are found in proteins."[111] Living organisms use left-handed amino acids exclusively. All nonliving processes leave *racemic* [50 percent] mixtures of left-handed and right-handed molecules (stereoisomers). How was it possible then for living things, which utilize left-handed

---

[110] James Darnell, Harvey Lodish, and David Baltimore, *Molecular Cell Biology*, p. 1128; *Darwin on Trial*, p. 104.
[111] *Molecular Cell Biology*, p. 1130.

amino acids exclusively, to evolve from the racemic mixture that was present in the prebiotic soup? Moreover, the scientists had to admit, "We have no way of knowing whether these laboratory reactions were the reactions that actually took place on primitive earth to establish life in cellular form."[112]

In *Origins*, the nontheist Robert Shapiro looks more carefully at the theory of prebiotic synthesis.[113] He points out that a simple organism requires more than just amino acids in order to exist. Of the many biological building materials needed for the development of living organisms—proteins, nucleic acids, polysaccharides, and lipids—none have ever been detected in a prebiotic synthesis experiment. Moreover, the building blocks of these basic constituents, such as nucleosides and sugars, have never been found in any significant amounts. And of the amino acids produced in the first Miller-Urey experiment, only alanine and glycine appear in any significant quantity (2.1 and 1.7 percent, respectively) with the next most abundant amino acid present at 0.026 percent. The likelihood that the prebiotic soup could sustain the formation of more complicated molecules, much less a complex organism like a bacterium, appears staggeringly low. Shapiro concludes: "The very best Miller-Urey chemistry, as we have seen, does not take us very far along the path to a living organism. A mixture of simple chemicals, even one enriched in a few amino acids, no more resembles a bacterium than a small pile of real and nonsense words, each written on an individual scrap of paper, resembles the complete works of Shakespeare."[114] Moreover, recent work by Thaxton, Bradley, and Olsen suggests that the prebiotic conditions postulated by Miller and Urey may be incorrect. The atmospheric conditions on primitive earth may actually have been hostile to the molecules that were produced in the experiment.[115]

But the idea that life evolved naturally is so appealing that some scientists will scarcely consider another view. George Wald, who received the Nobel Prize in Physiology and Medicine in 1967 for his

---

[112] *Molecular Cell Biology*, p. 1130.

[113] *Origins: A Skeptic's Guide to the Creation of Life on Earth*, pp. 98–116.

[114] *Origins: A Skeptic's Guide to the Creation of Life on Earth*, p. 116.

[115] See *The Mystery of Life's Origins*.

work on the biochemistry of vision, holds an attitude that is representative of many believers in naturalistic evolution. In a *Scientific American* article from 1954, Wald writes: "One has only to contemplate the magnitude of this task to concede that the spontaneous generation of a living organism is impossible. Yet here we are—as a result, I believe, of spontaneous generation."[116] Shapiro confirms this impossibility by a calculation of the odds. Using extremely reasonable assumptions about the simplest possible organism, replication times, the age of the universe, the number of possible simultaneous reactions that can occur, etc., Shapiro calculates the number of possible random attempts (trials) at spontaneous generation that could have taken place during the history of the earth as 2.5×10^{51}. Using calculations previously made by scientists Fred Hoyle and N. C. Wickramasinghe, Shapiro explains that the probability of a single bacterium arising by chance from an optimum collection of amino acids is 1 in $10^{40,000}$. This adverse probability far exceeds the number of possible trials (2.5×10^{51}); consequently, Shapiro concludes that spontaneous generation is extremely unlikely.[117] And this simple model assumes that only the formation of a suitable collection of proteins and enzymes is necessary for the creation of the bacterium. The additional requirements for DNA, RNA, cell walls, etc., were not considered in the calculation of odds. Calculations performed by other scientists using different models have yielded a theoretical probability for the spontaneous development of a complete bacterium as 1 in $10^{100,000,000,000}$.[118] Because the probabilities are so staggeringly low, many scientists have concluded that spontaneous generation of life is impossible.

There are other difficulties with the theory of prebiotic synthesis. DNA, RNA, and protein must work together as an integrated whole. Is it possible that the three different kinds of molecules could have emerged at the same time and the same place from inorganic compounds? Could they have spontaneously developed an ordered relationship with each other? Those probabilities are

---

[116] George Wald, "The Origin of Life," *Scientific American 190*: 45–53, 1954.
[117] *Origins: A Skeptic's Guide to the Creation of Life on Earth*, pp. 117–131.
[118] *The Creator and the Cosmos*, pp. 147–156; *Origins: A Skeptic's Guide to the Creation of Life on Earth*, p. 128.

remote. Therefore, as Johnson points out, "An evolutionary scenario must assume that this complex system evolved from a much simpler predecessor, probably employing at first only one of the three major constituents. Which came first, the nucleic acids (DNA or RNA) or the proteins? And how did the first living molecule function and evolve in the absence of the others?"[119]

Indeed, some scientists postulate that RNA may have been the first living molecule. There is some experimental evidence that suggest RNA, which functions as a genetic messenger in the translation and coding of proteins, can occasionally function as a protein enzyme and catalyze some chemical reactions. There is also evidence that RNA-to-RNA replication can occur. This has led some to suggest that DNA and proteins may have evolved from a primitive RNA-like molecule.

However, the formation of a single primordial molecule that is so versatile and complex that it could perform most or all of the functions of DNA, RNA, and proteins would, in principle, be no easier to explain than the formation of the three types of molecules. Moreover, there is no evidence that RNA has ever been produced in a prebiotic synthesis experiment.[120] Therefore, the RNA-first hypothesis has not made the problem any easier. And as Darnel and colleagues have said, "[T]he unsolved question, and the crux of the problem of precellular evolution, is how an *ordered* relationship between nucleic acids (RNA) and proteins began."[121] Thus there remain serious problems that render suspect any undue confidence in the theory of prebiotic synthesis.

Human Ancestors

The existence of fossils belonging to human ancestors that are 2 or 3 million years old has often been cited as evidence to deny the truth of the biblical record. Adam and Eve, as everyone knows, were created only a few thousand years ago. How can science and

---

[119] *Darwin on Trial*, p. 107; see also Michael Denton, *Evolution: A Theory in Crisis.*
[120] *The Creator and the Cosmos*, pp. 152–153.
[121] *Molecular Cell Biology*, p. 1131.

Christianity be reconciled on this point? We begin by recalling that all scientific methods of dating make assumptions that cannot be verified. Moreover, all scientific theories commit the fallacy of asserting the consequent and the fallacy of induction. Therefore, we cannot assume that the primitive age for these alleged human ancestors is correct.

Next, we consider the fossil record itself. First, the proposed fossils are themselves controversial. Few people are aware that most of the fossils of alleged human ancestors have been discredited for lack of evidence. The Piltdown Man (1912) was exposed as a hoax in 1953.[122] It remains an embarrassment to the scientific community that the fraudulent origin of the Piltdown fossil eluded detection for decades. The Nebraska Man (*Hesperopithecus*, 1922) was also once heralded as the missing link to man. Yet the entire creature was imaginatively reconstructed on the basis of a single tooth. That tooth was later found to belong to an extinct pig.[123] The Neanderthal Man (1856) has been classified and reclassified. Initially, he was thought to be an ancestor of modern man. However, the famous German pathologist Rudolf Virchow dismissed that claim and diagnosed the Neanderthal as a modern man who happened to suffer from rickets.[124] More recently, the fossil[125] and molecular[126] evidence has prompted scientists to reclassify the Neanderthal as a distinct nonhuman species without a direct link to our human ancestors. The famous Lucy (*Australopithecus afarensis*, 1974) is still considered a human ancestor; however, even that assumption is now being challenged.[127] Consequently, the list of fossils that remain viable candidates for human ancestry is considerably shorter than most people realize.[128]

---

[122] *Betrayers of the Truth*, pp. 119–122; William Fix, *The Bone Peddlers*, p. 12.
[123] *The Bone Peddlers*, p. 11.
[124] Roger Lewin, *Bones of Contention*, pp. 63–65.
[125] Zollikofer C. P. E., Ponce de León M. S., Martin R. D., and Stucki P., "Neanderthal Computer Skulls," *Nature* 375: 283–285, 1995.
[126] Hugh Ross, "Link with Neanderthals Cut by Computer," *Facts and Faith*, Volume 9, Number 3 (Reasons To Believe, P.O. Box 5978, Pasadena, CA 91117), p. 2, 1995.
[127] *The Bone Peddlers*, pp. 62–78.
[128] *The Bone Peddlers*, pp. 14–15.

Yet even this short list does not provide much evidence for human ancestry. Many forget that the fossil candidates are not classified as humans, *i.e., Homo sapiens*. Instead, scientists have given them names such as *Australopithecus afarensis, Australopithecus africanus, Homo habilis*, and *Homo erectus*. What can this mean except that some aspect of the fossil candidate differs significantly enough from the skeleton of a *Homo sapien* so as to prevent it from being categorized as a true modern human? If the reader will take the initiative to look at photographs of the skulls of these alleged human ancestors, he would see that they are obviously not modern humans.[129] Nevertheless, many paleontologists consider these creatures viable candidates for human ancestry for two primary reasons. First, the size of their skull suggests a larger cranial capacity than modern apes. Second, the structure of their lower extremity suggests that they may have been able to walk upright. However, larger cranial capacity does not prove humanity. (Just because a creature has a large brain does not mean that its brain performed the same function as ours.) Nor does the structural precondition for walking upright prove that these creatures actually did so.[130] All of the problems associated with establishing scientific truths and verifying prehuman events in history revisit paleontology with a vengeance.

But let us accept for the sake of argument that these bipedal, humanlike creatures actually did walk the earth millions of years ago and that the six days of creation were epochs in earth's history instead of literal twenty-four-hour periods. Does that conflict with the biblical account of the creation of man? Hardly. The animals that were created before Adam may well have included apes and other bipedal creatures capable of walking upright. However, as we have seen, a large cranial capacity and the ability to walk upright do not make such creatures human. Nor can other traits such as the use of simple tools conclusively demonstrate the humanity of bipedal creatures, since some animals are also known to make tools.[131] Some other criteria of humanity is needed, and that criteria has to be consistent with the biblical description in order for us to make a fair comparison.

[129] For example, compare the photographs found in *Bones of Contention*.
[130] *The Bone Peddlers*, pp. 7, 28–29; *Darwin on Trial*, pp. 83–85.
[131] *The Bone Peddlers*, pp. 6–7.

What is the clearest indication of humanity as described in Genesis? As Hugh Ross explains, the characteristic unique to Adam was his spiritual capacity.[132] Indeed, Adam had received the divine rational image, which enabled him to communicate and fellowship with his Creator. Thus he had the capacity for spiritual worship. This ability was present even after the Fall as men continued to worship either the true Creator or the false pagan deities. Evidence for the presence of spiritual capacities in proposed human ancestors may include the use of developed language or activities that indicate an acquaintance with abstract concepts. Thus, the presence of sophisticated painting or pottery at a site that contains fossils of alleged human ancestors might provide better evidence for humanity as defined in Genesis 1. (It would be *better* evidence but not *conclusive* evidence, because it would be impossible to prove that the creatures whose remains are present at a site were actually responsible for the paintings or the pottery.) Is there any evidence for such capacities in proposed human ancestors? And how long ago did they occur?

In France, recent discoveries of pottery and woven materials suggest that some of these capacities emerged in human beings approximately 25 to 30 thousand years ago.[133] In other studies, sophisticated art, religious relics, and musical instruments have been uncovered and dated from 30 to 50 thousand years ago.[134] (Some studies suggest that the ability to fashion advanced tools and relics may have emerged in human ancestors as early as 90 thousand years ago.[135, 136] However, these particular studies used controversial and experimental techniques for dating the samples.)

---

[132] Hugh Ross, "Art and Fabric Shed New Light on Human History," *Facts and Faith*, Volume 9, Number 3, pp. 1–2, 1995.

[133] Bruce Bower, "Stone Age Fabric Leaves Swatch Marks," *Science News 147:* 276, 1995.

[134] Bruce Bower, "When the Human Spirit Soared," *Science News 130:* 378–379, 1986.

[135] Brooks A. S., Helgren D. M., Cramer J. S. *et al*, "Dating and Context of Three Middle Stone Age Sites with Bone Points in the Upper Semliki Valley, Zaire," *Science 268:* 548–553, 1995.

[136] Yellen J. E., Brooks A. S., Cornelissen E. *et al*, "A Middle Stone Age Worked Bone Industry from Katanda, Upper Semliki Valley, Zaire," *Science 268:* 553–556, 1995.

Overall, the date generally accepted by scientists for the development of sophisticated, modern, and human behavior is 35 to 40 thousand years ago.[137] Moreover, the fossil remains found in these studies actually are classified as *Homo sapiens* and not as one of the alleged human ancestors. These archaeological findings have been corroborated by recent studies in molecular biology that suggest a common ancestry for human Y chromosomes occurred approximately 37 to 49 thousand years ago.[138,139] (Similar molecular studies may wind up ruling out the highly touted *Homo erectus* as one of the ancestors of *Homo sapiens*.[140])

Now of course all of these studies depend on scientific theories of dating that cannot be proven true; but, taken together, they suggest that sophisticated human behavior, of the kind consistent with the first pair of humans described in the Bible, appeared within a time frame that is consistent with that described in the Bible. How is this possible in light of Bishop Ussher's dating of Adam's creation at 4004 B.C.? First, we need to understand how Ussher obtained this date. Ussher back-calculated from the genealogies provided in the Bible. However, the Bible never claims that the genealogies are complete. For example, Matthew 1:8 states that Joram fathered Uzziah, but 1 Chronicles 3:11–12 documents three generations between Joram and Uzziah (Azariah). Perhaps the genealogies were never intended to describe only direct father-to-son relationships. Indeed, the Hebrew word for father (*ab*) can also mean grandfather, forefather, or ancestor.[141] For example, when God spoke to Jacob (the grandson of Abraham), he said, "I am the Lord, the God of your father Abraham and the God of Isaac; the land on which you lie, I will give it to you and to your

---

[137] A. Gibbons, "Old Dates for Modern Behavior," *Science* 268: 495–496, 1995.
[138] Whitfield L. S., Sulston J. E., and Goodfellow P. N., "Sequence Variation of the Human Y Chromosome," *Nature* 378: 379–380, 1995.
[139] Hugh Ross, "Searching for Adam," *Facts and Faith*, Volume 10, Number 1, p. 4, 1996.
[140] M. F. Hammer, "A Recent Common Ancestry for Human Y Chromosomes," *Nature* 378: 376–378, 1995.
[141] Vine, W. E., Unger, Merrill F., and William White, *Vine's Expository Dictionary of Biblical Words* (Nashville, TN: Thomas Nelson, 1985), Old Testament Section, p. 78.

descendants."[142] Here God refers to Abraham as Jacob's father when in fact Abraham was Jacob's grandfather. This shows that the word *ab* can at times mean grandfather or forefather. Moreover, as Ross points out, in Daniel 5:11, Belshazzar's mother refers to Nebuchadnezzar as Belshazzar's father, even though they were four generations apart and not even directly related.[143] Even Daniel refers to Nebuchadnezzar as Belshazzar's father (Daniel 5:18). Therefore, *ab* can mean forefather or ancestor. Because of these caveats, the date for the creation of Adam cannot be determined simply by adding the numbers given in the biblical genealogies. If the genealogies are anywhere from 10 to 80 percent complete then the date for the first *Homo sapien* (Adam) may be anywhere from 6 to 50 thousand years ago, well within the time frame suggested by the scientific evidence.

Conclusion

The conflict between science and Christianity disappears once we see that science never arrives at truth. The problems associated with scientific epistemology, not to mention the presence of naturalistic presuppositions in the mind of many scientists, should make readers wary of scientific claims to objectivity. Moreover, an examination of the scientific evidence on its own terms and merits has led us to the conclusion that science does not contradict the biblical account of creation. In fact, there is much that is consistent with the biblical description. Thus the denial of Christianity's claims to truth on the supposition that science nullifies them is without foundation.

---

[142] Genesis 28:13.

[143] Hugh Ross, "Biblical Evidence for Long Creation Days," short paper (Pasadena, CA: Reasons To Believe), p. 9. While I disagree with Ross about the six days of creation being epochs, I concur with his analysis of the recent date for human ancestors and the problems associated with genealogies.

11

BRIDGING THE CHASM

I wonder at the hardihood with which such persons undertake to tell about God. In a treatise addressed to infidels, they begin with a chapter proving the existence of God from the works of Nature . . . this only gives their readers ground for thinking that the proofs of our religion are very weak. . . . It is a remarkable fact that no canonical writer has ever used Nature to prove God.

Blaise Pascal, *Pensées*

I n part two of this book, we have considered Ayn Rand's philosophy as a comprehensive system. It was weighed in the balance, and found wanting.[1] Objectivism, which is both materialistic and empirical, cannot sustain a workable theory of knowledge. Consequently, its subsidiary theorems in ethics and politics have no logical foundation. Moreover, we encounter numerous contradictions in these practical branches of Rand's philosophy and find that she could neither justify her concept of a rational man *qua* man nor establish the principles of a limited government and the foundations for a free society.

In contrast, our brief construction of Christian theism, taking the approach of philosopher Gordon Clark, has shown that a consistent, noncontradictory philosophy may be derived from the axiom of revelation. In the tradition of Pascal, Clark never attempted to prove God's existence using the traditional arguments, for he recognized that all philosophies begin with presuppositions, and Christianity and secular philosophies have no presuppositions in common. (Other scholars, like C. S. Lewis and Francis Schaeffer, have also emphasized how these two worldviews stand completely opposite to each other in their presuppositions and, therefore, in their conclusions.[2]) Instead, what Clark accomplished in his several volumes was to show that the fundamental approaches of rationalism, empiricism, and even Kant's synthesis are all defective. They yield no truths at all, either in epistemology or morality. Nor could they give meaning to history and life. In contrast, all things become consistent when viewed from the vantage point of Christianity, that is, by accepting the axiom of revelation. Thus the God of Christianity is the *sine qua non* of all demonstration and truth. The only other option is skepticism and nihilism.

---

[1] Daniel 5:27.

[2] *Miracles*, pp. 3–11; *A Christian Manifesto*, pp. 17–30.

In the conclusion to *A Christian View of Men and Things*, Clark writes: "[I]t has been argued that Christianity is self-consistent, that it gives meaning to life and morality, and that it supports the existence of truth and the possibility of knowledge. Thus theism and atheism have been examined in considerable detail. It remains for each person to make his choice."[3] I hope that the contrast drawn between theism and atheism, Christianity and Objectivism, has been sufficiently compelling to help the reader make his choice. If not, he is encouraged to pursue the matter further by investigating the materials given in the bibliography.

In this chapter, I do not intend to go against Pascal's warning and attempt to prove God's existence from nature. But it is likely that many readers have at one time come across a discussion of the traditional proofs for God, and some have considered the apparent failure of such proofs as sufficient reason for not believing in God. Therefore, I think it would be helpful to say a few words about the utility and limitations of such arguments in order to remove any obstacles that might keep a person from considering the truth claims of Christianity.

To begin with, we should note that even if all of the traditional proofs for God's existence fail, God might still exist. In chapter 8, we saw how axiomatic systems include undecidable propositions. The existence of the God of Christianity may be true; however, the truth of that proposition may be undecidable and indemonstrable if one begins with the presuppositions of secular philosophy. Moreover, if the Christian position is true and man is a created being who can do nothing apart from his Creator, it is at least plausible that the creature can construct no argument to prove his Creator's existence unless the Creator reveals himself.[4] (In *Surprised by Joy*, C. S. Lewis points out that man's relationship to God resembles Hamlet's relationship to Shakespeare. Hamlet, within the play that bears his name, could never learn of Shakespeare's existence unless Shakespeare reveals himself. Unless Shakespeare writes a part for himself in the drama and introduces himself to Hamlet, Ham-

---

[3] *A Christian View of Men and Things*, p. 218.
[4] John 15:5.

let could never know what Shakespeare was like. Lewis explains: "The 'Shakespeare' within the play would of course be at once Shakespeare and one of Shakespeare's creatures. It would bear some analogy to the Incarnation."[5]) That is why Christianity is acknowledged as a system based on God's revelation to man and not based on man's ability to reach or prove God. Thus, if Clark's arguments are correct, the God of Christianity may not be in need of demonstration, but may in fact be the *sine qua non* presupposition of all rational demonstration.

Antitheism: The Universal Negative

It should be noted at the outset that the position of antitheism is logically indefensible. How can any person, limited in knowledge and experience, know enough to proclaim the universal negative "There is no God"? I was once naive enough to make this claim. However, such a statement presupposes omniscience and omnipotence on the part of the one making the assertion. Indeed, it is an absurd presumption, but this is precisely what I at one time claimed to know. It was also what Ayn Rand claimed to know.

During a television interview in 1979 on *Donahue*, Phil Donahue sought to clarify Rand's position with regard to her atheism.[6]

> DONAHUE: You do not accept the existence of a god. . . . Now the reason you don't is because you can't prove that such an entity or being or energy exists.
> RAND: I can't, nor can anyone else. . . . There is no proof.
> DONAHUE: Therefore you've concluded there isn't one. . . . [But] you can't prove there isn't [a god].
> RAND: You are never called upon to prove a negative. That is a law of logic.

Notice, Rand denied God's existence because, in her estimation, all of the traditional arguments fail to prove God. In addition,

---

[5] *Surprised by Joy*, p. 227.
[6] *Donahue*, May 1979; tape on file with author.

she denied that a proof could ever be produced. Unfortunately, if any violation of the laws of logic has taken place, it is Ayn Rand who has violated them. The statements she made are in the form of a universal negative, and if a person wishes to assert a universal negative, he is obligated to prove it.

Let us address Rand's two statements. First, God may exist despite the failure of the traditional arguments and despite the failure of *any* future arguments to prove God. God may simply choose not to be found or not to allow his existence to be proven. Second, a valid proof for God's existence may *someday* be produced. How does Rand know it could never be produced? Thus we see that a universal negative does not become true merely because there is insufficient evidence for the positive assertion. Indeed, Donahue was perceptive enough to ask Rand, "Why don't you say 'I don't know' rather than 'I'm sure there isn't'?"[7] It is perfectly acceptable to say "I don't want to believe in the Christian God" or "I don't know"; it is quite another matter to assert the universal negative "There is no God."

Rand replied: "Because you can't accept even as a hypothesis something for which there is no evidence. . . . It has to be either reason or faith. I am against God for the reason that I don't want to destroy reason. . . . [Faith] gives men permission to function irrationally." However, it is interesting that Rand herself accepted the validity of the senses without evidence or proof.[8] Moreover, we have seen how accepting the hypothesis of Christian theism solves many of the problems in philosophy that Objectivism cannot. There seems to be sufficient reason for at least considering the hypothesis. Moreover, sufficient evidence has been produced for the rationality of biblical Christianity based on Reformational principles.[9] And Kierkegaard's irrationalism is a poor example of Christianity. But after all of these superficial objections have been answered, we are still left with Rand's bold assertion of a universal negative. And she is obligated to either prove the impossibility of God's existence

---

[7] *Donahue*, May 1979; tape on file with author.
[8] See chapter 8 on reason and reality.
[9] See chapter 8 on reason and reality.

or temper her statement by saying "I don't believe there is a God," instead of "There is no God." Furthermore, Rand may not believe in the God of Christianity, but it is impossible for her or anyone else to believe in no god. As John Robbins points out in *Without a Prayer*, even Rand believed in the twin gods of indestructible matter and autonomous individual reason.[10]

Along these lines of discussion, it is noteworthy that one of the popular expositors of atheism in Libertarian and Objectivist circles, George Smith, has advocated a softer version of atheism. His writings influenced my early views on the subject. In *Atheism: The Case against God*, Smith claims that atheism is simply the absence of belief in a god:

> *Atheism, in its basic form, is not a belief: it is the absence of belief.* An atheist is not primarily a person who *believes* that a god does *not* exist; rather, he does *not believe* in the existence of a god.[11]

> When the atheist is seen as a person who lacks belief in a god, it becomes clear that he is not obligated to "prove" anything. The atheist *qua* atheist does not believe anything requiring demonstration; the designation of "atheist" tells us, not what he believes to be true, but what he does *not* believe to be true. If others wish for him to accept the existence of a god, it is their responsibility to argue for the truth of theism—but the atheist is not similarly required to argue for the truth of atheism.[12]

Smith further subdivides atheists into two camps. An *implicit* atheist is one who simply lacks belief in a god (he is the person described in the paragraph quoted above), while an *explicit* atheist is one who *rejects* belief in a god. The explicit atheist is also known as an *antitheist*.[13] Such a person will often specifically state "God does not exist" or "There is no God." He may even come up with reasons why the existence of God is impossible. Therefore, we may

---

[10] *Without a Prayer*, pp. 108–143; see also chapter 8 on reason and reality.
[11] *Atheism: The Case against God*, p. 7.
[12] *Atheism: The Case against God*, p. 16.
[13] *Atheism: The Case against God*, p. 17.

regard both Ayn Rand and George Smith as antitheists. Smith seems to be saying that all atheists are implicit atheists first, and some are secondarily antitheists. And because an atheist is always an implicit atheist first—and as an implicit atheist he does not assert the universal negative "There is no God"—he has thereby relieved himself of the burden of having to prove that God does not exist. The onus, Smith feels, is instead on the theist to produce positive evidence for God. He sees atheism as the default alternative to theism. If theism lacks evidence or proof, then atheism must be true.

Moreover, Smith goes on to define what atheism is *not*. "*From the mere fact that a person is an atheist, one cannot infer that this person subscribes to any particular positive beliefs.*"[14] However, as Ravi Zacharias points out, this softer version of atheism, held by the likes of Smith and Bertrand Russell, which claims to hold no particular positive beliefs, is a misnomer.[15] In *Can Man Live without God?* Zacharias explains: "The word *atheism* comes from the Greek, which has two words conjoined. The *alpha* is the negative, and *theos* means 'God.' The atheistic position, whether you like it or not, posits the negation of God." Positing the negation of God is a positive belief. While Smith is correct to point out that not all atheists believe in the same philosophy, he is incorrect in supposing that an atheist, even an implicit atheist, advocates nothing in particular and that positing the negation of God does not imply certain philosophical attitudes or beliefs. Even an implicit atheist who does not specifically say "There is no God" must act as if there is no God and thereby act implicitly according to another worldview.

Indeed, in *The New Atheism and the Erosion of Freedom*, Robert Morey indicates some of the other problems associated with Smith's soft version of atheism.[16] First, if atheism is simply the absence of belief in God, how could Smith possibly make a case against God, as the subtitle of his book implies? To make a case against God, one would have to make some positive assertions and produce a

---

[14] *Atheism: The Case against God*, p. 21.
[15] *Can Man Live without God?* pp. 186–187.
[16] *The New Atheism and the Erosion of Freedom*, pp. 47–48.

set of valid arguments against God within some philosophical framework. Yet Smith claims to make no positive assertions. Second, Morey shows that Smith does indeed make positive assertions. His absence of belief in the Omnipotent Creator of Christianity has simply been replaced by other beliefs. The rejection of revealed truth, as we have seen, has to be replaced by some variety of secular epistemology. The rejection of man as a creature made in the image of God has to be replaced by some theory of naturalistic and mechanistic evolution. The rejection of biblical ethics has to be replaced by some other system of moral absolutes or else be reduced to moral relativism and nihilism. Smith, in fact, advocates an epistemological and ethical theory that he inherited from Objectivism.[17] And those theories have already been subjected to critical analysis in other parts of this book. Consequently, we see that atheism cannot mean the mere absence of theistic belief. It includes the assertion of positive beliefs. However, those assertions have to be justified. They are not true by default.

Nevertheless, the traditional arguments probably do fall short of proving God's existence. However, as we noted, their failure does not disprove God's reality. Moreover, as we shall see, even if God's existence could be proved, the mere statement "God exists" would not help us understand God very much. Is this God the Impersonal Being of pantheism, the Unmoved Mover of Aristotle, or the Omnipotent Creator of Christianity? As Gordon Clark and Francis Schaeffer have each pointed out, believing *what God is* is more important than believing *that God is*. For even if we could demonstrate the omnipotence and omniscience of God from the traditional proofs, it is doubtful that we could demonstrate the truth of the Trinity or the substitutionary death of Christ apart from accepting revelation. And those truths are essential to Christianity.

For me, the traditional arguments for God did not constitute a proof for God. However, they were cumulative in their influence in opening my mind to the possibility of God until such a time as I saw that all of life and philosophy made more sense with the God

---

[17] *Atheism: The Case against God*, pp. 130–147, 275–326.

of Christianity than without him.[18] It was then that I accepted the message of the gospel and the love and salvation that Christ offered to me. Implicitly, what I did was to accept the axiom of revelation and what the Scriptures revealed about God and his purposes for myself and for mankind.

In the remainder of this chapter, the traditional ontological, cosmological, contingency, and teleological/design arguments will be discussed. All of the arguments will be treated briefly with the exception of the teleological/design argument, which will be considered in some detail because of the subsidiary problem of prophecy.

The Ontological Argument

The ontological proof was produced by the rationalist Anselm (A.D. 1033–1109).[19] Anselm defined God as "a being than which nothing greater can be conceived. . . ." However, if such a being existed only in our minds, it would not be the greatest thing that could be conceived, because an even greater thing, one which existed both in the mind and in reality, would then be conceivable. Now God is the greatest conceivable thing. And because his existence cannot be conceived not to exist, he must exist not only in the mind but in reality also. Consequently, Anselm was persuaded that the ontological argument proved the existence of God.

However, Immanuel Kant, in his critique of the ontological proof, denied that God could not be conceived not to exist. One could annihilate God in thought, Kant supposed, by simply refusing to think about him. If God's existence in thought is not necessary, then neither is his existence in reality necessary. (Note that God's existence in reality does not have to be a sensible one. The square root of negative one is not a sensible object, but it exists.) With reference to Kant's critique, however, we may ask: Are there conditions under which it would be impossible to annihilate God in one's thought and for God's existence to be undeniably real?

---

[18] Compare other sections of this book, especially the epilogue.

[19] *Prosologium*, chapters 2 and 3, in Walter Kaufmann (editor), *Philosophic Classics*, pp. 522–523; Gordon Clark, *Three Types of Religious Philosophy*, pp. 33–44.

What if God, as Augustine said, is truth? Jesus said, "I am the way, and the truth, and the life; . . ."[20] John described Christ as the Omnipotent Creator and Logic (*Logos*) through whom all things came into being: "In the beginning was the *Logos*, and the *Logos* was with God, and the *Logos* was God."[21] The Psalmist spoke with awe concerning the Creator, "Oh Lord, God of truth."[22] Logic and truth are real, even though they are not sensible realities that we can point to. Moreover, if God were truth and logic, and he imparted this divine rational image to man, then it would be impossible for man to annihilate God in thought. If a man thinks at all, he has to think using the laws of logic. For without logic, we could not even begin to think. As Clark writes, "[God] exists so truly that he cannot even be conceived not to exist."[23]

Anselm's ontological argument may not be convincing to everyone. Perhaps one may even accuse Anselm and Augustine of surreptitiously characterizing God as truth and logic; however, those descriptions of God were already present in the revelation of the Scriptures long before these theologians attempted to systematize them. What this discussion shows is that the Christian conception of God as truth and logic is at least consistent with the ontological argument. Under these conditions, God cannot be annihilated in thought; therefore, he exists. This provides at least some breathing room for considering the God of Christianity.

The Cosmological Argument

The cosmological argument, also known as the first-cause argument, was summarized most ably by Thomas Aquinas (A.D. 1225–1274). In *Summa Theologica*, he attempts to prove the existence of God in five ways. One of those ways is the argument from motion. However, Aquinas's argument has several defects that have been

---

[20] John 14:6.

[21] John 1:1.

[22] Psalm 31:5.

[23] *Three Types of Religious Philosophy*, p. 39. Of course, if a person chooses not to think using the laws of logic, then he speaks irrationally and his arguments have no validity.

extensively elaborated by believers and nonbelievers. One of those defects is the occurrence of circular reasoning. Consider his argument for God as an Aristotelian type of prime mover. Every object that is moved has to be moved by another, says Aquinas. "If that by which it is moved be itself moved, then this also must needs be moved by another, and that by another again. But this cannot go on to infinity, *because then there would be no first mover*, . . . Therefore it is necessary to arrive at a first mover, moved by no other; and this everyone understands to be God" (emphasis added).[24] Does not this passage assume that there must be a first mover? Hence, the reasoning is circular.

However, Smith objects to the first-cause argument on other grounds. To him, the idea of causality only makes sense in the context of physical existence. Moreover, it makes no sense to him to posit an "unknowable" being (God) as the cause of the material universe. "A causal primary, on the other hand, is the metaphysical basis for the concept of causality. It does not require explanation, because it makes explanation possible; it is the basis of all causal interactions. Existence, the causal primary, is presupposed by all causal processes—all motion and change—and therefore must be regarded as existing eternally."[25]

Several things may be said with regard to Smith's objection. First, Smith, an empiricist and Objectivist, at least in his metaphysics and epistemology, simply begs the question as to what existence is. As we saw in chapter 8, the axiom "existence exists" is essentially meaningless. Moreover, it is impossible to argue that the existence of the physical universe rules out the existence of an immaterial reality like God. Therefore, if "existence" includes the existence of the physical universe as well as the existence of an immaterial God, then God causing the physical universe to exist does make sense, because both God and the physical universe are part of "existence." Advocates of the cosmological argument do in fact assert the existence of God and claim that an

[24] *Summa Theologica*, Part One, Question Two, Third Article, "Whether God Exists?" in *Philosophic Classics*, p. 527.
[25] *Atheism: The Case against God*, p. 241.

existing God is the "causal primary" who causes other entities to exist.[26] Second, contrary to Smith's assertion that theists posit an "unknowable being" as the cause of the universe, Christianity affirms that God is knowable through the revelation of the Scriptures.[27]

Smith, following in Nathaniel Branden's footsteps, also suggests that since theists require a causal explanation for the universe and for existence as a whole, atheists ought to ask Christians for a causal explanation of God.[28] A couple of things may be said in response to Smith's suggestion. First, nothing in the definition of the physical universe requires its eternal existence, whereas the Scriptures from which we derive our knowledge of God defines God as eternally existing. Second, from a scientific perspective, the entire space-time continuum does appear to have had a beginning. We saw this in the last chapter. The physical universe is not eternal, and time itself had a beginning. Thus we have evidence that suggests the physical universe requires an explanation, but we have no evidence that an immaterial God requires a cause.

In conclusion, our consideration of the cosmological argument has emphasized the importance of presuppositions and axioms. Atheists like Rand, Branden, and Smith assume that material existence is all there is, and requires no explanation. And, of course, on this presupposition there is no God. But, as we have seen, then there is no thought or truth either.[29] Atheists posit a fundamental view of the universe that is *impersonal*. And the impersonal, as Francis Schaeffer says, can never offer an explanation for the *personal*.[30] Moreover, the presupposition that the physical universe

---

[26] See Robbins's excellent critique of Nathaniel Branden on this point in *Without a Prayer*, pp. 115–118.

[27] *Atheism: The Case against God*, p. 238.

[28] Nathaniel Branden, "Intellectual Ammunition Department," *The Objectivist Newsletter*, May 1962, p. 19; *Atheism: The Case against God*, p. 239.

[29] See chapter 8 on reason and reality.

[30] *Francis A. Schaeffer Trilogy*, Book Three: *He Is There and He Is Not Silent*, p. 283.

has always existed is itself doubtful. Therefore, there is reason to consider the Christian alternative.

The Contingency Argument

The contingency argument shares many of the characteristics of the cosmological argument. Its advocates argue from the *possible* nonexistence of the natural universe to the existence of a cause. As the Roman Catholic theologian Frederick Copleston stated in his celebrated debate with Bertrand Russell: "Why something rather than nothing, that is the question."

Russell replied, "[T]he concept of cause is not applicable to the total [universe]," and, therefore, "the universe is just there, and that's all."[31] Smith shares Russell's viewpoint and points out that the question asked by Copleston seems to be "loaded with theistic presuppositions. . . ." Again, Smith argues that the idea of *cause* or *explanation* makes no sense outside the context of existence. (However, empiricism has its own presuppositions, and it also faces difficulties when it attempts to explain causality within the context of existence.[32])

The ideas of contingency and necessity were introduced by Aristotle and championed by Aquinas. The essential question is: Does the universe contain *contingent* beings (entities which depend on other entities for their continued existence) that can only be explained by the existence of a *necessary* being (an entity whose existence requires no explanation)? Smith thinks that the contingency argument represents an artificial dichotomy between necessary and contingent existence. His own view is that "everything exists necessarily."[33] Advocates of the opposing view, Norman

---

[31] Bertrand Russell and F. C. Copleston, "A Debate on the Existence of God," *The Existence of God*, edited by John Hick (New York: Macmillan, 1964), p. 175 as quoted in *Atheism: The Case against God*, p. 249.

[32] Gordon Clark has pointed out that empiricism can never demonstrate causality. At best, it can demonstrate that one event follows another (as Hume also pointed out), but it can never guarantee that the event X will produce the event Y. Only God can guarantee the occurrence of X as well as Y (*Lord God of Truth*, pp. 23–27).

[33] *Atheism: The Case against God*, p. 251.

Geisler[34] and Ravi Zacharias[35] present a ten-step argument briefly summarized here.

1. Some things undeniably exist.
2. My nonexistence is possible.
3. Whatever has the possibility not to exist is currently caused to exist by another.
4. There cannot be an infinite regress of current causes of existence.
5. Therefore, a first uncaused cause of my current existence exists.
6. This uncaused cause must be infinite, unchanging, all-powerful, all-knowing, and all-perfect.
7. This infinitely perfect Being is appropriately called "God."
8. Therefore, God exists.
9. This God who exists is identical to the God described in the Christian Scriptures.
10. Therefore, the God described in the Bible exists.

The reader may wish to consider the details of this argument as found in Norman Geisler's *Christian Apologetics*. However, the argument is quite intricate and includes difficult and controversial ideas that we alluded to earlier. These include ideas of contingency (step 3), infinite regress (step 4), uncaused cause (step 5), and necessary characteristics of the uncaused cause (step 6). The reader will have to see if this intricate Aristotelian-Aquinas styled proof satisfies him.

I, for one, do not believe this proof is valid. Moreover, it seems to me, even if the transition from steps 1 through 8 of this particular contingency argument were otherwise correct, it would be difficult to move from step 8 to steps 9 and 10. For even if such a God as described in steps 1 through 8 exists, how could we argue that he was identical to the God described in the Scriptures? The God

[34] Norman L. Geisler, *Christian Apologetics* (Grand Rapids, MI: Baker, 1976), pp. 238–250.
[35] *Can Man Live without God?* pp. 190–191.

described in the Bible has many characteristics not attributed to him in the contingency argument. Again, examples include the Trinity and the Incarnation. Therefore, the God of the Bible and the God derived from the contingency proof are not identical. Indeed, how can we know anything about the God in the Bible apart from believing the claims of the Bible? If we do not appeal to the truth of the Bible, to the axiom of revelation, we have recourse only to what we think we can prove about God via the traditional arguments. Nevertheless, the contingency argument, like the cosmological argument, serves one important purpose, and that is to demonstrate the importance of presuppositions. The contingency of the universe is as valid a presupposition as the eternity of the universe. In fact, the contingency of the universe may be a more reasonable presupposition given the current scientific support for the big bang theory. However, the contingency of the universe raises questions about the possibility of a sustaining Creator of the universe, and that again makes room for considering the claims of Christianity.

The Design or Teleological Argument

Because of his watchmaker argument, William Paley (A.D. 1743–1805) is perhaps the most famous advocate of the argument from design. In *Natural Theology*, Paley asks us to imagine finding a watch on a pristine stretch of land.[36] Upon inspection of the watch, we see that it includes dials, springs, cogwheels, etc. Moreover, this mechanism appears to have a purpose. Surely, the presence of mechanism and purpose in the watch implies design and, therefore, a designer. Therefore, we conclude that the watch is a manmade object. But if a simple watch impresses us with the need for a designer, how much more should the evidence of complexity and contrivance in nature impress us with the need for a Grand Designer, God.

David Hume anticipated Paley's design argument by some thirty years. In one of his examples against the design argument, Hume

---

[36] William Paley, *Natural Theology: Selections*, edited by Frederick Ferré (Indianapolis, IN: Bobbs-Merrill, 1963), pp. 3–4 as quoted in William Lane Craig, *Reasonable Faith* (Wheaton, IL: Crossway Books, 1990), pp. 86–87.

asks how one can argue from the existence of both good and evil in the world to the existence of an afterlife where justice will ultimately be rectified. The hypothetical theist replies with an analogy. The universe is a half-finished house, and God is a builder of houses. A half-finished house implies that there is a builder who will return to complete what he has begun. Therefore, God will ultimately right the wrongs of this world. This analogy did not satisfy Hume. He argues that experience may help provide a connection between houses that are built and the builders who built them, but experience cannot tell us that a half-finished house will in fact be completed in the future. Indeed, we have seen builders who later returned to complete half-finished houses, but we have also seen half-finished houses deserted and left half built. Moreover, we have not experienced half-finished universes initiated by God, nor have we seen half-finished universes that God later returned to complete. Using this and other examples, Hume shows that the design argument is incomplete and inconclusive.[37]

Using the example of Paley's watch, Smith also argues that we recognize a watch as an object of human design only because we are already familiar with objects that have been designed by men.[38] It is only this familiarity that allows us to identify the watch, and not the rock lying next to it, as a work of human contrivance. (Indeed, Paley subverts his own design argument by contrasting the watch with the rock. The rock, he acknowledges, is a natural object that could have lain there forever. Logically then, Paley could not later claim that he saw in the rock and in the natural universe some evidence of design that implied a Designer.) Moreover, let us suppose that some advanced alien civilization has the ability to manufacture items that are indistinguishable from things we call natural objects, like trees and flowers. However, because we are unfamiliar with the industrial activities of this alien civilization and have not seen them manufacturing trees and flowers, we do not recognize evidence of de-

---

[37] *Enquiries Concerning Human Understanding and Concerning the Principles of Morals*, Section XI, pp. 132–148; Gordon Clark, *Thales to Dewey*, pp. 389–391.
[38] *Atheism: The Case against God*, pp. 266–269.

sign when we encounter trees and flowers. Therefore, it would be difficult to argue for the existence of the alien civilization on the basis of intricacies we observe in trees and flowers. Similarly, since we are unfamiliar with God's design in nature and have never seen him manufacturing trees and flowers, we cannot infer God's existence from the complexities we observe in nature. Smith concludes: "[O]ne must know that a god exists before one can say that nature exhibits design."[39]

Once again, the conflict arises from irreconcilable presuppositions. Both sides argue in a circle. For the theist who uses the design argument, his reasoning goes something like this:

PREMISE: There is a God, a Grand Designer.
CONCLUSION: Therefore, the intricacies exhibited in nature are the result of God's design.
PREMISE: Nature exhibits intricacies. Intricacies imply design by a Designer.
CONCLUSION: Therefore, there is a God, a Grand Designer.

However, the atheist also has presuppositions. His reasoning is as follows:

PREMISE: There is no God.
CONCLUSION: Therefore, nature may be complex but does not exhibit design.
PREMISE: Nature exhibits complexity but does not exhibit design.
CONCLUSION: Therefore, there is no designer and no God.

The two sides have reached an impasse.

To an atheist who holds firmly to this position, even the most compelling evidences for the *anthropic principle*—the growing recognition among scientists that the universe exhibits an incredible fine-tuning of conditions that makes the existence of intelligent life on earth possible and which may be most plausibly explained

---

[39] *Atheism: The Case against God*, p. 267.

by the existence of a personal Creator—means nothing.[40,41] Nor is it likely that the immense improbability of life evolving by chance, as we saw in the last chapter, will persuade him.[42] As C. S. Lewis

---

[40] Richard Swinburne, "Argument from the Fine-Tuning of the Universe," *Physical Cosmology and Philosophy*, edited by John Leslie (New York: Macmillan, 1991), p. 165 as cited in Hugh Ross, *The Creator and the Cosmos*, pp. 125–126.

[41] William Lane Craig, "Barrow and Tipler on the Anthropic Principle versus Divine Design," *British Journal of Philosophy and Science* 38: 392, 1988 as quoted in *The Creator and the Cosmos*, pp. 125–126.

[42] Smith argues against using probabilities in considering design (*Atheism: The Case against God*, pp. 270–271). Just because the probabilities for an event are extremely low, that does not make it impossible. In fact, if the probability for an event occurring in history is defined as the ratio of that one event to the sum total of all events in history, then the probability of any particular event occurring in history is infinitesimal. Consequently, Smith supposes that arguments against evolution, which utilize probability calculations, are faulty. Smith also uses an example given by W. T. Stace (*Religion and the Modern Mind* [Philadelphia, PA: J.B. Lippincott, 1952], p. 86 as quoted in *Atheism*, p. 271). A tile is blown off a roof and kills a man. The chances of that particular event occurring, out of all the events that occur in history, is infinitesimal, but it happened. Similarly, evolution, however small its probability may be, happened. But Smith's argument is fallacious. First of all, Smith assumes that evolution is an event that has occurred in history. How does he know this? We have seen people struck and killed by flying roof tiles, but no one has ever seen a single biologically active molecule (such as a protein) spontaneously self-assemble from the prebiotic soup. No one has ever been able to produce a single biologically active molecule under the primordial conditions hypothesized by scientists. And no one has ever seen one species evolve naturally from another species. Moreover, scientists calculate the probability for the evolution of life on the basis of theoretical considerations (see chapter 10, section on prebiotic soup and probabilities). They do not calculate it on the basis of event probabilities in history. Moreover, the roof tile example is not entirely analogous to evolution. Of course the probability of a *particular* roof tile striking and killing a *particular* man is infinitesimal, just as the probability of any event occurring in history is infinitesimal. But, notice, we do not calculate the actuarial probabilities of a man being killed by a flying roof tile in this manner. The calculations are performed in the following manner. We estimate the failure rate of roof tiles. We estimate the probability of a flying roof tile hitting a man. We estimate the probability of a man dying after being struck by a flying object. Using all of these estimates, we can then calculate the lifetime probability of a man being killed by a flying roof tile. Even if this latter probability were extremely remote, say, 1 in 100 trillion (10^{14}), the probability for the spontaneous genera-

observes, "If we hold a philosophy which excludes the supernatural, this is what we always shall say."[43]

The two sides have reached an impasse. Is there any way we can possibly bridge the gap? Two thoughts come to mind. First, I would suggest that the nonbeliever take God, the theistic presupposition, as a hypothetical starting point. As we saw earlier, Clark has shown that consistency is maintained in philosophy when all things are viewed from the perspective and hypothesis of Christian theism. Now we can do the same thing by entertaining the hypothesis of God when considering design. The nonbeliever is not asked to accept the design argument as proof for God. However, he is asked to consider the implications of belief in God with regard to all of the philosophical issues we have discussed in this book and also with regard to the issue of design. Is it more likely that we came into being without design or with design? That is a question each person will have to answer for himself.

The second issue has to do with an objection to Paley's argument that we alluded to earlier. We saw design in Paley's watch because we have had some experience with men and the objects that they contrive. However, we have not experienced this kind of connection between an alien civilization and the natural objects—trees and flowers—that they contrive. Nor have we experienced this kind of connection between God and the universe that he created.

However, we would recognize the *possibility* of an alien civilization manufacturing trees and flowers *if* we had some book or manual that informed us of their activities. We would then be familiar with that possibility and be able to consider the hypothesis, even if we did not immediately believe it. (Indeed, knowledge of man's ability to make things also need not occur through direct observation; it can be learned through books.) The analogy to the

---

tion of a bacterium is vastly more improbable (1 in $10^{100,000,000,000}$). That is why scientists regard spontaneous generation and evolution as impossible.
[43] *Miracles*, p. 3.

Bible is striking. We have not personally observed God creating the universe, but suppose we look upon the Bible as a possible source of familiarity and experience with God and his creative works. Even if we do not immediately accept the Bible as true, the information contained therein recommends that we consider the hypothesis of the Christian God as Creator.

Prophecy as Design

As we think about nature and the question of design, we should also recognize that the Bible itself may be considered a part of nature and evidence for design. Let us accept *arguendo* that man is the product of mindless evolution. It follows then that anything created by man is ultimately a product of nature. That includes the Bible. What if the Bible, the product of creatures of mindless evolution, exhibits design? However, the design it exhibits is not merely design in the sense of great literature or some kind of coding and regularity as exhibited by the DNA in our cells. The Bible also exhibits design in terms of its prophetic predictions. But how can a product of mindless evolution predict the future? This is a difficult question to answer. An astronomy textbook, also a product of man and nature, may help us predict the next eclipse on the basis of previous observations, and *Atlas Shrugged* may, in a very general way, predict a blackout along the eastern seaboard as a sign of the imminent collapse of an increasingly mixed economy.[44] But neither book has predicted specific events in history regarding specific persons at specific times and places like the Bible. Can such evidence for design be dismissed as mere complexities in nature? Or, do they suggest the existence of a supernatural agency directing the course of human history?

Regarding predictive prophecies, atheists like Smith have said, "[M]any of these attempts at prophecy are of such an obscure nature that any of a variety of events could be interpreted as fulfillment."[45] Moreover, he asserts that "many alleged prophecies

---

[44] "Is Atlas Shrugging?" *Capitalism: The Unknown Ideal*, p. 166.
[45] *Atheism: The Case against God*, p. 207.

(especially those which are predicted and fulfilled in the same Old Testament book) were manufactured after the fact in question." For example, Moses, the author of Genesis, records a prophecy given to Abraham by God which states that the Hebrew nation would be enslaved by the Egyptians for four hundred years and afterward be delivered from that yoke of bondage.[46] However, Moses also describes the fulfillment of the prophecy in Exodus, another book that he authored. Since Moses wrote both the prophecy and its fulfillment, it is suggested that his testimony is unreliable. Perhaps Moses was eager to fulfill the prophecy and thus verify his own claims about God. As another example, Matthew reports that the prophecy of the virgin birth of the Messiah (Savior) was fulfilled in Mary and the Christ child, Jesus. But aside from accepting Matthew's truthful testimony and Mary's honesty and integrity, who today could verify that Mary was actually a virgin? Such questions are valid ones indeed, and they deserve a response.

First, even though some prophecies are obscure, many others are easily understood. Smith has simply picked some of the more obscure ones. Or, as we shall soon see, he has chosen not to pursue their implications more carefully. Second, fulfillment of a prophecy within the books written by a single prophet does not prove the prophecy false unless one asserts the impossibility of a prophet speaking the truth of God. The same consideration applies to prophecies predicted by one biblical author and verified by another biblical author. Unless one denies the possibility of God speaking the prediction to one author and fulfilling the prophecy in the presence of another author, such prophecies are not inherently impossible. However, such a claim on the part of the skeptic reveals his own naturalistic biases against the possibility of prophecy and ignores all the reasons a Hebrew prophet would have for speaking truthfully, not the least of which was the death penalty that was imposed on anyone who prophesied falsely.[47] Thus, Moses' prophetic predictions are possible; however, it will be difficult to prove them conclusively from a nontheistic starting point. But as a matter

[46] Genesis 15:13–14.
[47] Deuteronomy 18:20–22.

of principle, we do not attempt to prove the Bible or its prophecies by historical verification. (Those who wish to consider the integrity, reliability, and historical accuracy of the biblical documents may consult the references listed in the footnote.[48]) We accept the axiom of revelation (that God has spoken truthfully in the Bible) first, and all of the prophecies contained therein follow by deductive inference. Nevertheless, it will be helpful to consider a few

---

[48] An excellent starting place for investigating the historical reliability of the Bible is the book *Evidence That Demands a Verdict* by Josh McDowell. See Volume I, pp. 39–78. It is commonly supposed that the Scriptures are unreliable because we simply do not know what was originally written. It is presumed that transmission errors have corrupted the copies we have of the original documents. On the contrary, the Scriptures are the best-attested writings of antiquity. For example, the time span between the writing of the Scriptures and the first extant copy is a mere twenty-five years for the New Testament. Homer's *Iliad*, by comparison, spans 500 years between the original and the extant copy. There are also more copies of the New Testament (24,000) than any other writing of antiquity. The *Iliad* runs a distant second with only 643 copies. In addition, only forty lines of the New Testament are questioned, whereas 764 lines of the *Iliad* are in dispute. None of the disputed passages in the New Testament have a bearing on any major doctrine. The Old Testament was transcribed with extreme care. Transcription was not allowed to be performed from memory. Other safeguards were built into the process to prevent transcription errors. For example, the number of times that each letter of the alphabet appears in each book was ascertained prior to transcription. If there was a discrepancy between the number of occurrences of each letter in the alphabet between the copy and the original, the copy was destroyed and the transcription process begun anew. Consider how reliable this process was. A comparison of the Isaiah Scroll from the Dead Sea Scrolls (c. 125 B.C.) with the Isaiah text from the earliest extant copy of the Hebrew Bible (c. A.D. 900) shows that the Isaiah Scroll is "identical with our standard Hebrew Bible in more than 95 percent of the text. The 5 percent of variation consisted chiefly of obvious slips of the pen and variations in spelling" (Gleason Archer, *A Survey of Old Testament Introduction* [Chicago, IL: Moody Press, 1964], p. 19). A thousand years' worth of transcription resulted in no significant alteration of the Bible. As for internal consistency and extrabiblical evidence for the historical events described in both the New and the Old Testament, the reader will have to investigate further. Accuracy in these matters do not prove God, but they do remove doubts about the reliability of the Bible. By the standards of secular archaeologists and historians, the Bible is the most reliable document of antiquity. See also F. F. Bruce, *The New Testament Documents: Are They Reliable?* (Grand Rapids, MI: William B. Eerdmans, 1990).

prophecies that can be analyzed historically. Perhaps the historical accuracy of the biblical predictions may provide sufficient evidence of design for the skeptic to consider the truth claims of Christianity.

First, we need to take a slight detour and address some misleading criticisms of biblical prophecies. Examples of such misrepresentations may be found in *Atheism: The Case against God* by George Smith and in *The Selfish Gene* by Richard Dawkins. As a first example, both of these authors attempt to discredit the prophecy of the virgin birth by citing internal contradictions. The prophet Isaiah had foretold the miraculous birth of Jesus seven hundred years before it came to pass: "Behold a virgin will be with child and bear a son, and she will call His name Immanuel" (Isa. 7:14). However, Dawkins alleges that the Hebrew word *almah* used in Isaiah's prophecy "undisputedly means 'young woman,' with no implication of virginity."[49] Isaiah, both Smith and Dawkins argue, would have used *bethulah* if he had intended the word to mean "virgin."[50] Clearly then, the New Testament writer Matthew misinterpreted the Hebrew word for "young woman" and mistranslated it as "virgin," or *parthenos*, in the Greek. Or, perhaps Matthew blindly followed the Septuagint (the pre-Christian Greek translation of the Old Testament), which allegedly made the same mistake in translating *almah* as *parthenos*. Moreover, Dawkins claims, "It is widely accepted among Christian scholars that the story of the virgin birth of Jesus was a late interpolation, put in presumably by Greek-speaking disciples in order that the (mistranslated) prophecy should be seen to be fulfilled."[51]

Unfortunately Dawkins is mistaken, and his scholarship is sorely lacking. First, had he bothered to examine a Hebrew lexicon—Dawkins cites no scholarly source to substantiate his definitions of *almah* and *bethulah,* while Smith cites the commentary portion of the *Interpreter's Bible,* which is not as conclusive as he would like us to believe—he would have seen that *almah* can in-

[49] *The Selfish Gene*, p. 270.
[50] *Atheism: The Case against God*, pp. 207–208.
[51] *The Selfish Gene*, p. 270.

deed mean "virgin." Let me quote from *Vine's Expository Dictionary of Biblical Words:*

> That *almah* can mean "virgin" is quite clear in Song of Sol. 6:8: "There are threescore queens, and fourscore concubines, and virgins [NASB, 'maidens'] without number." Thus all the women in the court are described. The word *almah* represents those who are eligible for marriage but are neither wives (queens) nor concubines. These "virgins" all loved the king and longed to be chosen to be with him (to be his bride), even as did the Shulam[m]ite who became his bride (1:3–4). In Gen. 24:43 the word describes Rebekah, of whom it is said in Gen. 24:16 that she was a "maiden" with whom no man had had relations. Solomon wrote that the process of wooing a woman was mysterious to him (Prov. 30:19). Certainly in that day a man ordinarily wooed one whom he considered to be a "virgin." . . . Thus *almah* appears to be used more of the concept "virgin" than that of "maiden," yet always of a woman who had not borne a child. This makes it the ideal word to be used in Isa. 7:14, since the word *bet[h]ulah* emphasizes virility more than virginity (although it is used with both emphases, too).[52]

Thus *almah* implies virginity in Isaiah's prophecy. It was a better word to use than *bethulah*, and the New Testament writer Matthew was accurate both in his translation and his understanding. (I might add that it would not be much of a sign or miracle for a woman to give birth who was not also a virgin.) Moreover, when Dawkins refers to the wide acceptance of his view among "Christian" scholars, I wonder which Christians he is referring to? He provides no names or sources to substantiate his claim. Indeed, liberal theologians have all but abandoned the truth of the Scriptures and adapted it to conform to their own unscriptural purposes. Given equal time, a list of Christian scholars who oppose Dawkins's position could easily be produced. Thus Dawkins's assertions not only fail to convict the biblical prophecy of internal contradiction, but they also betray his own biases.

---

[52] Vine, W. E., Unger, Merrill F., and William White, *Vine's Expository Dictionary of Biblical Words* (Nashville, TN: Thomas Nelson, 1985), Old Testament Section, pp. 276–277.

Smith goes on to criticize a number of other prophecies. For example, he thinks an obvious instance of mistaken prophecy can be found in Jesus' promise that the Second Coming would occur during the lifetime of his followers. Smith writes:

> For instance, Matthew 24:29–34 [Revised Standard Version] reads, in part:
>
> ²⁹Immediately after the tribulation of those days the sun will be darkened, and the moon will not give its light, and the stars will fall from heaven . . .³⁰then will appear . . . the Son of man coming on the clouds of heaven with power and great glory. . . . ³⁴Truly, I say to you, *this generation will not pass away till all these things take place.* (Emphasis added [by Smith].)[53]

I have quoted Smith verbatim. The ellipses are his, but the verse numbers were supplied by me. Smith is to be congratulated for acknowledging that he has quoted the passage "in part." Other writers have not been as obliging.[54] However, why did Smith leave out verses 31 through 33? Are these verses not important or relevant to the prophecy? Here are the missing verses:

> ³¹And He will send forth His angels with a great trumpet and they will gather together His elect from the four winds, from one end of the sky to the other. ³²Now learn the parable from the fig tree: when its branch has already become tender, and puts forth its leaves, you know that summer is near; ³³even so you too, when you see all these things, recognize that He is near, right at the door. ³⁴Truly I say to you, this generation will not pass away until all these things take place.

In the missing verses, Jesus tells the disciples the specific sign that indicates his imminent return. He had already given a number of signs at the beginning of the chapter, but the final sign he gives is the parable of the fig tree. When the fig tree puts forth its leaves, then and only then will the return of the Messiah occur

---

[53] *Atheism: The Case against God*, pp. 209–210.
[54] See chapter 5 for Nathaniel Branden's selective quotation of 1 Corinthians 7.

within the lifetime of those who observed the sign. What is the fig tree?

Here is one possible explanation. The fig tree often symbolizes the nation of Israel in the Scriptures. For example, in Joel 1:6–7, the prophet laments Israel's destruction by foreign invaders. He says, "My fig tree splinters." Could it be that Jesus knew of the impending destruction of Jerusalem in A.D. 70 and the subsequent dispersion of the Jews for nineteen hundred years? The rebirth of the nation of Israel in 1948 may very well represent the blossoming of the fig tree that Jesus spoke of, and perhaps it is *our* generation that will see his coming. However, this interpretation of the fig tree symbol is not conclusive, and it is not accepted by all. Nevertheless, it is a principle of prophecy that the various passages bearing on the same event have to be considered together. In Luke 21:24–28, Jesus prophesies that Jerusalem would be destroyed and controlled by non-Jews until the end times. Within a generation after his death and resurrection, that did in fact occur. Only after the Six-Day War in 1967, did Jerusalem revert to Israeli sovereignty. This after nearly nineteen hundred years of non-Jewish control. Again, the end could not have come in the lifetime of Jesus' disciples, because this prophecy had not yet been fulfilled. Moreover, Jesus had promised earlier, in Matthew 24:14, that he would not return until the message of the gospel had been preached to every nation on earth. (The assignment to preach to every nation is known as the Great Commission.) The word *nations* refers not only to specific countries, but to the thousands of population groups throughout the world, each with their own language or dialect. It is only in recent years that the fulfillment of the Great Commission has become an imminent possibility, as the work of Bible translation progresses at an accelerated pace. And the timing coincides with the rebirth of Israel as a nation and the return of Jerusalem to Jewish control. All of these factors actually lend credence to the prophecy that Smith sought to discredit.

Nevertheless, Smith continues with his criticism.[55] One of Jesus' other prophecies, Smith alleges, also promises the coming of his

---

[55] *Atheism: The Case against God*, p. 210.

kingdom during the lifetime of his followers. "Truly I say to you, there are some of those who are standing here who shall not taste death until they see the kingdom of God after it has come with power" (Mark 9:1). According to Smith, this prediction is obviously false because the Second Coming did not occur during the disciples' lifetime. However, notice that Jesus was not referring to the Second Coming as in Matthew 24:3–31. He simply said that the kingdom of God would come with power. What is the kingdom of God? In Mark 9:1, and in Luke 9:27 and Matthew 16:28 where the promise is repeated, this prediction made by Jesus is immediately followed by the Transfiguration event. Clearly then, the coming of God's kingdom with a visible manifestation of power referred to the Transfiguration, not the Second Coming.

Perhaps Smith thought that Jesus was promising a reinstatement of political and economic power to the nation of Israel or the ushering in of the final Messianic kingdom. This was a common misconception among the Jews of the first century, but clearly it was not what Christ meant.[56] Moreover, even if the Transfiguration were not the event that Jesus was predicting in Mark 9:1 and he meant something else by "the kingdom of God," we should realize that the kingdom of God exists on many levels, and Jesus could have been referring to one of those. Many people do not understand this. God's kingdom is established in the hearts of men as soon as they believe (John 3:3; Luke 17:21). They are immediately translated in the spiritual realm from the kingdom of darkness to the kingdom of light. God's kingdom may come with demonstrations of physical healing or deliverance from bondage (Luke 10:9). The growth of the early church after Pentecost is often cited as an example of the expansion of God's earthly kingdom (Acts 1:8). All of these events may take place well before the final coming of God's kingdom (Hebrews 10:12–13). Yet Smith conveniently ignores all of this and states quite confidently: "In conclusion, the Bible shows no traces whatsoever of supernatural influence. Quite the contrary, it is obviously the product of superstitious men who, at times, were willing to deceive if it would

---

[56] Acts 1:6–8.

further their doctrines."[57] However, we must demure from this conclusion. On the contrary, we wonder if the Bible was right after all and if the difficulties Smith encountered were merely the result of his own inadequate understanding of the Bible.

Our detour into some of the typical misrepresentations of biblical prophecies has come to an end. To summarize, examples of prophecies that are fulfilled and authenticated within the Scriptures do not necessarily imply the falsehood of such prophecies. If the prophecies are not contradictory, as the example of the virgin birth shows, one can only reject such prophecies categorically by refusing to accept the possibility of revelation. Once the axiom of revelation, that God has indeed spoken and spoken the truth through his prophets, is accepted, the fulfillment of prophecies in the Scriptures logically follows.

Nevertheless, there are many biblical prophecies whose fulfillment can be considered from a historical perspective and not merely a philosophical one. These prophecies span several hundred years of history from the time they were given to the time when they were fulfilled, and the original prophet had no way of knowing that they would be fulfilled. The Jews would not have dared to alter the Word of God as given through these prophets, and the fulfillment of these prophecies, as verified by both Christian and non-Christian sources, would have been very difficult to contrive. Josh McDowell provides an excellent summary of some of these prophecies in his book *Evidence That Demands a Verdict*.[58] All of the examples that he uses are prophecies spoken by Old Testament prophets. Although these prophecies were recorded at an earlier date in history, they are generally acknowledged to have been written down by the years 280 to 250 B.C., when the entire Old Testament was translated into the Greek. Thus, this date serves as the minimum age for all of the prophecies. The prophecies are precise both in their descriptions of events and the timing of those events. Consequently, the fulfillment of these prophecies serves as

---

[57] *Atheism: The Case against God*, pp. 210–211.
[58] *Evidence That Demands a Verdict*, Volume I, pp. 166–175, 267–323.

remarkable testimony to the reliability of the writers who claimed to speak for the God of truth.

I will mention only two such prophecies. The first is Daniel's prophecy of the 70 weeks:

> Seventy weeks have been decreed for your people and your holy city, to finish the transgression, to make an end of sin, to make atonement for iniquity, to bring in everlasting righteousness, to seal up vision and prophecy, and to anoint the most holy place.
>
> So you are to know and discern that from the issuing of a decree to restore and rebuild Jerusalem until Messiah the Prince there will be seven weeks and sixty-two weeks; it will be built again, with plaza and moat, even in times of distress.
>
> Then after the sixty-two weeks the Messiah will be cut off and have nothing, and the people of the prince who is to come will destroy the city and the sanctuary. And its end will come with a flood; even to the end there will be war; desolations are determined. (Dan. 9:24–26)

Daniel lived from approximately 605 to 538 B.C. Prior to speaking forth this prophecy about the Messiah, he had already predicted the fall of the Babylonian Empire as well as the sequential rise to power of the Medes, the Persians, and the Greeks under Alexander the Great. If we accept the prophecies as having been written during Daniel's lifetime, then his detailed predictions concerning the rise of the Greek Empire and its subsequent division into four kingdoms (336 to 323 B.C.) are simply astonishing, because it was indeed what occurred historically.[59] However, Daniel's prophecy about the coming of Messiah is even more impressive.[60] The prophecy clearly defines seventy weeks as a period of time. It is subdivided into seven weeks, sixty-two weeks, and one week. The context of Daniel 9 implies that each day of the week stands for one year. Therefore, one week of years equals seven years, and seven weeks of years equals forty-nine years, etc. Now, from the "decree to *restore and rebuild* Jerusalem until Messiah the Prince

---

[59] Daniel 8.
[60] *Evidence That Demands a Verdict*, Volume I, pp. 168–175.

there will be seven weeks and sixty-two weeks" (emphasis added). That is, approximately 483 years (69 x 7) would pass from the decree for Jerusalem's restoration to the arrival of Messiah. Now King Artaxerxes gave permission for Nehemiah to rebuild Jerusalem "in the month of Nisan, in the twentieth year of King Artaxerxes," *i.e.,* March of 444 B.C.[61] Therefore, a total of 483 years was supposed to pass between 444 B.C. and the coming of Messiah. Adjusting for the fact that the Hebrew year consists of 360 days instead of 365.25 days for our solar year, the passage of 483 Hebrew years brings us from 444 B.C. to the approximate time of Jesus' public ministry (A.D. 29–33 by our solar calendar). Moreover, Daniel predicted that the Messiah would be cut off and afterward a people would come and utterly destroy Jerusalem and the temple. Jesus was crucified, and in A.D. 70 the Romans destroyed Jerusalem and its temple.

Another prophecy that is difficult to ignore is found in Jeremiah 31:38–40. The Book of Jeremiah was written between 626 and 586 B.C., and this prophecy describes the rebuilding and expansion of Jerusalem:

> "Behold, days are coming," declares the Lord, "when the city shall be rebuilt for the Lord from the Tower of Hananel to the Corner Gate. And the measuring line shall go out farther straight ahead to the hill Gareb; then it will turn to Goah. And the whole valley of the dead bodies and of the ashes, and all the fields as far as the brook Kidron, to the corner of the Horse Gate toward the east, shall be holy to the Lord; it shall not be plucked up, or overthrown anymore forever."[62]

As McDowell points out, the specific order of Jerusalem's expansion from 1880–1935 exactly matches the nine steps predicted by Jeremiah's prophecy.[63]

These two examples of prophecy and their fulfillment suggest that there is something remarkable indeed about the Bible. How-

---

[61] Nehemiah 2:1–9.
[62] Jeremiah 31:38–40.
[63] *Evidence That Demands a Verdict,* Volume I, pp. 311–314.

ever, there is a limit to this kind of evidence. First, the nonbeliever might argue that this only verifies the particular prophecy or historical event in question, it does not verify the rest of the prophet's message about God. While the objection is valid, it would be rather difficult, or at least inconsistent, to accept only part of what a prophet claims to be divine revelation while rejecting the rest. Second, the objection might be raised that the fulfillment of these prophecies is merely a coincidence. It may even be the work of religious zealots who deliberately attempt to fulfill the prophecies themselves. For example, Jesus may have put himself in a position to be crucified just to fulfill the prophecy. However, this objection faces several difficulties. It is one thing to proclaim yourself the Messiah. It is quite another thing to have actually convinced a significant number of the early disciples much less a significant portion of the human race that you are indeed the Messiah. Moreover, there were other personalities just before the time of Jesus who claimed to be someone great, but nothing came of the movements they led.[64]

Indeed, look at just a few of the items that a person would have to fulfill in order to qualify as the Messiah. First, he would have to arouse the anger of the religious authorities by claiming equality with God. Second, he would have to perform enough signs and wonders over a sustained period of time to convince the people of his Messiahship. Third, he would have to arrange the circumstances of his life and death to fit in with all of the prophecies proclaimed by the Hebrew prophets. He would have to accomplish all of this while exhibiting great wisdom and clarity of mind. Few people would follow a person who appeared genuinely insane. Nor would authorities try so hard to discredit someone who was obviously deranged. Moreover, it is a well-known occurrence that people who feign mental illness by calling themselves Jesus Christ make a marvelous recovery when you remind them that Jesus was nailed to the cross and crucified. And Jesus could have spared himself torture and death by retracting his claims. Indeed, the very basis of the Christian faith is the death and resurrection of the Messiah. If his disciples had not actually witnessed his resurrection, then they suffered unnecessary

[64] Acts 5:34–39.

torture and death for a lie that they knew to be a lie. Finally, the claim of Jesus to be the Messiah cannot be divorced from the fact that Jerusalem and its temple were indeed destroyed some forty years after his death. After this event, no one else could legitimately claim to be Messiah. The Messiah, according to Daniel, had to arrive before the destruction of the city and the temple. Could a small band of believers, committed to the nonviolent preaching of the gospel, have succeeded in inciting the Roman Empire to destroy the city just to fulfill their prophecy? With regard to the prophecy of Jerusalem's expansion, it is obvious that the plan could have been thwarted by just a few people who insisted on building in a different direction. And the British government that supervised Palestine during 1880–1935 was probably not filled with orthodox believers bent on fulfilling ancient prophecies about Jerusalem. Thus the difficulties of fulfilling prophecies by human contrivance should be obvious. The cooperation of too many people and the confluence of too many circumstances out of man's control are required.

But alas, the person who does not want to believe that God exists will simply deny the possibility of fulfilled prophecies. They may take the position, as I once did, that prophecies do not happen because there is no God. But once again, we have a circular argument. What C. S. Lewis said bears repetition: "If we hold a philosophy which excludes the supernatural, this is what we always shall say."[65] Again, presuppositions come into play. No conclusive proof for God's existence comes from the fulfillment of prophecy. However, we have shown the failure of several critics to convict biblical prophecies of internal contradiction, and we have examined some prophecies that cannot be easily dismissed as coincidences. The interested reader is therefore encouraged to further investigate the historical accuracy and integrity of the Scriptures. It may, along with the conclusions derived from our discussion earlier in this chapter, provide further impetus for considering the Christian worldview.

---

[65] *Miracles*, p. 3.

12

EPILOGUE:

IN THE NAME OF THE BEST WITHIN US

EDDIE: The minister said last Sunday that we must always reach for the best within us. What do you suppose is the best within us?
DAGNY: I don't know.
EDDIE: We'll have to find out.

Atlas Shrugged

With the drawing of this Love and the voice of this Calling
We shall not cease from exploration
And the end of all our exploring
Will be to arrive where we started
And know the place for the first time.

T. S. Eliot, "Little Gidding"

As our journey through the fiction and philosophy of Ayn Rand draws to a close, we have learned and considered much together. Philosophy is as comprehensive as life and affects the totality of our being. That is why Rand has influenced so many. For these reasons, our exploration has been extensive. It was unavoidable, indeed, inevitable. But it has been neither a prodigal nor a futile search. There is a purpose and a conclusion. In the words of T. S. Eliot, "[T]he end of all our exploring will be to arrive where we started / And know the place for the first time."[1] Let me conclude then by sharing the story of where it first began for me.

As I leaned my head against the cabin wall, I saw rain drops dance their way across the windowpane. Turbulence made this the roughest flight that I had ever experienced, but I was dozing off to sleep from the weariness of the journey. I was returning to Baltimore from what I hoped was a successful medical school interview in Boston in December of 1987. Whatever the outcome of my application to Harvard, I had already been accepted by another prestigious institution. I told myself that I need not worry.

As I entered that netherland between consciousness and sleep, I found myself wondering about the meaning of it all. I was twenty years old. I had accomplished much. My future looked to be as challenging and fulfilling as I could have hoped for. But as the winter winds of the northeast corridor shoved the plane incessantly, I wondered what would happen if the plane crashed and I perished. All those years of dedicated study and effort wasted. What would be the meaning of it all? As a nonbeliever once said, "The

---

[1] T. S. Eliot, "Little Gidding," from *The Four Quartets* (New York: Harcourt Brace Jovanovich, 1971), p. 59.

universe won't stop and hold a funeral for you if you die tomorrow; life is what we make of it." But even that seemed too optimistic. What meaning could there be in all of our lives if ultimately we were destined to be food for the worms? With that comforting thought, I fell asleep.

As it turned out, my plane arrived safely in Baltimore, and my application to Harvard was successful. All was well, and the anxious thoughts that plagued me on the plane seemed to disappear. During my last semester at Hopkins, I was able to relax somewhat from the rigors of academic work. I found time to reacquaint myself with some of the poetry that I had learned to love in high school. One of the selections was the sonnet "Death Be Not Proud" by John Donne. As I read the final couplet—"One short sleep past, we wake eternally / And death shall be no more; Death, thou shalt die"—I realized that the words which had stirred my heart so many years ago spoke of ideas to which I had no right philosophically. Objectivism did not provide for an eternity of life after death. Death *could* be proud because ultimately it triumphed over human life. If I wanted to be consistent, I would have to do away with my childish sentiments.

During my first year in medical school, I confronted death once again in the anatomy laboratory. As the noxious fumes from the formaldehyde tickled my nostrils, I wondered about the person whose preserved corpse I was now dissecting. What is a person, really? What did we mean by this person's consciousness and personality? Where did it come from, and where will it go when life ends? From my Objectivist and atheistic point of view, I had to conclude that a person ceases to exist with death. Consciousness and the human personality dissolve into the material elements from which they arose. I asked myself, *Were all of this person's dreams and accomplishments for naught? Were his thoughts and feelings merely a transient epiphenomenon of the material universe?* From dust man came; to dust he returned. What meaning of life could possibly be derived from this perspective?

These questions became even more pressing as I began to have doubts regarding the truth of Rand's philosophy. Indeed, why even strive for the Objectivist vision of man as a heroic rational being when life was destined for a meaningless conclusion? Whatever sense of achievement I might attain in life, whatever good I might do, and whatever memory of me that may live on in the minds of others, these were illusions that ultimately dissipate into nothing. For death comes to us all. As Bertrand Russell writes so poignantly:

> Brief and powerless is Man's life; on him and all his race the slow, sure doom falls pitiless and dark. Blind to good and evil, reckless of destruction, omnipotent matter rolls on its relentless way; for Man, condemned today to lose his dearest, tomorrow himself to pass through the gate of darkness, it remains only to cherish, ere yet the blow falls, the lofty thoughts that ennoble his little day; . . . proudly defiant of the irresistible forces that tolerate, for a moment, his knowledge and his condemnation, to sustain alone, a weary but unyielding Atlas, the world that his own ideals have fashioned despite the trampling march of unconscious power.[2]

Eventually I came to realize that Objectivism had no answer to Russell's pessimism about a world without God. Atlas would not only shrug, but ultimately he would collapse in weariness and die. Nothing could prevent that. Whatever inspiration we may draw from Rand's portrayal of the heroic, the meaning of life was not to be found in her philosophy.

I was prepared to accept this dismal view of reality. I thought I might be able to maintain a heroic posture in the midst of this nihilism. But how could I remain committed to my ideals when I knew that truth was an illusion and that Objectivism was no more valid than the next philosophy? Perhaps the best course in life was one of moral relativism, pragmatism, and compromise. Was there an alternative to this futility? Into this morass of darkness and confusion came the light and clarity of Christ's message. And in that message, I found what Objectivism could not provide. Chris-

---

[2] Bertrand Russell, "A Free Man's Worship," *Why I Am Not a Christian* (New York: Simon and Schuster, 1957), pp. 115–116.

tianity gives meaning to life. It offers a basis for morality and a reason to strive for the ideal in all of life's pursuits. Truth and knowledge are possible. They are graciously revealed by a loving God who has also provided the means by which men may be reconciled to their Creator through the death of his Son. All of Christianity represented a rescue for me. One night in February of 1989, alone in my dorm room at Harvard's Vanderbilt Hall, I received Christ as my Savior.

After I became a Christian, I was reminded of the moments on that night years ago, just after I finished reading *Atlas Shrugged* for the first time. It seemed to me that a still, small voice spoke these words within me: *"One day you will find out why this is wrong."* Even though those words gave me pause, I was too caught up in the excitement of Rand's fiction to heed them. I see now that they were words of warning from a Heavenly Father who wanted to steer his child clear of danger. I cannot help but wonder how many others have also heard the warnings but decided to ignore them in their pursuit of Objectivism. How many years of hopeless existence could have been avoided if only we had paid attention? It is not too late to stand still and listen.

Coming to know Christ was the first step in a long succession of changes that took place in my life. By his grace, Christ loosed me from the chains that bound me. I have never felt more alive, because he is Life itself. I have never felt more free, because he is the Truth that set me free. I have never felt more certain, because he showed me the Way to fulfillment. And because he first loved me, I am free to show compassion, mercy, and love toward others. God fulfilled what he had promised through the prophet Ezekiel, "I will give you a new heart and put a new spirit within you; and I will remove the heart of stone from your flesh and give you a heart of flesh."[3]

Christ summoned me to a complete break with the course of my former life, and I realized I had to renounce the oath that John Galt took at the start of his battle. It was an oath that I had come to identify with. "I swear—by my life and my love of it—that I will

---

[3] Ezekiel 36:26.

never live for the sake of another man, nor ask another man to live for mine."[4] Those words that once held such power over my life now seemed shallow and empty by comparison with the richness and fullness of life in Christ. Jesus said, "Whoever wishes to save his life shall lose it; but whoever loses his life for My sake shall find it."[5] As I began to live my life for God, he gave me immeasurably more than I could ever have hoped for or dreamed possible. Moreover, I discovered that no man is an island unto himself. What we do, for better or for worse, affects everyone around us. None of us lives or dies to himself.[6] As I lived my life in relationship with God, I discovered the joy of living in fellowship with other believers. In the words of Elton Trueblood, "A society of loving souls, set free from the self-seeking struggle for personal prestige and from all unreality, would be something unutterably precious."[7]

The second part of Galt's oath also held special meaning for me. I took it as a point of pride that I would never ask another person to live for my sake. But eventually, I came to understand something that always seemed to have eluded Rand: Christ not only came to die for me, but he also came to live for me. The Eternal Word, the Son of God, came into our fallen realm from his throne above. And on the cross, he paid the penalty for my sins. He was resurrected to life by the power of God. And now, as the Scriptures say, he always lives to make intercession and pray for his people.[8] He came to earth to live for me.

In *Atlas Shrugged*, Eddie Willers asks, "What do you suppose is the best within us?" As a fourteen-year-old boy, I too wanted to find the answer to that question. I once thought I had found the answer in the philosophy of Ayn Rand. But I was mistaken and deceived. Along the way, I discovered that in order for us to reach for the best *within* us, we have to have the best *in* us. And it is

---

[4] *Atlas Shrugged*, p. 993.
[5] Matthew 16:25.
[6] Romans 14:7 (NKJV).
[7] Elton Trueblood, "Alternative to Futility," in *Finding God at Harvard*, edited by Kelly Monroe, p. 335.
[8] Hebrews 7:25; 2 Corinthians 5:15.

Christ, the fountainhead of all life and value, whom we so desperately need to dwell in us. For then he will be "able to do exceeding abundantly beyond all that we ask or think, according to the power that works within us."[9]

One night, it seemed to me, the God of all creation impressed these words upon my heart: *"Will you let me live for you, my child, you who are so keenly aware of your own failures and shortcomings? Will you let me come and penetrate every area of your life and restore it as only I can?"* Could it be that he is here now speaking those very words to you? Do you hear his invitation for you to come as a weary Atlas, to whom he longs to give his rest? "Come to Me, all who are weary and heavy-laden, and I will give you rest. Take My yoke upon you, and learn from Me, for I am gentle and humble in heart; and you shall find rest for your souls. For My yoke is easy, and My load is light."[10] So come. Today, if you hear his voice calling your name, come and learn. And you too shall find rest and come to know that place for the first time.

---

[9] Ephesians 3:20.
[10] Matthew 11:28–30.

BIBLIOGRAPHY

Aristotle. *The Basic Works of Aristotle*. Ed. Richard McKeon. Random House, New York, 1941.

Augustine, Aurelius. *City of God*. Volume 1. Trans. J. Healey. Ed. R. V. G. Tasker. J. M. Dent and Sons, London, 1945.

Barton, David. *The Myth of Separation*. WallBuilder Press, Aledo, Texas, 1992.

Binswanger, Harry (editor). *The Ayn Rand Lexicon: Objectivism from A to Z*. The New American Library, New York, 1986.

Blanshard, Brand. *The Nature of Thought*. Two Volumes. George Allen and Unwin, London, 1939.

Branden, Barbara. *The Passion of Ayn Rand*. Doubleday, Garden City, New York, 1986.

Branden, Nathaniel. *Breaking Free*. Bantam, New York, 1981 [1970].

———. *The Psychology of Romantic Love*. Bantam, New York, 1981 [1980].

———. *The Psychology of Self-Esteem*. Bantam, New York, 1971 [1969].

———. *Who Is Ayn Rand?* Random House, New York, 1962.

Broad, William and Nicholas Wade. *Betrayers of the Truth: Fraud and Deceit in the Halls of Science*. Simon and Schuster, New York, 1982.

Calvin, John. *Institutes of Christian Religion*. Trans. Henry Beveridge. William B. Eerdmans, Grand Rapids, Michigan, 1989.

Clark, Gordon H. *A Christian View of Men and Things*. Third Edition, The Trinity Foundation, Unicoi, Tennessee, 1998 [1952].

———. *Clark Speaks from the Grave*. The Trinity Foundation, Jefferson, Maryland, 1986.

———. *Colossians*. Second Edition, The Trinity Foundation, Jefferson, Maryland, 1989 [1979].

———. *Essays on Ethics and Politics*. The Trinity Foundation, Jefferson, Maryland, 1992.

———. *In Defense of Theology*. Mott Media, Milford, Michigan, 1984.

———. *An Introduction to Christian Philosophy*. Second Edition, The Trinity Foundation, Jefferson, Maryland, 1993 [1968].

———. *The Johannine Logos*. Second Edition, The Trinity Foundation, Jefferson, Maryland, 1989 [1972].

——— and Aurelius Augustine. *Lord God of Truth and Concerning the Teacher*. Second Edition, The Trinity Foundation, Hobbs, New Mexico, 1994 [1986].

Clark, Gordon H. *The Philosophy of Science and Belief in God*. Second Edition, The Trinity Foundation, Jefferson, Maryland, 1987 [1964].

———. *Religion, Reason and Revelation*. Second Edition, The Trinity Foundation, Hobbs, New Mexico, 1995 [1961].

———. *Thales to Dewey*. Second Edition, The Trinity Foundation, Jefferson, Maryland, 1989 [1957].

———. *Three Types of Religious Philosophy*. Second Edition, The Trinity Foundation, Jefferson, Maryland, 1989 [1973].

———. *The Trinity*. Second Edition, The Trinity Foundation, Jefferson, Maryland, 1990 [1985].

Darnell, James E., Lodish, Harvey F., and David Baltimore. *Molecular Cell Biology*. Scientific American Books, New York, 1986.

Davies, Paul. *The Last Three Minutes*. BasicBooks, Harper Collins, New York, 1994.

——— and John Gribbin. *The Matter Myth*. Touchstone, Simon and Schuster, New York, 1992.

Dawkins, Richard. *The Selfish Gene*. Oxford University Press, Oxford, 1989.

Den Uyl, Douglas J. and Douglas B. Rasmussen (editors). *The Philosophic Thought of Ayn Rand*. University of Illinois Press, Urbana and Chicago, 1984.

Dietze, Gottfried. *In Defense of Property*. Henry Regnery Company, Chicago, Illinois, 1963.

Eire, Carlos M. N. *War against the Idols: The Reformation of Worship from Erasmus to Calvin*. Cambridge University Press, Cambridge, England, 1986.

Fix, William R. *The Bone Peddlers: Selling Evolution*. Macmillan, New York, 1984.

Gladstein, Mimi Reisel. *The Ayn Rand Companion*. Greenwood Press, Westport, Connecticut, 1984.

Halliday, David and Robert Resnick. *Physics*. John Wiley and Sons, New York, 1978.

Harriman, David (editor). *Journals of Ayn Rand*. Dutton, New York, 1997.

Hawking, Stephen W. *A Brief History of Time*. Bantam Books, Toronto, 1988.

Hobbes, Thomas. *Leviathan*. Dutton and Company, New York, 1950.

Hofstadter, Douglas R. *Gödel Escher Bach: An Eternal Golden Braid*, Vintage Books, New York, 1979.

Hume, David. *Enquiries Concerning the Human Understanding and Concerning the Principles of Morals*. Ed. L. A. Selby-Bigge. Second Edition, Oxford University Press, Oxford, 1902.

———. *The Philosophy of David Hume*. Ed. V. C. Chappell. The Modern Library, Random House, New York, 1963.

———. *A Treatise of Human Nature*. Volume 1. J. M. Dent and Sons, London, 1911.

Hyneman, Charles S. and Donald S. Lutz. *American Political Writing during the Founding Era, 1760–1805*. Two Volumes. Liberty Press, Indianapolis, Indiana, 1983.

Jaki, Stanley L. *Science and Creation: From Eternal Cycles to an Oscillating Universe*. Science History Publications, New York, 1974.

Jastrow, Robert. *God and the Astronomers*. W. W. Norton, New York, 1978.

Joad, C. E. M. *Guide to Philosophy*. Dover, New York, 1957 [1936].

Johnson, Philip E. *Darwin on Trial*. Second Edition, InterVarsity Press, Downers Grove, Illinois, 1993 [1991].

Jones, W. T. *A History of Western Philosophy*. Second Revised Edition in Five Volumes. Harcourt Brace Jovanovich, New York, 1969 [1952].

Kaufmann, Walter (editor). *Philosophic Classics. Volume 1: Thales to Ockham*. Second Edition, Prentice Hall, Englewood Cliffs, New Jersey, 1968.

Kennedy, D. James and Jerry Newcombe. *What If Jesus Had Never Been Born?* Thomas Nelson, Nashville, Tennessee, 1994.

Lakatos, Imre and Alan Musgrave (editors). *Criticism and the Growth of Knowledge: Proceedings of the International Colloquium in the Philosophy of Science, London, 1965*. Cambridge University Press, Cambridge, England, 1970.

Leakey, Richard E. and Roger Lewin. *Origins*. Dutton, New York, 1977.

Lewin, Roger. *Bones of Contention: Controversies in the Search for Human Origins*. Simon and Schuster, New York, 1987.

Lewis, C. S. *Miracles*. Macmillan, New York, 1978 [1947].

———. *Surprised by Joy: The Shape of My Early Life*. Harcourt, Brace and World, New York, 1955.

———. *The Weight of Glory*. Revised Expanded Edition, Macmillan, New York, 1980 [1949].

MacIntyre, Alasdair C. *After Virtue: A Study in Moral Theory*. Second Edition, University of Notre Dame Press, Notre Dame, Indiana, 1984 [1981].

Mahan, Bruce H. *University Chemistry*. Third Edition, Addison-Wesley, Reading, Massachusetts, 1975 [1969].

McDowell, Josh. *Evidence That Demands a Verdict*. Volume 1. Here's Life Publishers, San Bernardino, California, 1979 [1972].

Merrill, Ronald E. *The Ideas of Ayn Rand*. Open Court, La Salle, Illinois, 1991.

Monroe, Kelly (editor). *Finding God at Harvard: Spiritual Journeys of Thinking Christians*. Harper Collins/Zondervan, Grand Rapids, Michigan, 1996.

Morey, Robert A. *The New Atheism and the Erosion of Freedom*. Bethany House, Minneapolis, Minnesota, 1986.

Newbigin, Lesslie. *Foolishness to the Greeks: The Gospel and Western Culture*. William B. Eerdmans, Grand Rapids, Michigan, 1986.

O'Neill, William F. *With Charity toward None: An Analysis of Ayn Rand's Philosophy*. Littlefield, Adams and Co., Totowa, New Jersey, 1977 [1971].

Peikoff, Leonard. *Objectivism: The Philosophy of Ayn Rand*. Paperback Edition, Meridian Books, New York, 1993 [1991].

———. *The Ominous Parallels: The End of Freedom in America*. Stein and Day, Briarcliff Manor, New York, 1982.

Popper, Karl R. *Conjectures and Refutations: The Growth of Scientific Knowledge*. Fifth Revised Edition, Routledge, New York, 1989 [1963].

Rand, Ayn. *Atlas Shrugged*. Paperback Edition, The New American Library, New York, 1957.

———. *The Ayn Rand Letter*. Volumes 1–4, 1971–1976. Reprinted by Palo Alto Book Service, Palo Alto, California, 1979.

———. *Capitalism: The Unknown Ideal*. Paperback Edition, The New American Library, New York, 1967.

———. *For the New Intellectual*. Paperback Edition, The New American Library, New York, 1961.

———. *The Fountainhead*. Paperback Edition, The New American Library, New York, 1971 [1943].

———. *Introduction to Objectivist Epistemology*. Paperback Edition, The New American Library, New York, 1979.

———. *The New Left: The Anti-Industrial Revolution*. Second Revised Paperback Edition, The New American Library, 1975 [1971].

———. *The Objectivist*. Volumes 5–10, 1966–1971. Reprinted by Palo Alto Book Service, Palo Alto, California, 1982.

————. *The Objectivist Newsletter.* Volumes 1–4, 1962–1965. Reprinted by Palo Alto Book Service, Palo Alto, California, 1967.

————. *Philosophy: Who Needs It.* Bobbs-Merrill Company, New York, 1982.

————. *The Romantic Manifesto.* Second Revised Paperback Edition, The New American Library, New York, 1975 [1971].

————. *The Virtue of Selfishness: A New Concept of Egoism.* Paperback Edition, The New American Library, New York, 1964.

————. *We the Living.* Paperback Edition, The New American Library, New York, 1959 [1936].

Rauschning, Herman. Preface. *The Ten Commandments: Ten Short Novels of Hitler's War against the Moral Code.* Ed. Armin L. Robinson. Simon and Schuster, New York, 1943.

Robbins, John W. *Without a Prayer: Ayn Rand and the Close of Her System.* The Trinity Foundation, Hobbs, New Mexico, 1997.

Rosner, Bernard. *Fundamentals of Biostatistics.* Second Edition, Prindle, Weber, and Schmidt, Boston, Massachusetts, 1986.

Ross, Hugh. *The Creator and the Cosmos.* Second Edition, NavPress, Colorado Springs, Colorado, 1995 [1993].

Rothbard, Murray N. *For a New Liberty: The Libertarian Manifesto.* Revised Edition, Collier Books/Macmillan, New York, 1978 [1973].

Sandoz, Ellis (editor). *Political Sermons of the American Founding Era, 1730–1805.* Liberty Press, Indianapolis, Indiana, 1991.

Schaeffer, Francis A. *A Christian Manifesto.* Crossway Books, Westchester, Illinois, 1981.

————. *Francis A. Schaeffer Trilogy.* Crossway Books, Westchester, Illinois, 1990.

————. *How Should We Then Live? The Rise and Decline of Western Thought and Culture.* Fleming H. Revell, Old Tappan, New Jersey, 1976.

Shapiro, Robert. *Origins: A Skeptic's Guide to the Creation of Life on Earth.* Summit Books, New York, 1986.

Shermer, Michael. *Why People Believe Weird Things: Pseudoscience, Superstition, and Other Confusions of Our Time.* W. H. Freeman, New York, 1997.

Smith, George. *Atheism: The Case against God.* Prometheus Books, Buffalo, New York, 1979.

Thaxton, Charles B., Bradley, Walter L., and Roger L. Olsen. *The Mystery of Life's Origin: Reassessing Current Theories.* Philosophical Library, New York, 1984.

Tocqueville, Alexis de. *Democracy in America.* Two Volumes. Trans. Henry Reeve. Arlington House, New Rochelle, New York, 1965.

Weber, Max. *The Protestant Ethic and the Spirit of Capitalism.* Trans. Talcott Parsons. Charles Scribner's Sons, New York, 1958.

Weizsäcker, Carl-Friedrich von. *The Relevance of Science: Creation and Cosmogony.* Harper and Row, New York, 1964.

Whitehead, Alfred North. *Alfred North Whitehead: An Anthology.* Macmillan, New York, 1953.

Windelband, Wilhelm. *A History of Philosophy.* Two Volumes. Trans. James H. Tufts. Harper Torchbook Edition, Harper and Row, New York, 1958 [1901].

Zacharias, Ravi. *Can Man Live without God?* Word Publishing, Dallas, Texas, 1994.

INDEX

To order additional copies of

Reconsidering
AYN RAND

Order through your local bookstore, or
have your credit card ready and call

(800) 917-BOOK

To order by mail, send check or money order for
$25.95 (Hardcover) / $16.95 (Softcover)
plus shipping and handling* to

Books Etc.
PO Box 4888
Seattle, WA 98104

*Shipping and handling is $3.95 for the
first book and $1.00 for each additional book.
Washington residents please add 8.6% sales tax.
Please allow 2 to 3 weeks for delivery

Prices subject to change without notice.